Creating the American Century

In his last work before his death in 2014, American historian Martin J. Sklar analyzes the influence of early twentieth-century foreign policy makers, focusing on modernization, global development, and the meaning of the "American century." Calling this group of government officials and their advisers – including business leaders and economists – the "founders of US foreign policy," Sklar examines their perspective on America's role in shaping human progress from cycles of empires to transnational post-imperialism. Sklar traces how this thinking both anticipated and generated the course of history from the Spanish–American War to World War II, through the Cold War and its outcome, and to post-9/11 global conflicts. The "founders'" legacy is interpreted in Wilson's Fourteen Points, Henry Luce's 1941 "American Century" *Life* editorial, and foreign policy formulation to the present. Showing how modernization has evolved, Sklar discusses capitalism and socialism in relation to modern democracy in the US and to emergent globalizing forces.

Martin J. Sklar (1935–2014) was an American historian best known for originating the concepts of corporate liberalism, the disaccumulation of capital, and the capitalist/socialist mix. His books include *The Corporate Reconstruction of American Capitalism, 1890–1916: The Market, the Law and Politics* (Cambridge, 1988) and *The United States as a Developing Country: Studies in US History in the Progressive Era and the 1920s* (Cambridge, 1992). Sklar was the founding editor of several journals and a former Professor of History at Bucknell University.

Creating the American Century

*The Ideas and Legacies of America's
Twentieth-Century Foreign Policy Founders*

MARTIN J. SKLAR

CAMBRIDGE
UNIVERSITY PRESS

CAMBRIDGE
UNIVERSITY PRESS

University Printing House, Cambridge CB2 8BS, United Kingdom

One Liberty Plaza, Twentieth Floor, New York, NY 10006, USA

477 Williamstown Road, Port Melbourne, VIC 3207, Australia

4843/24, 2nd Floor, Ansari Road, Daryaganj, Delhi – 110002, India

79 Anson Road, #06-04/06, Singapore 079906

Cambridge University Press is part of the University of Cambridge.

It furthers the University's mission by disseminating knowledge in the pursuit of education, learning, and research at the highest international levels of excellence.

www.cambridge.org
Information on this title: www.cambridge.org/9781108419475
DOI: 10.1017/9781108302968

First published 2017

Printed in the United States of America by Sheridan Books, Inc.

A catalogue record for this publication is available from the British Library.

Library of Congress Cataloging-in-Publication Data

NAMES: Sklar, Martin J., 1935- author.
TITLE: Creating the American century : the ideas and legacies of America's twentieth-century foreign policy founders / Martin J. Sklar.
DESCRIPTION: Cambridge ; New York, NY : University Printing House, 2017. | Includes bibliographical references and index.
IDENTIFIERS: LCCN 2017035939| ISBN 9781108419475 (hardback) | ISBN 9781108409247 (paperback)
SUBJECTS: LCSH: United States—Foreign relations—20th century. | United States—Foreign relations—20th century—Philosophy.
CLASSIFICATION: LCC E744 .S566 2017 | DDC 327.73009/04—dc23 LC record available at https://lccn.loc.gov/2017035939

ISBN 978-1-108-41947-5 Hardback
ISBN 978-1-108-40924-7 Paperback

Five Secretaries of State, 2005–1902:
Back to the Future

Development, transparency, and democracy reinforce each other. That is why the spread of freedom under the rule of law is our best hope for progress . . . this is a time of unprecedented opportunity for the transatlantic Alliance. If we make the pursuit of global freedom the organizing principle of the twenty-first century, we will achieve historic global advances for justice and prosperity, for liberty and peace. But a global agenda requires a global partnership . . . history does not just happen; it is made.

Condoleezza Rice, 2005

The fascinating thing, when you have served in this office [Secretary of State] is . . . that, however different one's approach when one enters, one comes to be united in a realization that the national interest of the United States is not something that can be invented in every administration. The national interest of the United States in the search for peace and progress in the world has some fundamental aspects to it. And so we are driven back to certain core principles.

Henry Kissinger, 1997

For the bigger part of the [twentieth] century, the world had witnessed a titanic struggle between two visions of the future. Both were revolutionary: one based on freedom and flexibility, the other based on central power and control . . . It was as though a gigantic experiment had been conducted and the world was the laboratory. One group of countries had organized themselves through totalitarian and repressive government, with . . . an economy planned and managed from the center . . . The other group of countries organized political life more or less openly, with the rule of law and elected leaders and with economic systems based on markets, incentives, and private property . . . The situation in foreign affairs [by the end of the 1980s] had been transformed in one of the truly revolutionary periods in the international politics of the century. A sea change of immense importance had occurred.

George P. Shultz, 1993

In the nineteenth century an international system of sorts not only kept the peace for a century but also provided highly successful economic working agreements. It brought about the industrialization of Europe and of many other parts of the world – our own country, for one . . . This was accomplished by the export of capital, primarily by Great Britain, but also by all of Western Europe . . . a system for the export of capital, much greater than our present . . . efforts, is necessary. The system has been destroyed which expanded the power of Western Europe . . . One to replace it will be devised, managed, and largely (but not wholly) financed by the United States; otherwise, it is likely to be provided by the Soviet Union, under circumstances destructive of our own power.

Dean Acheson, 1958

The "debtor nation" has become the chief creditor nation. The financial center of the world, which required thousands of years to journey from the Euphrates to the Thames and the Seine, seems passing to the Hudson between daybreak and dark.

Every young and growing people has to meet, at moments, the problem of its destiny . . . The fathers are dead; the prophets are silent; the questions are new, and have no answer but in time . . . The past gives no clue to the future. The fathers, where are they? And the prophets, do they live forever? We are ourselves the fathers! We are ourselves the prophets! The questions that are put to us we must answer without delay, without help – for the sphinx allows no one to pass.

John Hay, 1902

Contents

Acknowledgments

For their historical perspective and judgment, I am deeply grateful to Lewis Bateman and Ronald Radosh. My thanks also to Margot Goldsmith, who brought peerless precision to reading the manuscript for continuity, and to Steven Schrier, who provided essential computer expertise.

I would like to thank Deborah Gershenowitz of Cambridge University Press for her sensitive editing of this book and Robert Judkins for his thoughtful direction of its production. I am grateful also to Kristina Deusch for editorial assistance, Jennifer Miles Davis for copy-editing, Geetha Williams for typesetting, Juliet Stanton for proofreading, and Roger Bennett for the index.

For their support and encouragement, I am indebted to Norton Wheeler and Judith Sklar.

Nao Hauser

Prelude: American Century and World Revolution

On February 22, 1902, the 170th anniversary of the birth of George Washington, Frank A. Vanderlip delivered an address to the Commercial Club of Chicago titled, "The Americanization of the World." The Chicago financial editor-journalist, who in 1897 became assistant secretary of the Treasury in the McKinley administration, had directed the financing of the war against Spain under the eminent Chicago banker and close friend and mentor Secretary of the Treasury Lyman J. Gage. Vanderlip was now vice-president of the Rockefeller-aligned National City Bank of New York, protégé of Wall Street titan James Stillman, and in 1909 would succeed Stillman as the bank's president. Vanderlip personified an intersecting of the spheres of intellect, government, and modern business in US foreign-policy making. On this occasion, he spoke to the assembled Chicago business, political, and civic leaders about his recent travels for the bank in Europe and England, and perspectives they cast upon the US role in world affairs.

Vanderlip reported the belief circulating among the knowledgeable and powerful across the Atlantic that the twentieth century would see "the Americanization of the world." It was a phrase, he noted, "fine, round, full sounding," that originated not "in the mouth of a bumptious Yankee, but was coined by a keen Englishman," whom Vanderlip described as the "Radical of the Radicals," the renowned editor of the journal *Review of Reviews*, William T. Stead, whose book, bearing the "full sounding" phrase as its title, was about to be published. Among Stead's "extravagant predictions regarding our future," Vanderlip said, were the Briton's "assertions that we are to dominate not only the industrial and commercial situations, but political events also, and even that England's greatest hope lies in frankly throwing in her lot with the Americans."[1]

Indicating how seriously held, across the Atlantic, was this idea of American ascendancy, Vanderlip noted that "at the opposite extreme of political life in England," the editor of what he identified as "Great Britain's most conservative and influential newspaper" (probably the *Times* of London) told Vanderlip: "The thing that I see in the political future is the United States of the world. The century which has just closed is Great Britain's. The century which has just begun is yours. The growth and progress of America are irresistible."[2]

Vanderlip gave it as his "firmest conviction in America's ultimate destiny" that the Britons were right: "The twentieth century is America's century . . . we are to be the dominating influence in the industrial affairs of the world," he stated, "we may come to a dominating position in the financial affairs of the world in time . . . [and] we are rapidly coming to a dominating political position." The "Americanization of the world" meant "industrial progress . . . commercial invasion . . . growth, development, the conquest of markets and the extension of influence." America's global "commercial invasion" was a necessary function of its own national "industrial development," which had brought the US "to a point where the world's markets are of prime importance to us." As these trends continued, and as "we shall occupy easily the commanding position in many of the world's industrial fields," Vanderlip said, it "needs no prophet to see that we have before us a role of tremendous importance" in world affairs. "All this new power . . . carries with it new responsibilities, as power always carries responsibility." Americans, therefore, could not "look soberly at the conditions which have developed . . . without recognizing that we have come to an entirely new era in the national life."[3]

The world need not fear its Americanization, because, Vanderlip explained, in "gaining that predominance we will advance all other people with us," while at the same time "we have been and will be enlightened and advanced by every point of superiority which any other people possess." It followed that America's "broadening influence in industry, finance, and politics will carry to the other nations of the earth, not defeat . . . but will bring to them all better methods, better conditions, better standards, higher political ideals, and finer conceptions of liberty and good government." The rise of the US, in other words, would mean not the fall of others, but the rise of all. Global human progress would succeed to the age-old cycles of history. The US, in short, was a nation of universal significance. "All mankind is joint heir to this heritage and the whole world will ultimately be the richer." Indeed, only insofar as Americanization really did have this universal meaning "will the American spirit become predominant."[4]

Regarding ways and means, Vanderlip designated the nascent American large corporation as the basic agency of global Americanization: "I believe in the great corporation. I believe there is no more effective way for us to impress ourselves on the trade situation of the world than through these great industrial units that can project into the world's markets the strength of their commercial position with irresistible force." Not by arms, but by the "revolutionary changes" inherent in global economic development, would Americanization conquer. "There may be bruises caused in the first readjustments which are a part of such revolutionary changes," but they "will be forgotten in the material benefit the readjustment will ultimately bring." Vanderlip acknowledged that "we may ourselves have the larger share" of the world's developing wealth, but still its growth would be "great enough to permit substantial benefit" for all countries. In summarizing what he called "the American ideal" inspiriting the world's Americanization, Vanderlip stated: "A victory of the best methods in industry, commerce, and finance; an ascendancy because of the best and fairest understanding between capital and labor; a triumph of the highest ideals of liberty and of political duty and responsibility – that is what I conceive we should mean by the Americanization of the world."[5]

Vanderlip's address to the Commercial Club of Chicago on that Washington's birthday of 1902 may help us to realize that when Henry R. Luce in 1941 published his essay, "The American Century," in the February 17 issue of his mass circulation *Life* magazine – a date exactly between the birthdates of Lincoln and Washington – he was engaging his editorial heart and mind in a US foreign-policy "tradition" already four decades old, not merely in the phrase but in a policy-making substance.[6] In 1902, Vanderlip, like President Theodore Roosevelt, was looking forward to a beckoning future with an optimism strongly current in the US, and at odds with a troubled pessimism, a gnawing fear of a Western decline and decay, prominent in European, and even in some American, intellectual circles. In 1941, Luce was joining another President Roosevelt in recalling the US to its proper role in world history, at odds with a US recovering from economic depression and comforted in a psychic worldly withdrawal; at odds as well with a world succumbing to a regnant German and Japanese imperialism. In 1902, Vanderlip, like TR, was welcoming the impending birth of an American Century; in 1941, Luce, like FDR, was seeking to rejuvenate an American Century from premature senescence and demise.

Luce's essay may be understood as part of a movement, submerged and on the defensive in the 1930s, to recall the US to its global mission, its "Manifest Duty," as Luce phrased it (in place of the older "Manifest Destiny"), against the "virus of isolationist sterility," which had "so deeply infected an influential section of the Republican Party." Luce emphasized the Anglo-American alliance in world affairs, with the US as senior partner, and now with Britain's full assent. He correlated an Americanizing globalization with both worldwide social democratic reform and the modernizing and preservation of US democracy itself: "The Party in power [Democratic Party] is the one which for long years has been most sympathetic to all manner of socialist doctrines and collectivist trends . . . the fear [among antiwar isolationists] that the United States will be driven to a national socialism, as a result of cataclysmic circumstances [i.e., a great war] and contrary to the free will of the American people, is an entirely justifiable fear." Nevertheless: "It can be said, with reason, that great social reforms were necessary in order to bring democracy up-to-date in the greatest of democracies." At the same time, neither President Franklin D. Roosevelt, nor the Republicans, nor the American people at large, were able to "make American democracy work successfully on a narrow, materialistic, and nationalistic basis . . . Our only chance now to make it work is in terms of a vital international economy and in terms of an international moral order." In this context, Luce explained, "In 1919 we had a golden opportunity . . . unprecedented in all history, to assume the leadership of the world . . . Wilson mishandled it . . . We bungled it in the 1920s and in the confusions of the 1930s we killed it . . . [but] with the help of all of us, Roosevelt must succeed where Wilson failed." Further: "This objective is Franklin Roosevelt's great opportunity . . . to go down in history as the greatest rather than the last of American Presidents . . . Under him and with his leadership we can make isolationism as dead an issue as slavery, and we can make a truly *American* internationalism something as natural to us in our time as the airplane and the radio" [Luce's italic].

As with Vanderlip, so with Luce, an American internationalism meant that the twentieth century was to be "a revolutionary century," not only "in science and industry," but also "in politics and the structure of society." It therefore meant "a revolutionary epoch," and "the world revolution." The very survival of US liberal democracy depended upon it; that is, the preservation and sustained vitality of US liberal democracy had become a function of world revolution: "For only as we go out to meet and solve for our time the problems of the world revolution, can we know how to reestablish our constitutional democracy for another 50 or 100 years." The American Century meant not the internationalism, or empire, of Rome, the Vatican, Genghis Khan, the Ottoman Empire, Imperial China, not that of Lenin or Hitler, nor even that of nineteenth-century Britain (these are all on Luce's list), but the internationalism of "our Bill of Rights, our Declaration of Independence, our Constitution, our magnificent industrial products, our technical skills," and "an internationalism of the people, by the people, and for the people." That is, it meant the universalization of democracy, human rights, liberty and equality, and progressive evolution, as understood in the modern Western political tradition, and in this sense, if "the world of the twentieth century . . . [were] to come to life in any nobility of health and vigor," it had to be "to a significant degree an American Century."

Whatever the differences of time and circumstances, and hence of wordage, style, and angle of appeal, the substantive similarities between the Luce and Vanderlip statements are striking, and particularly the themes of the US–UK alignment, progressive political and economic development, universality, world revolution, and the US as the driving force of world revolution. It may occur to the reader, as it has long occurred to this writer, that the agenda of US twentieth to twenty-first-century expansionism, imperialism, and internationalism has a distinct *left-wing* character, and moreover, that expansionism, imperialism, and internationalism have more strongly correlated with the Left side of US politics than the Right side through most of the nation's history. (Think about it.)

Nevertheless, more is required to acknowledge the authenticity of a foreign-policy tradition and comprehend its meaning than even striking similarities in two statements, impressive as they may be in source and content, thirty-nine years apart. With this in mind, instead of applying from hindsight, or retrofitting, a preferred present-day meaning of "American Century" to past and current affairs, let us proceed *from* the past *to* the present in search of a historically evolving meaning in actual US foreign-policy making, and accordingly go back to policy-relevant thinking among US policy-forming leaders at the time around the turn of the twentieth century, when the US entered upon a new era in national and world affairs.

A consideration of this thinking, and its manifestation in policy and events, may serve to indicate a need, or at least a motive, to pursue further inquiry into a set of interrelated questions: (1) the extent to which early twentieth-century US foreign-policy thinking *anticipated* major trends in twentieth-century world politics and the challenges and choices these trends would pose to US foreign-policy makers; (2) the extent to which the general trend of world politics and the US role in world affairs during the course of the twentieth century may have *realized* basic objectives in the thinking of early twentieth-century policy-forming US leaders; (3) the extent to which, more than having anticipated, this early twentieth-century thinking may indeed have *generated* and *shaped*, major trends and the general course of twentieth-century world affairs; (4) the extent to which, in other words, the US was not merely *reactive*, but decisively *proactive*, in world affairs; and (5) the extent to which the US role was deliberately and authentically revolutionary, or indeed the decisively revolutionary force, in world affairs. The inquiry may accordingly shed more light on the extent to which, and in what ways, the term, "American Century," may usefully help to describe, other than ironically, satirically, pejoratively, ornamentally, or triumphally, the course of world affairs during the twentieth century, and equally, if not more so, their prevalent trends in the twenty-first.

In both Vanderlip's usage and Luce's are to be found two ways in which the "American Century" could play on the stage of world history: first, in that of the US becoming the leading, dominating, or "hegemonic" world power, as with Britain in the nineteenth century; and second, whether with or without a US hegemony, in that of twentieth-century world affairs increasingly and ultimately evolving in accordance with long-term US foreign-policy initiatives and objectives. A less dramatic, or less journalistic, way of stating the matter, a consideration of this thinking may reveal strong threads of continuity in the US role in world affairs from the 1890s to the 1990s and beyond, weaving into coherent patterns alike of historical continuity and epochal departures.

The thinking under consideration here, of which Vanderlip's and Luce's may be taken as representative extracts, ranged more broadly and ran more deeply than indicated by interpretations associated with such thematic terms as "Social-Darwin imperialism," "end-of-the-frontier expansionism," "TR realism," and "Wilsonian idealism." It was a trend of thought that was crystallizing and coming to prominence among US policy-forming leaders in the years around the turn of the twentieth century and the early years of the new century before World War I. Intellectually appealing as these other interpretations have been, if we cast the arc of our inquiry at a wider angle to include a larger universe of policy-forming intellect and activity, other, more vitally formative and enduring dimensions of thought may become visible.[7]

It makes some substantial difference to conceive this thinking not as a fixed paradigm, but as a *set of thinking*, itself plastic and evolving, consisting in turn of components themselves varying and evolving, and which as a whole undergoes, as in the case of the individual's passage from birth and infancy to adulthood and maturity, continuous change in both responding to, and making, historical circumstances, and through that change, maintaining and realizing an essential identity.

The set of thinking, as it emerged around the turn of the twentieth century and in the early years of the century before World War I, may be found expressed in publications, state papers, and private papers, of such US leading figures as, in alphabetical order, and far from a complete list of eligibles, the following: Brooks Adams, Henry Carter Adams, A. Piatt Andrew, William J. Calhoun, John Bates Clark, Charles A. Conant, Herbert Croly, Henry P. Davison, Charles Denby, Lewis D. Einstein, Frederic Emory, John Foord, Arthur Twining Hadley, Hugh H. Hanna, John Hay, David J. Hill, Jacob Hollander, Edward M. House, Francis M. Huntington-Wilson, Jeremiah W. Jenks, Edwin W. Kemmerer, Philander C. Knox, J. Laurence Laughlin, Henry Cabot Lodge, Alfred Thayer Mahan, William McKinley, Edward S. Meade, Walter Hines Page, George W. Perkins, John R. Procter, Paul S. Reinsch, George E. Roberts, Theodore Roosevelt, Elihu Root, Leo S. Rowe, Edwin R. A. Seligman, Leslie M. Shaw, Sidney Sherwood, Herbert Knox Smith, Henry L. Stimson, Willard D. Straight, William Howard Taft, Frank A. Vanderlip, William English Walling, Paul Warburg, Frederick Wells Williams, Woodrow Wilson, Leonard Wood, Carroll D. Wright. Many more names could be added to the list.

Names such as these will suggest to those familiar with the US history at the time that the persons engaged in the set of thinking here under discussion included, in a large proportion, senior national political leaders, advisers to them, and appointees to national policy-forming or policy-implementing offices and commissions – that is, persons not merely exerting influence, or indirectly affecting policy, in some indeterminate degree, but directly engaged in its formulation and implementation.

As individuals and ensemble, they represented an emergent *social-institutional milieu*, interconnecting spheres of government, business, intellect, the law, journalism, civic association, the military, and higher education, in which individuals often worked in more than one of the spheres, either serially or simultaneously. The new milieu included a growing corps of *service savants*, who although increasingly academia-based by 1900, were not yet as commonly so as by the later twentieth century, and who engaged as professional experts, not merely as elite citizens, in policy formulation and implementation. In other words, they represented expanding and intersecting spheres of policy-forming activity, which in the US at the time involved a growing number and a social density sufficient to forming a qualitatively new critical mass in US society, politics, and government. It was an early crystallization of a social-institutional milieu, which, while encompassing many subsidiary disagreements and varied perspectives, involved mutual acknowledgment and liaison, and a shared set of thinking, as a matter of professional dignity, obligation, and routine, or as Secretary of State George P. Shultz has phrased it, an "institutional memory," grounded in what Secretary of State Henry Kissinger has referred to as "core principles." Increasingly, the milieu functioned both to generate and to shape policy making, day-to-day and over the long run. As an emergent social-institutional milieu, it was becoming, in effect, a new "tradition" or "establishment" in foreign-policy making, having roots in evolving class relations and in past experience and traditions, but also embarking on distinctive departures corresponding with the passage from one era of US history to another, or as Vanderlip had phrased it, to "an entirely new era in the national life."[8]

One of the implications of this is that it is fundamentally mistaken, or *ahistorical* – that is, not grounded empirically and contextually in the actual historical circumstances and events – to think about, or explain, the course of US foreign-policy making in terms decisively of a singular president or a handful of "influentials," or "Wise Men," or in terms of categories like (TR) Realism vs. (Wilsonian) Idealism, Isolationism vs. Internationalism, Liberalism vs. Conservatism, and more recently, Multilateralists vs. Unilateralists, Hawks vs. Doves, Hard Power vs. Soft Power, Right-wingers vs. Liberals, Neo-Conservatives vs. Realists, and so on. All these perhaps there were, but if so, as subordinate and ephemeral variables of an evolving social-institutional milieu forming and imposing an "institutional memory," embedded in "core principles," and working in a concrete historical context.[9]

The set of thinking under consideration here was in essence historical in method and content. This is quite apart from whether or not one considers the thinking to be "good history," or agrees or disagrees with it. It sought to comprehend the present as a result of the past, and on that basis to anticipate the probable course of history in the future. In this way, by in effect defining the present historical era in terms of its past derivation and feasible future tendencies, leaders could know, or at least decide with greater confidence, *what is to be done*, that is, what objectives and policies, short- and long-term, were possible, desirable, or necessary, and what was to be abandoned, changed, or rejected.

This runs counter to a widely held view that Americans are ahistorical in mentality and culture, or as it is often jocularly put, that they have a short – perhaps one-week – memory span. If so, it would truly make Americans "exceptional," and indeed, it is a way of disparaging Americans and, in effect, dehumanizing them. Actually, and counterintuitive to some readers as this may be (whatever the case in recent years, to which we return at the end of the book), Americans in general, and especially the politically and civically engaged citizenry and their leaders, have been among the *most* historically conscious of the world's peoples. Americans have been a people so little self-contained, so little formed or unified, *as a nation*, by remote common habitat, ethnicity, religion, custom, or legendary tradition, that thinking historically about their nation and its place in the world has been a matter of identity itself, of success and survival, of life and death. The more "rooted" a people, the more their identity may be a matter of kin, fixed legend, place-specific time, and timeless place, and less a matter of the flow, causal relations, purpose, and meaning of historical ideas and events across place and time. The more "rootless" a people, the more historically minded they will think and act, if they are to form a coherent society, nation, and civilization, and the stronger the tendency to combine a national identity with a universal-human history.

Progeny of Abraham, for example, those who became the Jews, "rootless" and wandering, then in bondage, then again wandering, emigrants and immigrants, over four centuries, and becoming a "mixed multitude" (Exodus 12: 38–41), fighting among themselves and conquering others, before becoming a settled nation, *invented* history, the *Old Testament* – along with the Talmud their Covenant with God, with the past, with one another, and with the future, a people of the just law, constantly disputing, interpreting, and changing the law, and keeping it all the same. The first great secular historians and lawmakers came from among peripatetic, emigrating, imperial Greeks and Romans of antiquity seeking to forge a common (cosmopolitan) civic identity.[10] Christianity, arising among the Jews, was early spread by peregrinating evangelizers – emigrants and immigrants – a universal religious identity, sown and grown in earthly time and events, across and among the many Greek, Roman, and "barbarian" peoples, societies, and cultures. Western civilization: rooted in the interplay of the "rootless" Judeo-Christian, Hellenic, and Roman traditions – faith and reason, law and history.

It is not without significance, and it is worthy of contemplation, that US identity begins with wandering "Old Testament" Protestants, heirs also to the Greek and Roman heritage, establishing a new Zion in a new Promised Land, with its city upon a hill and country-Whig soul – both the sacred and the profane. At the heart of American national identity are the Declaration of Independence and the Constitution – the national Covenant, along with its history and jurisprudence, the "Old Testament" and rule of law, a law always made and remade, interpreted and reinterpreted, always changing and always the same – a Republic, "one nation, under God, indivisible, with liberty and justice for all," a people not so much law-*abiding* as law-making, law-changing, law-keeping, and law-centered: a people engaged in a continual creative tension and rejuvenating dialogue between original intent and changing circumstances, between "the fathers" and "the sons," between a prior necessity and free will, between universal truths and variable principles, between constancy and progress, between the prophets and the practicalists, between present and past and future – in short, the very stuff of the historical mind. Historical discourse becomes, for the people of Abraham Lincoln, as with the people of Abraham, the core of US national identity, of US civilization. The nation of immigrants (including those held in bondage and emancipated), the nation of wanderers – from abroad and thence within and abroad again (new frontiers and open doors) – is a nation peculiarly of *historical* identity, and it forms the vital substance of its culture, its politics, its very coherence as a society. Hence, the lure of "multiculturalism" – really multiple *mono*culturalisms – and disdain of teaching and learning a *national* history, resonate among those who seek the *dis*-integration, the vanquishing, or the disappearance, of the United States.[11]

The set of thinking considered here placed US affairs in the context of the nation's own past history and development, in that of world history, and not only in that of contemporary world history but also in that of the history of the world – human history – from ancient times. It was *not* "American Exceptionalist" in kind. It viewed US history, however unique in some ways, as with every society, as nevertheless exemplary of universal-human evolutionary norms, patterns, or laws. On the universal-human scale, according to the thinking, US history represented a relatively advanced stage of evolution or development attained, for *historical* reasons, by "Anglo-Saxon" or Anglo-American and some other western European and transatlantic societies – those designated as exemplifying

"Western Civilization" – but a stage of development that was of universal access, and that therefore other societies, given the right historical conditions, were attaining to (for example, Japan), or would attain to, sooner or later.

The set of thinking may best be recognized both as rooted in the prophetic religio-historical tradition, and as a member of the growing body of nineteenth- to twentieth-century Euro-American cumulative-evolutionary thought, and on that account, as being in principle universal in application, that is, in principle, not racially, ethnically, or nationally exclusive, however much it acquired, in the usage of various thinkers and policy makers, the taint and corruption of racism or a "Eurocentric" chauvinism. It ranked stages of human history on a scale of lesser to greater development, lesser to greater advancement, less modern to more modern civilization, in accordance with cumulative-evolutionary premises. In this regard, there were essential similarities between the Americans here referred to – let us call them the American Twentieth-Century *Foreign Policy Founders* – and such nineteenth-century "Old World" thinkers as George W. F. Hegel, Saint-Simon, Auguste Comte, Alexis de Tocqueville, John Stuart Mill, Karl Marx, Herbert Spencer, Henry Maine, Wilhelm Roscher, Gustav Schmoller, and Walter Bagehot. The later historical stages, exemplified by Britain, parts of western Europe, the United States, and some others, ranked as more advanced, consisting as they did of a more modern and higher civilization than the earlier stages, which if extending into modern times exemplified decadence and backwardness (for example, the Ottoman Empire, the Qing Empire of China, the czarist Russian Empire, Mughal India, the Spanish Empire, Ethiopia). Still, the countries of the later, higher stage displayed to the lesser developed societies, and by implication, to the world at large, their future, that is, if they happened to evolve along modern lines, or chose to do so, or were made to do so. As Marx said of Germany's future, in its relation to the more industrialized Britain of the mid-nineteenth century: "*De te fabula narratur!* [the story is about you] . . . The country that is more developed industrially only shows, to the less developed, the image of its own future."[12]

The set of thinking, accordingly, brought into common usage, in both scholarly and political spheres, in the US, a discourse and concepts regarding the classification of societies corresponding with their evolutionary progress, associated with such terms as "modern," "pre-modern," "advanced," "backward," "development," "developed country," "undeveloped country," "less developed country." The discourse and concepts correlated closely with a transatlantic scholarly trend of thought that eventually came to be systematized and known as modernization theory.[13]

The set of thinking included perspectives that rendered world history since ancient times as understandable in terms of an evolving succession of predominant empires, which in rising and declining made their contributions to a process of cumulative human development. These perspectives resided in studies and ideas that critically explicated, assessed, and affirmed modern empire, as having some characteristics in common with past empire, but as having acquired other characteristics that substantially differentiated a more advanced modern empire from past modern and pre-modern empire: the term *imperialism*, instead of empire, more forcefully denoted dynamic or developmental processes of evolving sociocultural interrelations, rather than an inert or static entity, and hence came into some more common usage in the 1890s and early twentieth century.[14]

The differentiating characteristics of advanced modern imperialism could be viewed as holding the prospect of world history proceeding to a post-empire, or a post-imperialism, stage of development, and thus of humanity entering upon a profound departure in its historical development, one of epochal proportions, revolutionary both in substance and in implications – leading to a *novus ordo seclorum*.[15] Such a departure, or "exceptionalism," which some eighteenth-century US founders hopefully attributed to their new republic (in that case, a breaking of the Polybian cycle of political forms) could now be viewed as applicable not simply to one "exceptional" nation, but to a global humanity moving beyond the age-old evolution via the cyclical rise and decline of successive dominant empires, to a post-empire, noncyclical, and progressively evolving world order. This outlook was not an American Exceptionalism, not envisioning something outside or beyond universal processes, norms, or imperatives of historical evolution, even if the US might, by historical circumstance, be temporarily positioned to play an exceptional or uniquely singular role.

In this context, if the US was the most advanced of nations and poised to succeed to Britain's position in world affairs, the "American Century" held the prospect, first, of the US rising to the position of the leading or dominant world power, with a continuing global spread of "Americanization" – that is, "modernization" – which, second, by its very nature, would eventually make not only unnecessary, but also impossible, dictation by the US, or any single nation or group of nations, in world affairs, and hence inaugurate a post-imperialism world: a world liberated from cyclical repetition for a progressive universal-human evolution, in short, a new world order, a revolutionary evolution. Thus, the "American Century" as world revolution, and a twice-told tale: the second (post-imperialism) fulfilling by superseding the first (US as hegemonic). Twice-told also, in the *founders'* telling, and then in *history's* telling, in the play of actual events throughout the twentieth century and as they were tending in the twenty-first.

Far from the end of history, this "American Century" implied a continuation of history, even if, and precisely because, it represented a new phase of human evolution, even a new departure, but then, again, not an end of history, but at the least a progressive variation on the evolving cyclical pattern or, presumptively and preferably, an inauguration of a new, universalized stage of cumulative-evolution. It may be recalled that Marx did not believe that the socialism-communism he anticipated represented an *end* of history, but quite the contrary, a *beginning* of what may be considered a more fully human, or more authentically human, history, prepared for by the past and evolving, or developing, from it. This part of his thinking may be considered presumptuous, arrogant, naive, even silly, but it was not an end-of-history outlook. In the larger sense, the Americans were Marxian, and Marx was American. The US and the "American Century": the marriage of Locke and Marx, yielding the revolutionary trinity (once again, twice-told) of: (1) the laws of nature – and nature's God; (2) the social contract – and the Covenant; (3) historical evolution – and creative Reason and Law in the world (Logos), or, in the German – pace Hegel and Pope Benedict XVI – *Geistische Vernunft*.[16]

> Thus in Thy good time may infinite reason turn the tangle straight, and these crooked marks on a fragile leaf be not indeed.
>
> W. E. B. DuBois, 1903

Notes

1. "The Americanization of the World. An Address delivered before the Commercial Club of Chicago, February 22, 1902, by Frank A. Vanderlip, Vice-President of the National City Bank of New York" (Chicago: Rand McNally & Co., 1902), p. 2. A copy of this address, published as a fifteen-page pamphlet, is in the Vanderlip Papers, Rare Book and Manuscript Library, Butler Library, Columbia University, New York City. On the Spanish–American War financing, see Vanderlip's interesting and informative article, "Lessons of Our War Loan," *Forum*, XXVI (Sept. 1898), pp. 27–36. The National City Bank was a principal forerunner of today's Citibank within the larger Citigroup.

2. "Americanization of the World," p. 2.
3. Ibid., pp. 2, 4, 14. Cf. Vanderlip, *The American Commercial Invasion of Europe* (New York: Scribner's Sons, 1903).
4. "Americanization of the World," pp. 14, 15.
5. Ibid., pp. 14, 15.
6. Henry R. Luce, "The American Century," *Life*, vol. 10, February 17, 1941, pp. 61–65.
7. The application of the frontier-expansion-Open Door theme to a comprehensive interpretation of the history of twentieth-century US foreign relations was a major historiographical milestone, because it opened the way to new research and fresh perspectives of sustained viability and influence, for better or worse. It is proper and necessary to recognize William A. Williams here for his seminal work in this respect, for example, his now classic book, first published in 1959, *The Tragedy of American Diplomacy* (Cleveland: World Publishing Co., and subsequent editions by other publishers in various years). On his powerful impact on historical research and writing, especially at the University of Wisconsin, Madison, in the 1950s–1960s, see, e.g., Lloyd C. Gardner, ed., *Redefining the Past: Essays in Diplomatic History in Honor of William Appleman Williams* (Corvallis: Oregon State University Press, 1986), Part I: Essays by William G. Robbins, Bradford Perkins, Ivan R. Dee, and David W. Noble, pp. 3–62. Williams emphasized the prominence in American policy-forming thought of the idea of Empire – on seemingly everyone's tongue now, but at that time disdained in prevalent academic and intellectual discourse – an idea prominent also in this book, as the reader will see, in considering the thinking of US leaders about US and world history, but the treatment of the idea of Empire here is not entirely the same as that by Williams, nor that by those wagging their tongues with it today – or moving their cursors – leftward and rightward.
8. The phrase and concept "institutional memory," at George P. Shultz, *Turmoil and Triumph: My Years as Secretary of State* (New York: Scribner's Sons, 1993), pp. 33, 34. Henry Kissinger's point about "core principles" is at: "Foreign Policy Priorities on the Eve of the Twenty-First Century," *Third Annual Conference of Rice University's James A. Baker III Institute for Public Policy*, Houston, TX, October 16, 1997 (typed transcript), p. 16. The other conference participants included former Secretaries of State Baker and Warren Christopher, former President of the Soviet Union Mikhail Gorbachev, former US President George Bush, and, by videotape, Secretary of State Madeline Albright.
9. This is neither to disdain, deny, nor detract from the importance of eminent individuals ("great persons") and the roles they play, and have played, in history – in indelibly shaping historical events and trends – but rather to suggest they are best understood not as idiosyncratic, singular, or deus ex machina "forces," but rather as forceful leaders participating in a strongly based social-institutional milieu acquiring or already carrying a broad intellectual/moral authority, and hence a governing legitimacy, in the society at large. It is thus that their successes and failures may bring great benefits and tragedies, joys and sorrows, progressive advances and ruinous disasters, which would not be the case were they idiosyncratic or "exceptional."

10. Cf., e.g., William H. McNeill, *The Rise of the West: A History of the Human Community* (University of Chicago Press, 1963), pp. 193–194ff., re-development of Ionian (Greek) civilization and the creation of the polis, with similar currents shaping Roman civilization; and Nicholas Ostler, *Ad Infinitum: A Biography of Latin* (New York: Walker and Co., 2007), ch. 1, pp. 3–20.

11. Not *e pluribus unum*, but *ex uno multos*. From their standpoint, Barack Hussein Obama was their 2008 presidential candidate of choice, and his election signified the beginning of the end of the United States of America (Old Empire). Regarding the people of Abraham: ". . . the Old Testament writers . . . endowed history with immense importance, far greater importance than it had ever assumed in any previous culture. The God of Israel has made a pact, a covenant, with Israel; the working-out of this covenant year after year is history. [Par.] . . . the existence and purpose of man . . . becomes didactic and instructive about the future, with which the past is inseparably linked. The writing of history, then, became the driving force of action." Michael Grant, *The Ancient Historians* (New York: Scribner's, 1970; Barnes and Noble, ed., 1994), pp. 10–11, and see pp. 78–79. Also, McNeill, *The Rise of the West*, pp. 160, 161: "The historical writing of the Hebrews was infused with the religion of Yahweh, whose hand was seen guiding events . . . The biblical account of the exodus from Egypt is a striking example of the view that God revealed himself through history . . . [Par.] As a deity directing the course of history, Yahweh was unique in the Middle East . . . [Par.] The prophets became the pre-eminent spokesmen for the religion of Yahweh in early Hebrew society . . . [Par.] Yahweh controlled the destiny not only of his chosen people, but of all mankind . . . Thus the prophets expanded the idea that God revealed himself through history to make him supreme over all the world." My comment: a historical national identity combined with a universal-human history. Cf., also, Thomas Cahill, *The Gifts of the Jews* (New York: Anchor Books, Doubleday, 1998), esp. Introduction, and chs. 3–4, 6–7; Paul Johnson, *A History of the Jews* (New York: HarperCollins, 1998), pp. 16–20, 91–92; Ilana Pardes, "Imagining the Birth of Ancient Israel: National Metaphors in the Bible," in David Biale, ed., *Cultures of the Jews* (New York: Schocken Books, 2002), pp. 9–41, at pp. 9–12, and David Biale, "Introduction to Part One: Mediterranean Origins," in ibid., pp. 3–7; Paul K. Conkin and Roland N. Stromberg, *Heritage and Challenge: The History and Theory of History* (Wheeling, IL: Forum Press, 1989), pp. 3–6. Regarding the people of Abraham Lincoln, cf. Lincoln's 2nd Annual Message to Congress, December 1, 1862: "The dogmas of the quiet past, are inadequate to the stormy present . . . As our case is new, so we must think anew, and act anew. We must disenthrall ourselves, and then we shall save our country." Yet: "Fellow citizens, we cannot escape history . . . In giving freedom to the *slave* we assure freedom to the free . . . We shall nobly save or meanly lose, the last best, hope of earth." (Lincoln's italics, elisions mine, other punctuation *sic*.) And Gettysburg Address, November 19, 1863: "Four score and seven years ago [1776] our fathers brought forth on this continent, a new nation, conceived in Liberty, and dedicated to the proposition that all men are created equal." Yet: ". . . we here highly resolve that these dead shall not have died in vain – that this nation, under God, shall have a new

birth of freedom – and that government of the people, by the people, for the people, shall not perish from the earth." My comment: In keeping faith with God, the fathers, the old, and preserving the Covenant (Declaration of Independence, the Constitution), i.e., in knowing history and staying its course, not escaping it, we must think and act *anew*, be born again (new birth) in freedom. And as with Lincoln's Hay (prescript, above), we are now ourselves the fathers, the prophets – the makers of history and the historians – the questions are new and have no answer but *in time*: revolution in and with evolution, in and with history, not outside or erasing or forgetting it.

12. Karl Marx, "Preface to the First German Edition of the First Volume of *Capital*," in *Karl Marx and Frederick Engels, Selected Works in Two Volumes* (Moscow: FLPH, 1951), Vol. I, pp. 407–408.

13. In the usage of modernization theory, these rather socially mobile terms gradually displaced the older static terms, "civilized" and "uncivilized." Cf. M. J. Sklar, *The United States as a Developing Country* (Cambridge University Press, 1992), chs. I, II.

14. Among those whose historical writings comprehend this distinction between static entity and dynamic socio-cultural interrelations, or cultural diffusion, see in particular, Thomas Sowell, *Conquests and Cultures: An International History* (New York: Basic Books, 1998), chs. 1, 6, et passim.

15. For the pioneering work on post-imperialism and its relation to stages of historical development, see the writings of Richard L. Sklar, as displayed, e.g., in *African Politics in Postimperial Times: The Essays of Richard L. Sklar*, ed. Toyin Falola (Trenton, NJ: Africa World Press, 2002); and see David G. Becker and Richard L. Sklar, eds., *Postimperialism and World Politics* (Westport, CT: Praeger, 1999); and D. G. Becker *et al.*, eds., *Postimperialism: International Capitalism and Development in the Late Twentieth Century* (Boulder and London: Lynne Rienner Publishers, 1987).

16. Or, the marriage of Old World Locke/Smith/Mill and Hegel/Marx/Bagehot, yielding the New. The ahistorical, literalistic, and abstract-logical mode of understanding, in matters of this sort, is either/or; the historical, metaphorical, and evolutionary-logical mode is both/and. *Geistische Vernunft* may be translated as: Living (evolving) Reason in the world, i.e., in world history; hence, human history as a coherent, and ultimately universal, process of cumulative-evolution, and thus as progressively developmental, and in terms of the prophetic religio-historical tradition, redemptive and salvational. The (1), (2), (3) of the "revolutionary trinity" in the text above, has its analogue in (1) the Father, (2) the Son(s), and (3) the Holy Spirit.

PART ONE

ORIGINS

CHAPTER I

The Philippines, China, and US Global Objectives (The Conant Factor)

One of the most important [results of the Spanish–American War] is the friendly relations which have been established with England. Another is the expulsion of Spain from this hemisphere. Another is our entrance into the Pacific by the annexation of Hawaii and our securing a foothold . . . in the East [Manila] . . . Lastly, we have risen to be one of the great world powers . . . We are certainly going to have a very powerful navy.

Senator Henry Cabot Lodge (1898)[1]

SETTING THE STAGE

In the several years after the military victory over Spain in April–August 1898, the US government engaged in a course of action in the Philippines directly related to broader global objectives. These global objectives, and particularly those related to China, formed the operative context of the US engagement in the Philippines.

The outcome of the Spanish–American War, including closer working relations with Britain and the projection of a sustained US military force in the Caribbean and East Asia, placed the US in a new position in world politics. It was now a nation with hemispheric *and* global interests that were not, as in the past, largely inchoate and prospective, but tangible and immediate, and, therefore, strategic and compelling, both to the other great powers, and in its own day-to-day policy planning.

The US went to war against Spain explicitly over the situation in Cuba, but its first formidable military strike was Admiral George Dewey's naval victory at Manila, on May 1, 1898, six days after the formal US declaration of war, and almost two months *before* major US combat in Cuba.[2] For over three centuries, since the 1560s, the Spanish Empire had connected the New World – particularly the Caribbean and Mexico – with East Asia. The US now succeeded to the control of that connection, which along with the Spanish Empire had been withering away, and poised itself to rehabilitate and transform the connection into a vital sinew of a new global system.[3] As Theodore Roosevelt stated, with the Manila victory already in hand, and as his "Rough Riders" embarked with the US armed force from Florida to Cuba: "It is a great historical expedition . . . [and] if we are allowed to succeed . . . we [will] have scored the first great triumph in what will be a world movement."[4]

In its defeat of Spain, its military occupation of Cuba, its annexations of Puerto Rico, Guam, Hawaii, and Wake Island, its Pago Pago base at Samoa, its Midway Island possession (since 1867), its campaign of conquest and annexation in the Philippines, its now more realizable isthmian-canal intent, its growing battleship navy, and its huge, diversified, and industrializing economy, the US acquired both the reality and the prestige of world-power ranking, and particularly in Asian affairs. From London, as early as July 1898, US Ambassador, not yet secretary of state, John Hay observed to President William McKinley, "We have never in all our history had the standing in the world we have now."[5]

The new US strategic position and rising world-power prestige played dramatically on the global stage in a wink of the historical eye, with President Theodore Roosevelt's mediation in the ending of the Russo–Japanese War, in 1905. But in scarcely a blink, the new US position played diplomatically in Secretary of State Hay's "Open Door" notes regarding China, in 1899–1900, which those recipient powers that since 1897 had been hardening their spheres-of-influence claims, could not now simply ignore. It played diplomatically, also, in the renegotiated US–UK (Hay–Pauncefote) treaty giving exclusive US control and fortification of a Central American isthmian canal that would connect US Atlantic and Gulf Coast ports with Far Eastern Asia by a route shorter than Britain's connection via the Strait of Gibraltar and the Suez Canal. The new US position also played, once again militarily, with the impressive US participation in the multination intervention in China against the anti-foreign Boxers, during the late spring, summer, and fall of 1900. In due course, the powers made policy-bending adjustments to the "Open Door" notes, softening their spheres of influence, and receding from inclinations to partition and divide China among themselves, a la Africa.[6]

As a result of the new US strategic position, the "Open Door" notes, and the anti-Boxer intervention, the US, in making only a minor monetary claim in the multination Boxer-damages indemnity imposed upon

China, sat at the table, with a heightened moral tone, and a stronger hand, as one of the major "Indemnity Powers" in China's affairs. With US military power now projected along a line of Pacific bases in Hawaii, Midway, Samoa, Wake, Guam, and the Philippines, it was not lost to the notice of military and political leaders of the other great powers, and of China itself, that the initial US military expedition dispatched to Tientsin and Peking against the Boxers came directly from patrolling US warships (marines) and from infantry and artillery units engaged in the conquest of the Philippines. The latter deployment temporarily weakened US military forces in the Philippines, to the chagrin of the Army command under General Arthur MacArthur, but it demonstrated with a signal eloquence the order of priority embodied in US policy in East Asia.[7]

It may be less abstractly counterfactual than a factual historical inference to say: no Spanish–American War; no large US military presence in the Philippines; no chain of US Pacific naval bases; no "Open Door" notes of consequential impact; no significant US engagement in China's affairs before World War I; and, feasibly, no continuing existence of a greater China.

The US interest in China, the Caribbean–Pacific connection, and the global implications, led the McKinley administration to a strategic determination to preempt another great power – in particular, Germany or Japan – from controlling the Philippines in whole or in part, directly or indirectly, which would thereby jeopardize or prevent a US base at Manila, and accordingly, to the decision (with Britain's encouragement) to conquer and annex the entire archipelago. In taking possession of the Philippines, the US government pursued not only military-strategic, but also political-economic, objectives, and implemented social, economic, and governmental reforms in the islands, which, combined with its new world-power standing, provided both a model and a lever for US initiatives beyond the Philippines – in China, in East Asia, and thence on a global scale.

US policy makers conceived their objectives in the Philippines in the larger global framework, which combined interoceanic strategic planning with a sustained commitment to opening nonindustrial societies to, and making them essential components of, an ongoing process of worldwide modernizing development deemed vital to the industrial societies' own continuing development. Central to this larger framework was preventing an imperialist dismemberment of China, preserving its unified national entity, and attaining a leading US participation in China's development. In practical terms, this larger global framework meant tying China and other nonindustrial societies into an international system of capitalist investment and trade, and initiating within these societies requisite and facilitative governmental, fiscal, legal, educational, and social reforms. It implied revolutionary transformations in "traditional" and largely non-bourgeois societies – or in recent phrasing, modern nation-building. In this sense, as well as the strategic, US policy in the Philippines was a part of the formation of US global policy, what Senator Henry Cabot Lodge indeed called "the large policy," and what came to be regarded as the quest for an "Open Door" world, and as the substance of an "American Century."[8]

Although the conquest and annexation of the Philippines partook of the "old colonialism," the policies undertaken – with whatever degree or lack of success – bespoke a new imperialism, a new internationalism, of a modern industrial capitalism moving into a corporate-administered stage of development, and looking toward a post-imperialism age.[9]

THE MCKINLEY–ROOT FRAMEWORK OF DEVELOPMENT

President McKinley's instructions of April 7, 1900 to the Philippine Commission, appointed by the president as the impending US governing body in the islands, took the form of a long letter from the president to Secretary of War Elihu Root for transmission to the commission. A War Department sub-agency, the commission was headed by McKinley's fellow Ohio Republican, hitherto federal circuit court judge and *anti-annexationist*, William Howard Taft.[10] Root actually wrote the instructions. A skeptic may tend to glide over or ignore this kind of instrument as a routine formality, or worse, as an arrogant sham, but the instructions repay some detailed attention as embodying the developmental intent and correlative objectives of the new imperialism. Like the US Constitution itself, the instructions mandated a framework of both government and economic development. But in an imperial departure from previous constitutional tradition and practice, the instructions promulgated an organic law for a numerous people not expected to form a coequal state of the union, and not permitted to exercise the usual territorial powers of self-government.[11]

The instructions authorized the Taft commission to make "rules and orders, having the effect of law," on specified matters with fundamental modernizing implications: "the raising of revenue by taxes, customs, duties, and imposts"; "the appropriation and expenditure of public funds"; "the establishment of an educational system"; the inauguration of an "efficient civil service"; the establishment and organization of courts of law and of municipal and provincial governments; "and all other matters of a civil nature," including the appointment of officers at all levels.[12]

The instructions intended the commission to establish a form of government that ultimately would resemble that of the US, and thus be conducive to modern development and eventual self-government. In the distribution of powers, "following the example . . . of the United States," the Philippine central government "shall have no direct administration except of matters of purely general concern," and except for "supervision and control" necessary to security and "efficient administration." In local government, officers "are to be selected by the people." In the selection of officers of more extended jurisdiction, Filipinos were to be preferred but, because of the "many different degrees of civilization and varieties of custom and capacity" among them, it "will be necessary to fill some offices for the present with Americans," but eventually to be replaced by Filipinos. The instructions directed that "as soon as practicable," a civil service system be established as the basis of a modern salaried government bureaucracy.[13] Among the standards of proficiency, an "absolute and unconditional loyalty to the United States" was to be a prerequisite of "merit and fitness" for office. To assure loyalty, "absolute [the word again] and unhampered authority and power to remove and punish any officer deviating from that standard must at all times be retained in the hands of the central authority of the islands." The Lincoln "One-Tenth Plan" loyalty standard, deployed in the post-Civil War US South, was to be applied and enforced with respect to officeholders in the Philippines.[14]

The instructions anticipated conflict between modernization and tradition, as had also been the case in North–South relations before, during, and after the Civil War, and in relations and wars with Indians from colonial times – a strong leitmotif in US history. Philippine traditions should be recognized and respected, but not to the extent of obstructing modern development. The commissioners were to "bear in mind that the government which they are establishing is designed not for our satisfaction or for the expression of our theoretical views, but for the happiness, peace, and prosperity of the people of the Philippine Islands." Given an American idea of these terms – happiness, peace, and prosperity – although the measures adopted were to conform to the people's "customs, their habits, and even to their prejudices," nevertheless, they were to do so only "to the fullest extent consistent with the accomplishment of the indispensable requisites of just and effective government." On the meaning of this, the instructions were definitive and emphatic: the Philippine people "should be made plainly to understand, that there are certain great principles of government which have been made the basis of our government system, which we deem essential to the rule of law and the maintenance of individual freedom, and of which they have, unfortunately, been denied the experience possessed by us." Accordingly, there were "practical rules of government which we have found to be essential to the preservation of these great principles of liberty and law," and these rules and principles "must be established and maintained in their islands for the sake of their liberty and happiness, however much they may conflict with the customs or laws of procedure with which they are familiar."[15]

The instructions expressed confidence that these rules and principles would "inevitably within a short time command universal assent" among the Philippine people. Therefore, it directed, "Upon every division and branch of the government of the Philippines . . . must be imposed these inviolable rules": then followed a listing of rights and protections contained in the US Constitution, with the significant and explicit exception, for the duration, of the right of trial by jury and the right to bear arms (potent weapons in the Americans' own struggle for independence). Due-process protection of life, liberty, and property headed the list. The ban on the establishment of religion and the guarantee of the right of religious freedom interdicted the previous power of the Spanish Catholic Church in the Philippines, and at the same time they were equally adverse to Islamist dictation or establishment in southern parts of the islands.[16]

To deepen the secularization, democratization, and modernization of the social order, and for this purpose, to reduce Catholic and Islamic control of education, the instructions directed "that the separation between state and church shall be real, entire, and absolute" (the word again), and, while "no minister of religion shall be interfered with or molested, in following his calling," that nevertheless "no form of religion and no minister of religion shall be forced upon any community or upon any citizen of the islands." More than this, further, and proactively, "a system of primary education" shall be established "which shall be free to all, and which shall tend to fit the people for the duties of citizenship and for the ordinary avocations of a civilized community." Although educational instruction should be provided "in the first instance . . . in the language of the people," nevertheless, given "the great number of languages" among "the different tribes," it would be "especially important to the prosperity of the islands that a common medium of communication" be introduced, "and it is obviously desirable that this medium be English."[17]

Governor Taft explained the English-language policy as essential to US plans for Philippine development and self-government. In testimony before the Senate Committee on the Philippines, chaired by Republican Senator Henry Cabot Lodge of Massachusetts, Taft stated that "the teaching of English . . . is now being done throughout the islands" in the public school system and was integral to "our great hopes in elevating" the Philippine people. It was closely tied to the establishment of "a popular assembly" and hence to "the gradual growth of popular government," those Filipino males learning English becoming "at once," if adults, "entitled to vote." Public education in English also facilitated the Filipinos' "taking in modern ideas of popular government and individual liberty," and it thus served modernizing development in general. As Charles A. Conant, the US special commissioner for Philippine currency and banking reform, further explained in testimony before the House Committee on Insular Affairs, the Spanish Catholic friars "refrained from teaching them [the Filipinos] Spanish, but did teach them . . . Tagalog . . . the object being, of course, largely to prevent their coming in contact with the ideas of Western civilization, because there are very few if any books in Tagalog relating to . . . political-economy and to political conceptions." Taft summed it up in saying that with English as their "common language," and their "reading its literature . . . [and] becoming aware of the history of the English race," the Philippine people "will breathe in the spirit of Anglo-Saxon individualism."[18] *In lingua vince.*

Addressing modern economic development more specifically, the McKinley–Root instructions stipulated that government strongly protect property rights and nurture incentives to investment and enterprise. Taxes that "penalize or repress industry and enterprise are to be avoided." The commission was to abide by the provision of the Treaty of Paris of December 1898, for "the protection of all rights of property," as well as "the principle of our own Government which prohibits the taking of property without due process of law." The "welfare of the people" was to be "a paramount consideration," but it was to be "attained consistently with this rule of property right." In taking lands for public use, the commission should allow both "due legal procedure" and "due compensation." Here, however, the instructions gave the commission some wide latitude in the interests of facilitating development. Too meticulous a regard for due process might inhibit investment and enterprise. For example, the instructions authorized the commission to redistribute land from nonproductive to productive uses. The commission was to make a thorough investigation into "the titles of large tracts of land held or claimed by individuals or by religious orders," and into "the justice of the claims and complaints made against such landholders by the people," and to seek "a just settlement of the controversies and redress of the wrongs which have caused strife and bloodshed in the past." In carrying out this land reform to spur enterprise and development, the commission, while "enjoined to see that no injustice is done," was nevertheless directed to attain "substantial right and equity," if necessary by "disregarding technicalities so far as substantial right permits." Delineating in further detail the overall program of economic development, the instructions directed the commission to formulate and adopt appropriate "mining laws, homestead and land laws, general transportation laws, and banking and currency laws."[19]

The McKinley–Root instructions to the Philippine Commission amounted, in effect, to a "patent-office" blueprint for constructing what the Americans took to be the political-legal framework of a modern society and modern development. The essentials were all there: the protection of private property, of investment and enterprise, and of individual liberty, under a rule of law suited to capitalist market relations, the establishment of public schools, the inauguration of civil government with appropriate legislative and fiscal powers, with courts of law, and with a bureaucracy based on civil service norms, and provision for increasing Filipino participation in self-government. As Root and McKinley stated in more general terms, "The great agency to bring industrial activity and awaken enterprise and prosperity and contentment to the country of the Philippines must be, not a military government, but the same kind of individual enterprise which has built up our own country."[20]

Principles or ideals often described as "Wilsonian" in US foreign relations were already established policies, regarded as practical and realistic, in the time of McKinley, Hay, and Root, and continued to be so in the administrations of Theodore Roosevelt and William Howard Taft. By the time Woodrow Wilson became president in 1913, what historians and others have thought to be uniquely or newly "Wilsonian" – markets and modernizing development, universal rights, liberties, and rule of law, self-government, representative democracy, and an internationalism of open trading relations and intergovernment cooperation for development and peacekeeping – was already a "tradition" in US foreign-policy making, or an "antiquity," as Walter Bagehot (the supreme realist and one of Wilson's favorite political-historical thinkers) might have phrased it. In other words, Wilson and Col. Edward M. House were not originators, but practitioners, of an already established US policy framework, although at an early stage of its global application, and acting (as did prior and subsequent leaders) with a need and an opportunity for initiative, improvisation, and innovation that, in their case, went with the circumstances of historical beginnings – the US as a great world power. That need and opportunity were already in play with McKinley, Hay, Root, Roosevelt, Taft, and Philander C. Knox, but moved to a higher level and a broader national and world canvas by the time of Wilson and House, which coincided as it did with World War I. Had the Great War erupted earlier, what we think of as "Wilsonianism" could as well have presented itself as "McKinleyanism," "Hayianism," "Lodgianism," "Rootianism," "TRianism," or "Taftianism." Admittedly, "Wilsonianism" has the better ring.[21]

An anecdote concerning the appointment of Root as secretary of war illuminates the intent of US policy at the time. Upon Root's learning, in the summer of 1899, that President McKinley wanted to appoint him, the New York Republican proreform leader and partner in the patrician "Wall Street" law firm of Root and Cravath demurred that he knew "nothing about war . . . [and] nothing about the army." McKinley conveyed to Root that the president was "not looking for any one who knows anything about war or . . . about the army," but "a lawyer to direct the government of these Spanish islands." The War Department was to be, in effect, and indeed in fact, the new US colonial office. On that basis, Root accepted the appointment, and he made a study of leading writings on colonial governments, especially those under British law. He quipped to Attorney-General John W. Griggs that they were about to form the "new law firm of 'Griggs and Root, legal advisers to the President, colonial business a specialty.'"[22] The anecdote is well known among scholars and oft-repeated, but together with the substance of the McKinley–Root instructions to the Philippine Commission, inter alia, its significance for the theme here invites particular notice: McKinley's appointment of Root, and also of Taft, signified his understanding, and that of US policy makers in general, of the close relationship between a capitalistic market system and the appropriate political-legal rule of law. By the same token, it signified the commitment to fostering what they regarded as a regime of modernizing political-economic development in US colonial policy.

CONANT'S APPOINTMENT

The McKinley–Root framework of government and modern development lacked, not necessarily in its principles but in its provenance, a firm foundation in the Philippine people. While some Filipinos preferred not to be modernized at all, and some not exactly in the American meaning of the term, most of those who composed the leadership of the multifaceted nationalist movement did want modern national development. It was an essential reason for their rebellion against Spain. But many of them preferred to provide for it themselves through the establishment of national independence and their own processes of government.

Philippine resistance to annexation by the US proved a stubborn obstacle to American plans for development. It is by now a familiar matter of history that the real "Spanish–American" war in the East was not Admiral Dewey's quick victory over the Spanish naval and land forces at Manila. It was the war of conquest waged by the US against the Philippine national movement and its declared statehood and military forces. The war is nominally dated 1899–1902, but substantial combat persisted for another decade, and recurrent armed conflict continued in ensuing years.[23] The war ravaged the economy. Agriculture suffered from land damage and disuse as well as from drought, locusts, and plague. By late 1902, about 90 percent of the islands' carabao, the draft animal essential to rice cultivation, perished from hostilities, neglect, and disease. The bitter and often brutal conflict gutted the labor force with continuing effect, especially as a result of the US military policy of at times relocating village populations, and of high Philippine casualties, which, out of a total population of about 8–9 million, included over 200,000 killed, either directly by the war, or indirectly from war-related disease, pestilence, malnutrition, and social dislocation.[24]

Apart from the devastating impact of the war, and compounded by it, there remained the serious impediments to development common to pre-industrial and nonbourgeois societies in general, and some that were specific to Philippine society. Lands held by the Catholic friars, for example, containing some of the best cultivable soil in the islands, would be subject to redistribution.[25] Roads and railways would have to be built, and telegraph and telephone lines installed, to furnish the islands' economy with a transportation and communications system suited to modern development. New harbor facilities would have to be built. Sewage, sanitation, and waterworks awaited construction, improvement, or repair. A civil service system was to be installed. School buildings would have to be repaired, built, or acquired, teachers recruited and paid, books suited to the propagation of a modern curriculum and the English language commissioned and bought.[26]

All these programs and projects would require financing, the success of which would depend upon the establishment of appropriate government fiscal institutions and practices, and the availability of private, especially foreign, capital. The monetary and banking systems, accordingly, would have to be reformed and developed to attract American and other foreign investment, and to provide the financial and credit instruments necessary to the growth of modern market relations, including those peculiar to modern fiscal operations.[27] For this purpose, in the midst of the war in the Philippines, and in the face of congressional inaction on the subject, the McKinley administration, in the summer of 1901, appointed Charles A. Conant to the position of Special Commissioner for Currency and Banking in the Philippines.

Conant and Secretary of the Treasury Lyman J. Gage had already been associates in public affairs and politics. Each enjoyed a widely respected reputation: Gage as the renowned Chicago banker and reform-minded civic leader, builder, and president of the First National Bank of Chicago; Conant as the eminent banking and financial authority, journalist, Washington correspondent since 1889 of both the New York *Journal of Commerce and Commercial Bulletin* and the *Springfield Republican* (Massachusetts), prolific author of influential articles appearing in both general and scholarly publications, on domestic and international monetary, banking, and political-economic affairs, including the broader subjects of imperialism and world politics, and as the author of the internationally influential treatise, *A History of Modern Banks of Issue*, published in 1896. Both Gage and Conant had been Gold Democrats earlier in the 1890s, and now both were serving the Republican McKinley administration. During his work with the Indianapolis Monetary Commission (IMC) as advisory executive secretary, Conant joined IMC chair Hugh H. Hanna (prominent Indianapolis machinery manufacturer and banker) and their IMC colleagues in conferring frequently with President McKinley, Secretary Gage, other cabinet officers, and members of Congress, in the drafting of the Gold Standard Act of March 14, 1900.[28] Conant and Gage testified at congressional hearings, at times together, in the political mobilization led by the IMC and the McKinley administration that resulted in the passage of the act.[29]

In the fall of 1900, just after the multipower military intervention had lifted the Boxer siege of the legations in Peking, Secretary of War Root requested advice from Gage on Philippine monetary and banking affairs. Gage consulted Conant. Conant prepared a short, five-page letter-memorandum to Gage, which Gage relayed to Root. The following summer, 1901, Root sent Conant to the Philippines as special commissioner for currency and banking.[30]

Root's review of Conant's credentials in his letter of introduction to Taft, in July 1901, is of interest for what the secretary chose to include, because it indicates a significant sphere of mutual acknowledgment, liaison, and shared bodies of assumptions, ideas, and knowledge. He told Taft that Conant had been "for some years" the Washington correspondent of the New York *Journal of Commerce*, that he had "made a special study of banking and finance," and that he was the author of both *A History of Modern Banks of Issue* and *The United States in the Orient*, the latter being the collection of essays, published as a volume the previous year, on the relation between modern capitalism and imperialism, and its implications for world politics and US foreign-policy making. Root also noted that Conant had "written frequently on financial and economic subjects for the leading periodicals and economic quarterlies," and that he had been "connected with the Executive Committee of the Indianapolis Monetary Commission, which had so much to do with the enactment of the gold standard act of March 1900." Root informed Taft that Conant "enjoys to a high degree the confidence of the Secretary of the Treasury [Gage], who consulted him last year when called upon by me for advice regarding the coinage question raised by your report." Conant was to "consult with you and report to me," Root told Taft, concerning a plan for a Philippine monetary and banking system, although it was "of course desired that the conclusions reached be such as you approve."[31]

CONANT'S MISSION

Conant's letter-memorandum to Gage in October 1900, had addressed (1) the general problem he defined as the dislocation of exchange relations between the industrial gold-currency and the agrarian silver-currency countries of the world; and (2) the specific problem of a temporary scarcity in the Philippines of Mexican silver currency, which had long served as a principal circulating medium in East Asia, and had become the archipelago's major circulating currency.

The general dislocation of exchange relations stemmed from silver's steady long-term decline in gold value – about 50 percent – since the 1870s, silver's incessant short-term fluctuations in gold value, and the resulting instability of exchange ratios between silver- and gold-based monetary units. Silver depreciation inhibited the export of goods, services, and capital from the industrial to the nonindustrial countries, by making the exported goods and services more expensive in local currency, and by the risk of losing capital, profit, and salary when funds accrued in local silver currencies were exchanged for gold currencies. Silver depreciation also disrupted government fiscal operations by making it more difficult for the local government to pay gold obligations with revenues collected in local currencies; it thereby had the correlated effect of burdening economic activity with higher taxes, and retarding development projects by increasing the risk of default in repayment of loans, and in any case by raising the cost of borrowing and diminishing access to investment funds in capital markets.

As to the specific problem, the swelling exchange activity in northern China, during the powers' military intervention against the Boxers, temporarily interrupted the long-term trend with a sudden rise in the gold value of silver currency in eastern Asia. As the demand for the Mexican dollar, and its value, rose in northern China, the coin drained from the Philippines to the mainland, and this in turn enhanced its scarcity and value in the islands.[32] The branches of the two British banks in the Philippines – the Hongkong and Shanghai Banking Corporation (today's HSBC), and the Chartered Bank of India, Australia and China – which had previously agreed to exchange two Mexican dollars for one US gold dollar, now demanded more than one US dollar (about US$1.04), and the Spanish-Filipino Bank (Spanish Catholic Church-owned) and the Manila merchants followed suit, thereby diminishing the purchasing power of US soldiers, officials, and civil servants, and burdening government fiscal operations in the Philippines.[33]

In either the general or the specific case, instability of currency exchange was the problem. In advising Gage, Conant noted that "a proper solution" would both "provide an adequate supply of money" and "establish a fixed relation between the money of the islands and gold." For this twofold purpose, Conant recommended in outline the system he would later work out in detail – a Philippine silver currency tied to gold at a fixed value, not a gold standard as such, but what he and others designated a gold-exchange standard. A direct gold standard, he believed, would yield a high-value monetary unit unsuited to the lower scale of prices and wages in a nonindustrial society like the Philippines. Conant cited, as successful examples of the gold-exchange standard, the currency systems that had recently evolved and become institutionalized in British India and had been placed in use since the 1870s in Java of the Netherlands East Indies.[34]

From Manila, Governor Taft had been repeatedly reporting to Secretary Root on the urgency of currency reform. Root approved, and sent to Taft, Secretary Gage's gold-exchange recommendation based upon Conant's memorandum. Taft agreed with Conant's plan, telling Root, it "should take effect promptly."[35]

Congress, however, could not yet be brought to act further on Philippine affairs. The Boxer crisis subsided, and silver currency resumed its long-term decline in gold value, with its disruptive impact on trade, investment, and government fiscal operations. By the summer of 1901, the War Department and the Philippine Commission were still urgently seeking a remedy. Conant advised Lt. Col. Clarence R. Edwards, chief of the War Department's Bureau of Insular Affairs (effectively, the new colonial office), that the Philippine monetary system "should be dealt with by definite legislation" by Congress, to "enable capitalists to know in what form of money debts would be contracted and discharged," because until "certainty is established by law, prudent investors will be chary of venturing their capital largely in the islands." Permanent monetary stability was "absolutely essential to invite large investments and the projection of railroads, manufacturing enterprises and other measures for the rapid development of the islands."[36]

Conant noted that his gold-exchange plan already had the approval of Gage, Root, and the Philippine Commission, that "the principles" of the system were well known, and that therefore there really was no technical need for a "special investigation." Nevertheless, for *political* reasons, Conant advised, it would be useful and probably necessary to send "a trained observer" to the Philippines, who would gather detailed information on the ground, draw up "a special report" suited to "concentrating the attention of Congress," and "appear before the proper Committees of Congress, explain his project, and answer questions." Such an expert would have with Congress "at least an appearance of greater authority" than a department officer "who had not made local inquiries on the subject." In effect, Conant here wrote his own instructions for his mission to the Philippines.[37]

Conant arrived in Manila on September 6, 1901, and began work extending over the next six weeks. This period coincided in its first days with the assassination of President McKinley (who was shot and wounded at the Pan-American Exposition in Buffalo, New York, on September 6, and died on September 14), and the accession of Theodore Roosevelt to the presidency. During this time of national trauma in the US and intensive military conflict in the Philippines, Conant proceeded with his work.[38]

On September 17, Conant began conferences with Philippine Commissioner Henry C. Ide, who was serving as Secretary of Finance and Justice of the Philippine government (note the combined office). On the basis of Conant's plan, together they drafted the provisions of currency and banking legislation. On September 23 and 24, Conant held hearings, at which representatives of the banks in Manila testified. The next day, Conant met with the Philippine Commission to complete in detail the currency bill, and on the following morning, September 26, they completed the banking bill.

By September 28, Governor Taft informed Conant that he, Taft, had written to Secretary Root that the Commission approved "in principle and in detail" both the currency and banking measures as drafted in the previous days' sessions, and subsequently it officially endorsed them in its annual report to the secretary of war.

Conant then went to Hong Kong where he met with Sir Thomas Jackson, head of the Hongkong and Shanghai Banking Corporation, F. H. Whitehead, head of the Hong Kong branch of the Chartered Bank, and other officers of the two banks, to discuss, as Conant put it, "general monetary conditions in the East," and to elicit their views, and solicit their banks' cooperation, respecting Philippine monetary and fiscal affairs. Conant departed Hong Kong on October 7 and arrived back in Manila on October 9, and he resumed advisory work with the Philippine Commission until October 16, when he departed for Japan.

In 1897, the Japanese government had converted the nation's monetary standard from silver to gold, financing the change with the indemnity extracted from China (200 million Haikwan Taels, about US$100 million) after the Sino-Japanese War of 1894–1895. In his capacity as an emissary of the US government, Conant wanted to confer with Japanese government and financial leaders about their experience with the monetary conversion and its impact on Japan's international trade and inflow of foreign capital, and also about Japan's prospective trade relations with the Philippines. On October 29, he held talks in Tokyo with Minister of Finance Count Matsukata Masayoshi, with other government officials, and with vice-governor of the Bank of Japan Korekiyo Takahashi, who in ensuing years would serve at different times as Japan's minister of finance and prime minister. Conant returned to the US from Japan, arriving in Washington, DC, on November 21, 1901, where he submitted his report, drafted on the voyage home, to Secretary Root.

These ostensibly tedious details of Conant's itinerary, ready access, and activity, among high government and financial officers indicate his senior standing in the policy-making function. His work, without specific instructions, at Manila, under the jurisdiction of the War Department, and his discussions at rather short notice, at Hong Kong and Tokyo, in foreign countries, and thus under the jurisdiction of the State Department, indicated an acknowledgment of his authority among the high Philippine and foreign leaders, and bespoke the implicit consent, and therefore the confidence, of Secretaries Root and Hay, of Governor Taft, and, by implication, of Presidents McKinley and Roosevelt.

Toward the end of Conant's work in Manila, Taft wrote to Root that he had "no doubt" that Conant would be "exceedingly useful" in helping to get congressional approval of the currency and banking measures, and that in addition, Conant "would be very efficient in giving us information in respect to other legislation." (Conant had advised the commission also on tariff and other matters, while in Manila.) In dealing with Congress in general, and with "the prominent members of the House and Senate," Taft confided, "Any arrangement that you [Root] think it wise to make with him of course we should be glad to carry out," for, Conant had been "exceedingly useful to us in the matter of coinage and banking and is a remarkably clear headed writer."[39]

CONANT'S REPORT: DEVELOPMENTAL
CAPITALIST IMPERIALISM

Conant's itinerary indicated the broader international context of his Philippine mission. On the one hand, the colony's affairs could not be addressed most effectively without reference to larger international relations. On the other, Philippine affairs formed an important component of a general US objective of constructing a global system of investment and trade that could expand and deepen markets for industrial countries' surplus goods and capital through the political-economic development of nonindustrial countries and their evolution toward becoming modern societies. In addressing the specific Philippine situation, Conant's report to Secretary Root also embodied the larger general objective.

The report may be read as a short treatise on the economic development of an undeveloped, or less developed, country (in that now-familiar term): the monetary, banking, financial, and fiscal infrastructure that industrial capitalist countries needed to install in nonindustrial and largely noncapitalist countries to place the latter on the road to becoming modern "market societies." This was the substance of the developmental imperialism distinctive to modern industrializing capitalism advocated by Conant, whether or not this new imperialism took the form of annexationist colonialism – itself a form becoming inessential to the substance. Conant dealt in detail with basic monetary and banking conditions of such modernization, and these in turn as key components of linkage into an international investment system, upon which sustained modern development depended. In providing the means of exchange, credit, investment, and trade, modern monetary and banking facilities at the same time implied the establishment of corresponding laws and institutions appropriate to securing property rights and contractual and other market relations, along with a government itself under the law and willing and able to make and enforce the appropriate laws and adopt complementary fiscal and administrative practices – the establishment, in short, of the rule of law.[40]

The parallels – or lines of continuity – with post-World War II events are evident: from Bretton Woods' IMF and World Bank, to GATT and the WTO, from the political-legal-economic restructurings in post-war Germany and Japan, to post-Cold War restructurings in Russia, eastern Europe, and China, from negotiations and arrangements made with respect to the monetary, banking, and fiscal crises in the 1990s in Mexico, southeast Asia, Russia, and South America, to attempts at institutional reforms and restructurings in Afghanistan, Central Asia, and Iraq, in 2002–2006. Many of the issues and reforms recently at hand, and at controversy, are essentially of the same kind as those addressed by US leaders about 100 years ago. They are the nuts and bolts, the contents and processes in detail, of those evolving trends in twentieth- and twenty-first-century world affairs often generally referred to as the "Open Door World," the "American Century," or "Globalization." Such terms as "developed," "less developed," "undeveloped," "civilized," "advanced," and "backward," as well as such terms as "modern," "pre-modern," "modernization," and "rule of law," which were taken to designate the extent of a society's equivalence or nonequivalence with modern industrial society, or, "the civilized world," came into routine use in public, scholarly, and policy-making discourse in the US, in the period of about the late 1890s and the early years of the twentieth century.[41]

In the immediate and longer-term shaping of twentieth-century US foreign-policy making, Conant ranked among the more influential and sophisticated thinkers who gave these terms, and related concepts, their meaning, currency, and impact. That is to say, he worked in leading government and nongovernment roles among those in the emerging social-institutional milieu that was reconceptualizing, reorienting, and reorganizing the modern US political economy and the US role in world affairs. In this work, he wrote policy-forming state papers, helped draft or promote laws in both domestic and international affairs, and published several books and countless articles, editorials, and essays in journalistic, trade, and scholarly publications. He engaged in continuous consulting, planning, and policy-forming activity at senior political and investment-banking levels, and he often testified before congressional committees. For more than a decade (1889–1901), he had also been one of the leading and well-connected Washington correspondents in financial, business, and political affairs, domestic and international.[42] He became an officer (1902–1906) of one of the larger New York investment banking houses, the Morton Trust Company (an analogue with today's Goldman Sachs), while continuing with his writings and his policy-forming work. As a matter of course, in these activities, Conant engaged in political, professional, intellectual, and personal relations with senior and lesser governmental, political, and business leaders, with editors of the prominent financial and business publications and the broader press, and with highly placed academic and nonacademic intellectuals, including those noted for their policy-related work in political-economy and monetary affairs, like Jeremiah W. Jenks of Cornell, J. Laurence Laughlin of the University of Chicago (who, with input from Conant, wrote the final report of the Indianapolis Monetary Commission), Arthur Twining Hadley (professor, then president) of Yale, Jacob Hollander of The Johns Hopkins University, Joseph F. Johnson of the University of Pennsylvania and later of the NYU School of Finance, Brooks Adams (fellow-Quincy-Bostonian and sometime Washingtonian), and Horace White, monetary authority and editor of the New York *Evening Post* (originally founded by Alexander Hamilton, today's *New York Post*). An understanding of US foreign-policy making in the years of Presidents McKinley, Roosevelt, Taft, and Wilson, without reference to Conant and his role, is like an understanding of US foreign-policy making in the years of Presidents Nixon and Ford without reference to Henry Kissinger and his role; and retrieving a fuller understanding of the earlier period, formative as it was, may enrich and deepen our understanding of the later.[43]

American leaders decided to annex the Philippine archipelago not for its own economic significance as such, much less for some abstract moral, religious, imperial-chauvinist, or dream-fed gratification, but as we have seen, for its strategic location, given its proximity to China, Japan, and southeastern Asia, that is, to the world's greatest arena of prospective modernizing development. Once the Central American isthmian canal were built, the Philippines with Manila would complete the chain of bases serving the projection of power and safeguarding the sea lanes connecting the East and Gulf Coasts of the United States, via the Caribbean

Sea, with the lands of the Pacific Ocean and East Asia. The Caribbean region, as Alfred Thayer Mahan was not alone in advising, would be America's Mediterranean Sea and Near East, in the sense that it would be its vital link to Asia via the isthmian canal, just as the Mediterranean and the Ottoman Near East were Britain's and Europe's vital link to Asia via the Suez Canal and the Near East land bridge. A world power had to be an Asian power, and, for the US, that required the link and the chain.[44]

Nevertheless, American leaders could not justify to themselves or, as they believed, to the world, grabbing a colony of such large dimensions simply to satisfy America's own strategic interests. If the motive for taking the Philippines was strategic, the justification in their own minds had to be developmental as well – contributing to the construction of the global system of modern political economy. This meant not only the strategic role of the Philippines in the work of construction, but also it meant bringing the benefits of modern capitalist development to the Philippines, which, in the Americans' view, necessarily included the blessings of liberty, education, and eventual democratic self-government. Hence the detail in the framework of Philippine government and socioeconomic development laid down in the McKinley–Root instructions to the Philippine Commission, and the viewpoint expressed in the instructions that such development would be the lasting justification of the American annexation.[45]

Conant's report, in embodying this developmental outlook, which he himself had been playing such a large role in formulating and disseminating, stated plainly that the recommended currency and banking institutions would "hold out the inducement to the large investment of American capital so essential to the prosperity of the country [the Philippines] and *the justification of American sovereignty* both to the people of the islands and the citizens of the United States."[46]

As before in his published writings and policy-forming activity, Conant noted that the monetary division of the world between the gold-standard industrial countries and the silver-standard nonindustrial countries obstructed the transfer of surplus capital from capital-rich to capital-scarce countries, interfered with the development of the non-industrial societies, and therefore also disrupted the continuing growth, development, and prosperity of the industrial societies. Worldwide development and prosperity required a global monetary system, and with it the spread of a strong banking and credit system, the prerequisite of which, in the current historical circumstances, was placing the currencies of the nonindustrial countries on a gold-based standard. Citing the recent experience of other less developed countries in their adopting a gold standard, particularly Russia in 1896, under Minister of Finance Count Sergei Witte's leadership, and Japan in 1897, Conant observed that just as thereafter "the influx of foreign capital was great and rapid" into both countries, with a corresponding invigoration of industrial development, so the installation of a Philippine gold-based currency "would promote the investment of capital in the Philippines and thereby stimulate their industrial progress." In general, Conant stated, "An important reason for the adoption of the gold standard by any undeveloped country is the inducement held out for the investment of capital there."[47]

Given a basic goal of modern progress, a silver currency in the Philippines without a fixed relation with gold, Conant held, was "hostile" not only "to the development of American trade" with the Philippines, but also therefore "to the best interests of the islands." Traders and investors did not want their capital or profits "swallowed up by fluctuations in the gold value of silver." This was part of the general problem of "the dislocation of exchanges" between the silver- and gold-currency countries, due to which "the accumulated capital of the great civilized countries has in recent years refused to seek investment in silver countries." If the congestion were to be relieved and development activity facilitated, Conant noted, "it is absolutely essential that monetary legislation, as well as that regarding the sanctity of contracts and the security of property, should be such as to attract the investors of these countries." Indeed, Conant emphasized, "The possession of a sound and sufficient currency is one of the most essential factors in the industrial progress of any community, because the state of the currency affects all classes of business transactions and every individual." Hence it was that, given the protection of contracts and property, "the proper regulation of the currency is more important than the regulations governing almost any other single branch of public administration or those affecting any one of several industries." Conant noted that as the "great majority of trading nations" had by then "adopted the gold standard," gold had become "by a process of natural selection . . . the money of international trade and the standard by which value is measured throughout almost the entire commercial world." It was, therefore, "one of the most important conditions of the progress of the islands that the currency system should be such as to attract American and foreign capital by the assurance that investments there can be realized upon at any time in the standard money of the world." The Philippine case, like that of Russia and Japan, exemplified the general proposition that, as Conant formulated it, "Experience has demonstrated that capital seeking investment can be attracted in no other way than by the adoption and maintenance of the gold standard."[48]

Historical context here is important in grasping, without anachronistic distortion, Conant's meaning and the substance of US policy embodied in Philippine currency and banking reform. As with his policy-making colleagues, Conant was historical and pragmatic in his economic thinking, not a doctrinal "gold bug." Still less was he an old-fashioned believer in "free-market" laissez-faire or in Say's-Law equilibriums (or Bastiat's harmonies), which he himself had taken a prominent lead in pointedly criticizing and rejecting as (1) out-of-date thinking in an age of the large-scale industrial economy with huge fixed investments and massive labor concentrations, and as (2) associated politically with obsolete Gladstonian Liberalism in Britain and equally obsolete Cleveland Democracy in the US. In a newer-fashioned phrasing, Conant's writings were "on the cutting edge" in his times, in treatment of the corporate reorganization of the property-production system, modern capital and credit markets, assets-based bank-note currency, central banking, the business cycle and crises, marginal-utility ("neo-classical") economic theory, and countercyclical monetary, banking, and fiscal policy. He was, indeed, a founder, in both thinking and activity, of the new "corporate-liberalism," or modern liberalism combining corporate-capitalism, imperialism, internationalism, post-imperialism, and social-democratic reform. In this sense, the erstwhile gold-Democrat Conant (like Lyman J. Gage and Franklin MacVeagh of Chicago) was a McKinley-Root-TR-Taft-Republican, and Woodrow Wilson was a Conant gold-Democrat (neither a Cleveland- nor a Bryan-Democrat).[49]

The key here, with respect to Philippine and broader global policy, was not the gold standard per se as an ontological absolute, but currency *convertibility* conducive to sustained long-term investment and development ("investments . . . can be realized upon at any time in the standard money of the world"). At that stage of history ("experience has demonstrated" – as a matter of "natural selection," that is, of evolutionary development), such convertibility required a gold-based currency – required in the sense that *in practice*, it could not be otherwise attained. Exchange fluctuations favored established short-term trading and its banking providers. Traders (both indigenous and foreign) could hedge against fluctuations, while the fluctuations also protected them against competitive, and especially developmental, investment, which could substantially change the patterns of trade. The banks profited from financing the trade and from hedging arbitrage. These interests of traders, their banks, and allied producers were hostile to the Conant-US program; their interests (and those of indigenous antimodernizing traditionalists) resided in sustained under-development corresponding with trading-production patterns of the older dynastic and commercial imperialism. The Conant-US program intended sustained development (including industrialization) through long-term investment and a transformative modernization.[50]

In more recent times, although gold remains a bellwether commodity, market development has been so great and so globally articulated as to be qualitatively new in depth and breadth, not only in goods, services, and capital, but also in money as such, so that an effectively reliable convertibility could and did become market-determined rather than gold-(precious-metal-) determined – but determined by a regulated, or admin-istered, market, not a "free market," regulated, that is, in part by parties in the market (e.g., options, derivatives, hedging arbitrage, holding secu-rities on various markets), and in part by cartel-like operations of central banks, and government fiscal actions, affecting interest rates and money supply. Global market-determined convertibility – the "market stand-ard," or the "information standard" – has become expressed in US dollar equivalency and serviced by US dollar reserves ("the standard money of the world") – although to some growing extent, expressed also in Euro equivalency, or in a market-currency basket, and conceivably in the not-too-distant future, in a yuan equivalency.[51] Sudden devaluations do occur with market-determined convertibility, as with the old silver–gold dichotomy, but by and large, the managed float, along with prolonged trade imbalances, persistent growth differentials among national econo-mies, interest-rate adjustments, sustained capital transfers, and local epi-sodic crises quarantined and treated by the IMF or by other international finance, have replaced metal (gold) shipment, steep price-deflation, trade balancing, and sharp widely spread investment–employment cycles. This pattern differs substantially from that of the gold-standard international system (with its "booms and busts") of the 1870s–1890s, and although it is fashionable to say that the world economy of that earlier period was equally or more global, the late twentieth-/early twenty-first-century glo-balization, in scale and scope, and in developmental impact *within* soci-eties around the world, is of a different order of magnitude and of kind altogether. How durable it is remains to be seen – although the earlier gold-standard system did not itself last very long, while having a lasting impact, both constructive and catastrophic.

A convertible, gold-based currency was a necessary condition of devel-opment, but to make it fully effective as a medium of circulation serving modern market development, Conant emphasized, the banking system also needed to be more highly developed. Two banking functions, in particular, he advised, were needed in the Philippines, namely, issuance of bank-notes fixed in value to the gold-based monetary standard, and mortgage banking. Each would play its part not only in smoothing and quickening the channels of monetary exchange, trade, and investment, but also, in so doing, in dissolving archaic, and encouraging the rise of modern, production and exchange relations.

Bank-Note Issue. In augmenting the money supply and accelerating the spread of money-exchange relations, "a flexible and unfettered bank-note currency," Conant advised, would be essential to modern development. Issued against commercial assets (bills of exchange), a bank-note currency "is capable of indefinite expansion as the demand increases," and by its very operation becomes a driving force of further modernization, in its function as "a necessary forerunner of the system of checks and deposit accounts – those more perfect forms of credit which tend to supersede it in advanced commercial communities." As Conant had elsewhere noted, "The refinement in the use of credit is a pretty accurate measure of national economic progress."[52]

Bank-note circulation was particularly effective in promoting modern market relations in "an agricultural community," Conant explained. "It tends to convert the wealth of the community [e.g., crops, seed, livestock, equipment, storage] into a transferable form in much the same manner in which the ownership of a mill or a railroad is converted into transferable subdivisions by the issue of stocks and bonds." It thereby contributes to dissolving older production relations of immobility and dependency – debt peonage and sharecropping: "When an agriculturist is paid for his products in bank-notes instead of a credit upon the store where he sells them, he is emancipated from the control of such stores and can make his purchases . . . upon the best terms." Instead of "a vassal of the factor or the storekeeper he becomes an independent purchaser in the open market. It requires no argument to demonstrate how greatly the farmer profits by such conditions." Freeing the farmer in this way, moreover, "the benefits do not end with him." Growing money-market exchange would bring a rise and spread of wage–labor relations and with them modernizing development in general. In possession of "money instead of store credits," the farmer can "pay his hands in money." They in turn can "make purchases under more favorable conditions than before and . . . contribute their share toward that larger and freer movement of both capital and credit and the stimulus to productive industry which in every country have followed the introduction of a sufficient and elastic system of bank-note currency."[53]

Mortgage Banking. In the absence of sufficient bank credit, Philippine cultivators were captives of a monopolistic marketing system controlled by finance companies that obstructed agricultural investment and development. Cultivators, as Conant explained, needed "the means of acquiring good seed, draft animals, and modern tools," for which a loan system was indispensable. The finance companies imposed usurious interest rates of 25–40 percent, and they also controlled the purchase and marketing of the crops at prices they fixed, thereby subjecting the cultivators to a double exploitation. Mortgage banking could supplant the finance companies with more plentiful loan capital at efficient rates of interest, and thereby join bank-note issue in freeing the cultivators from archaic debt, pricing, and marketing relations.[54]

Mortgage banking would further contribute to development by the oversight role that the modern bank routinely assumed with its borrowers. For example, Conant noted, although direct management of a sugar plantation "would not fall within the proper function of a bank," nevertheless "an enterprising American bank would probably find little difficulty in persuading American capitalists to undertake management under conditions which would ensure large profits and relieve the bank of serious risk." As with Americans so with Filipino cultivators and capitalists: they would work the lands "under modern conditions of culture – with improved machinery and without the crushing burden" of excessive interest rates. In serving modern development, a sound currency combined with bank-note issue and mortgage banking, Conant concluded, "will greatly relieve the present condition of borrowers in the Philippines," at the same time "afford profits far in excess of those which are usually earned" in the US, and therefore "will do much to promote the contentment of the [Philippine] people and consolidate American influence in the Philippines."[55] Modernizing economic development and successful US colonial authority went hand in hand.

Conant's currency and banking proposals assumed three essential conditions in the relations he anticipated between capital-surplus and capital-scarce countries: (1) corporations would serve as the prevalent agents of capital transfer; (2) the net flow of wealth, initially and for some time, would be *to* the less developed country, in the form mainly of capital goods associated with modern agricultural and industrializing development; (3) the currency system had to secure stability of exchange even with sustained current account deficits on the part of the less developed society.

Conant succinctly interrelated the three conditions: "If American capital comes to the Philippines in large amounts for investment," it would be "chiefly in the form of agricultural, mining, and manufacturing machinery, railway equipment and supplies for the maintenance of laborers" (including engineers and managers). "Investments of capital in undeveloped countries are inevitably made in these forms." It followed that "So long as these investments exceed the demands upon the islands there will be an excess of imports of merchandise, which will not require to be paid for by a countermovement of merchandise or gold." Rather, the return to the investors "will be in the form of printed certificates of bonds or shares, whose issue will not for the time being impose any burden for repayment of the principle upon the productive resources of the islands." Stability of exchange would remain secure, and the overall result would be that, "Contented with a small portion of the net produce of the islands in the form of interest, the whole body of investors, including those entering the market with new savings, will steadily send more to the islands than they take away." In this way of thinking, capitalist imperialism of the modern corporate type was by its very nature developmental.[56]

This was the distinctive mark of the new capitalist imperialism that Conant and his colleagues had in mind, in contrast with the older extractive, commercial, and settler imperialisms of the past. Thus, even with, or precisely because of, trade deficits involving massive imports from the industrial society, the security and stability afforded by appropriate government and laws, corporate enterprise, and a sound currency and banking system, "will tend to keep capital in the islands and encourage its continuous investment," as well as "the investment of the interest upon it in new enterprises." This would, in effect, mean "the continuous reinvestment of capital" in Philippine development. The general idea was not the extractive plunder of the colony's resources, nor the restriction of the colony's investment opportunities and activities, but the venting of the industrial society's surplus wealth upon the colony, with the growing capacity of the colony to develop modern market and class relations, augment its wealth, produce and diversely invest its own surplus, and increasingly assume the status of a modern developing country with growing functions of self-government. *Ex imperio postimperium.* Currency and banking reform was a critical component – a sine qua non – of the larger work of political and economic development.[57]

TESTIFYING

Beginning in late November 1901, Conant assumed the home-side of his mission. He worked with Root and the War Department, conferred with leaders of Congress and of public opinion, published supportive journalistic and scholarly articles of his own, arranged for publication of articles and editorials by others, and testified at congressional hearings. Governor Taft returned to the United States to do his part with Congress.[58]

On the last day of January, and during February 1902, Taft gave detailed testimony before the Senate Committee on the Philippines. Although chaired by the Republican internationalist and proimperialist Senator Lodge, the committee's members included Bryanite and Republican antiannexationists, as well as proannexationist Republicans and Democrats.[59]

Concerned as he was to prod Congress into passing an overall Philippine civil government act, it is significant that Taft devoted much of his testimony to matters of Philippine development – currency and banking, land disposal, agriculture, tariffs, road building, railroad construction, mining, corporation charters, franchises, and primary and vocational education. Taft also placed political and governmental questions in the context of Philippine development. He strongly emphasized that Philippine economic development, largely with US capital, was crucial to the *political* success of the US colonial administration. Explicitly and frequently, he cited Conant and drew upon his advice, ideas, and writings. For example, in discussing the currency and banking measures, and their importance to Philippine development, Taft specifically cited and discussed Conant's views, and directly told the senators that Secretary Root "was good enough to send us Mr. Conant who is a banking expert," and confirmed that Conant had drafted the currency and banking parts of the bill, which Taft and the whole Philippine Commission approved and hoped Congress would pass.[60]

Taft also relied on Conant for the larger picture of modern imperialism. Senator Charles A. Culberson, Texas Democrat and critic of the administration's Philippine policy, suggested that growing military costs threw doubt on the wisdom of annexing the Philippines. He noted that "the naval budget of Great Britain is so great" mainly due to "the number of colonies she has and their distance" from England. Taft conceded that although this was "a naval question," on which he was not an expert, "It may be that, having colonies, we shall require additional naval force," but given current world politics and the growing US interest in China and East Asia, he argued that "probably we should have a naval station there [Manila] at any rate, and that would require a naval force to protect it." All this, however, Taft held, was secondary to "the advantages that a country like England or a country like the United States would get from colonies of all descriptions," which were "not confined to mere trade . . . and are not measured by the mere cost of administration of the colonies." The main point, rather, was this: "The opportunities for investment under a secure government, under a friendly government, and the extension of those investments for the benefit not only of the islands or the colonies where the investments are made, but also for the benefit of the investors, is one exceedingly great," and, Taft added, "I do not know any place in which it is better shown than it is in the book of Mr. Conant on the United States in the Orient." As Conant had emphasized in his essays in the book, so now did Taft, that it was not simply trade that stood at the heart of modern imperialism, although trade could be expected to grow substantially, but the global extension of the modern capitalist investment system, or, in the specific case of the Philippines, as Taft phrased it, "the opportunity of investing surplus capital under the protection and security of your own Government."[61]

Senator Lodge invoked the strategic implications of great power rivalries, in arguing against Philippine independence at this time, but in addressing the question, Taft brought the matter back to Philippine development with US capital, as the major concern. Senator Lodge asked, "Do you think . . . we having withdrawn and a state of anarchy having arisen, it would probably lead to the partition of the islands among other powers?" Taft responded that it was "a question of opinion as to the interest which foreigners take in the islands," and that foreigners "whom I know in Manila" called the Philippines "the gems of the Orient." He noted the "interest that Japan has taken in the islands," and observed that other powers' intent in the Philippines "may be judged of by reference to the foreign capital invested there. The Germans have a great deal of capital [there]. The English have a good deal." Senator Louis E. McComas, Republican of Maryland, who had taught international law at the Georgetown University Law School, interjected, "What would happen to them if we withdrew?" Taft chose not to speculate on the action of other great powers, but instead centered his reply on the consequences for Philippine development. "Will not the insurrection come to an end; will not there be general peace and tranquility if you promise to give these people independence when they shall be fitted for it?" Put that way, Taft allowed, the proposition "seems to have a great deal of force." But the practical effect of even the promise of independence "would be exactly the opposite from that which the argument presupposes." Such a promise would "at once bring into a discussion of every issue the question whether now were not the people ready for independence," and that, Taft insisted, "would drive out capital; prevent capital from coming there; and upon the investment of capital, the building of railroads, the enlargement of the vision of the Filipino people, much of our hope of progress must depend."[62]

CONGRESS DISPOSES

Bringing Congress along on the Philippine currency and banking plans proved difficult. Congress included neither plan in the Philippine Civil Government Act that it did pass on July 1, 1902. Viewing the currency and banking proposals in some historical context may help better to understand the disposition of Congress.

The gold-exchange currency plan would establish, at a 32:1 ratio to gold, a silver peso fixed at a value of one-half US gold dollar, as the basic monetary unit of the Philippines. The new peso currency and the US dollar would have exclusive legal-tender status in the Philippines. The Philippine government would maintain the peso's fixed value, (1) by controlling and limiting the coinage, and (2) by providing for a sufficient gold-reserve fund held in Manila and New York. Payments of pesos for gold exchange (US dollars) would withdraw pesos from circulation in the Philippines, and conversely, payments of gold currency into the fund (or banks) for pesos would release them into circulation. In its international exchange transactions, the system would work automatically, as if it were a direct gold-standard system, in regulating the Philippine money supply, and keep the silver peso fixed at its par gold value.[63]

The banking plan would amend the US national banking law to allow national banks to issue circulating notes against commercial assets (bills of exchange). The existing law permitted national banks to issue such notes only against US government bonds. The plan would also amend the national banking law to allow a national bank to establish branches abroad (in the Philippines and anywhere else), and also, for purposes of international transactions, in the US. Under the existing law, national banks were not allowed to branch at all, neither in the US nor abroad. The banking proposals served two correlated purposes, namely, (1) that US banking and business capital should become globally competitive, and (2) that if the Open Door were to apply to the Philippines, US capital should be made globally competitive in this way in order to play a strong role in Philippine economic development, and not risk losing to foreign banks and capital control over the economy of the US' own colony.

Although the currency and banking proposals together applied to the Philippines, they also served the larger purpose of preparing for a more effective US engagement in constructing a new global system of investment and trade, and revising domestic US law and institutions for that purpose. Aside from their strategic role, the Philippines would serve as a component of the US engagement in the global system, as well as a catalyst of reform within the US. If Conant's gold-exchange currency plan were adopted, it could be invoked as a model for application to other nonindustrial countries, for example, China, in bringing them more strongly into the international investment system, with the US playing a leadership role. If the banking plan were also adopted, the Philippine component, although small, might nevertheless become a vital hinge on an open door through which US banking power, and the enterprise served by it, could flow to all points in Asia and indeed to other parts of the world as well. The Philippines would not only be a laboratory and a showcase for a globally relevant currency reform, but also a base for US capital in the Open Door world that US leaders were seeking to construct. The symbolism – or entelechy – in the spiral of historical events is arguably a sign of the Providential (or Intelligent Design): from the Spanish Inquisition and expulsion of Islam, to a Spanish world ascendancy and the Habsburg King Philip II (hence, Philippines), the doomed Armada, and the subsequent British world ascendancy, to US birth from the British Empire, US expulsion of Bourbon Spain from North America (Louisiana, Florida), the Caribbean (Cuba, Puerto Rico), and the Pacific (the Philippines, Guam), US accession to the Philippines and containment there of both Catholic and Islamic power, and thickening US engagement with Mexico, to US alignment in world affairs with Victorian/Edwardian Britain against "old Europe" (Habsburgs, Bourbons, Hohenzollerns), and an emerging US world ascendancy.

In spite of the concerted efforts of Conant, Taft, Root, and the War Department, their Philippine currency and banking plans – whatever the case with world-historical entelechy – found a cold reception in Congress. The currency plan drew the hostility of silver interests and political silverites or inflationists, on the one hand, who wanted a Philippine silver-standard currency on a 16:1 basis, and of gold-standard purists, on the other, who wanted to extend the US currency system directly to the Philippines, as had been done with Puerto Rico and Hawaii, and thus without usefulness in broader global currency reform. The gold–silver battles in US politics, moreover, were still fresh in the public mind, and however much seemingly settled by the Gold Standard Act of 1900 and McKinley's second victory over Bryan later that year, continued to touch raw ideological nerves and inflame party politics. The banking plan encountered an intractable resistance from foes of a central bank system and more generally of centralized banking power, which, they believed, assets-currency bank-notes and branch banking would facilitate. These adverse views were widespread across party lines. They were strengthened by Conant's association with the plans (indeed, authorship), because he was well known as a leading advocate in domestic affairs of the gold standard, assets currency, branch banking, and the establishment of a central-bank system. Opponents of the plan in Congress, many of them chafing at their defeat in the money wars, were not prepared to change the national banking law at this time, and especially not in a direction being strongly pressed by gold-standard, "sound currency," advocates. They were particularly determined not to permit the accomplishment through the back door of colonial legislation what could not yet be attained through the front door of domestic banking legislation. Whatever the case with the Open Door, these two doors would remain shut. In words of recent usage, they would not let the imperialist tail wag the national dog.[64]

It was from political discretion, therefore, that neither Senator Lodge, as chair of the Senate Committee on the Philippines, nor Representative Henry A. Cooper, Republican of Illinois, as chair of the House Committee on Insular Affairs, would lend his name to Conant's draft bill on Philippine currency and banking. It went to Congress, on January 7, 1902, not with the prestige of a Lodge–Cooper bill, which Conant had hoped it might, but simply as a War Department bill that was also strongly urged upon Congress by the Philippine government, and was known to have been drafted in its essentials by Conant. Its legislative prospects, accordingly, were not bright.[65]

If the bill's currency part was warmly controversial in Congress, the banking part was too hot to handle. In the heat, Conant replaced assets- with bond-based note-issue. It was not enough. Leaders in both houses severed the banking section entirely from the draft legislation and buried it in committee. They indirectly dealt with banking facilities in the Philippines by the section in the Civil Government Act providing for a general chartering, franchising, and regulatory authority for the Philippine government. US national banks were thereby effectively excluded from operating in the Philippines, leaving the field to foreign banks, and to state-chartered and local Philippine-chartered banks.

Conant did not get the revision of the national banking law that he sought, but as US commissioner and special adviser to Governor Taft, for whom he subsequently drafted the Philippine banking legislation adopted under authority of the Civil Government Act, he did get from Congress, indirectly, the authority to give banks in the Philippines the power to issue assets currency and to establish branches both within the Philippines and elsewhere abroad. Conant, in effect, became Congress's designated lawmaker on banking in the Philippines and, by implication, worldwide outside the US. The state-chartered (Connecticut) International Banking Corporation (IBC), with its head office at No. 1 Wall Street, New York, with branches in Washington, DC, and San Francisco, and with a London office (at Threadneedle House, Bishopsgate), became the major US bank in the Philippines, competing against the Hongkong and Shanghai, the Chartered, and the Spanish-Filipino banks. The IBC established branches not only in Manila and Cebu in the Philippines, but also in Hong Kong, Canton, and Shanghai in China, in Singapore, in Calcutta and Bombay in India, in Yokohama and Kobe in Japan, in Mexico City and Monterrey in Mexico, and in Panama City in Panama. It also became the official fiscal agent of the US government in the Philippines, in China (particularly in handling the US portion of the indemnity funds), and in the Republic of Panama. The IBC became, in effect, the major US colonial bank, and Conant pointedly admonished its executives, if they wished to retain their bank's fiscal-agency status, not to put narrow commercial banking interests above broader US development objectives in the Philippines and globally. The Philippine government later chartered an Agricultural (mortgage) Bank (opened 1908–1909) along the lines Conant had recommended. But US-owned banking operations established in the Philippines were not great enough in prestige and capital to become the international banking base that Conant had in mind. US international banking power on that scale would have to await the passage of the Federal Reserve Act of 1913, permitting national banks to issue assets currency and to branch abroad (but not to branch within the US), an act that Conant played no negligible part in helping to formulate and pass.[66]

Congress included nothing at all in the Civil Government Act on a currency system for the Philippines, except to grant the Philippine government power to mint fractional coins (a power that Taft did not use, asking derisively, fractional of *what?*). Until February 1903, Congress was as little disposed to pass currency legislation along the lines proposed in the Conant plan as it had been to pass the banking legislation. International circumstances, however, involving falling silver prices and the prospect of extending the proposed Philippine gold-exchange model to other countries, in particular to Mexico and China, led to a shift of position in Congress sufficient to accomplish passage of the currency section of the original bill in essentially the form drawn by Conant, and known as the Philippine Coinage Act of March 2, 1903.[67]

The very next day, March 3, 1903, Congress passed a bill, previously sent in by President Roosevelt and Secretary of State Hay, for the establishment and funding of the Commission on International Exchange (CIE). Its mission was twofold: (1) to help Mexico convert its time-honored silver-currency system into a new gold-exchange system; and (2) with the Mexican government's cooperation, to negotiate with the major European powers, Japan, and China, on a plan for Chinese currency reform along similar lines. Upon passage of the CIE bill, Secretary Hay, in consultation with President Roosevelt, Secretary of War Root, and Secretary of the Treasury Leslie M. Shaw, appointed a three-member commission composed of the recent head of the Indianapolis Monetary Commission Hugh H. Hanna to serve as CIE chair, Conant (the two having worked together in the IMC), and Cornell professor of political-economy Jeremiah W. Jenks, a close adviser of Roosevelt since the latter's New York days, an expert in both corporate and monetary affairs, recently returned to the US from a mission as special commissioner of the War Department (Root) to investigate economic and monetary conditions in the Dutch and English colonies of eastern Asia, and who in that capacity and subsequently had already been working with Conant and Governor Taft on the Philippine gold-exchange currency project.[68]

What had happened to cause this dramatic turn of events?

US PHILIPPINE POLICY AND GLOBAL OBJECTIVES

In the previous summer and fall of 1902, Conant was still serving, at Root's request, as Special Commissioner of the War Department for Philippine affairs, but now from his new position, in New York City, since March 1902, as an executive (treasurer) of the Morton Trust Company, one of the larger Wall Street investment banking houses (former Republican US Vice-President Levi P. Morton, president), for which Root, in private life, acted as general counsel. Root and Conant continued to consult regularly, Root when in New York City conferring at times with Conant at the Morton Trust offices. In his dual government/banking capacity, Conant conducted talks on monetary and related affairs with leading New York bankers, with officers of the Guggenheims' American Smelting and Refining Company and of other "silver interests in the East" (as he designated them, meaning in New York), and with Mexican and Chinese government officers. From the summer to November of 1902, the London price of silver went into a precipitous 30 percent fall. During this time, too, there were increasing indications that Britain, having earlier placed India's rupee on a gold-exchange basis, was now moving toward expelling the Mexican silver dollar and establishing a gold-based currency in the Straits Settlements, including Singapore, and in the Federated Malay States, and that France might do the same in Indo-China. The silver interests and their congressional allies, who had effectively helped block the Philippine gold-exchange plan, now changed to supporting it as promising a steady source of demand for silver for coinage, especially if investment and trade were to increase with a widespread installation of the gold-exchange currency system, and therefore as a likely force for firming and stabilizing silver prices.[69]

In mid-November 1902, Conant alerted Secretary of State Hay "regarding a project which is receiving serious consideration by financiers here [New York] for the establishment of the gold standard in China." Conant added, "You will appreciate the great importance to trade of bringing the monetary system of China into harmony with that of the rest of the world." He arranged for a consultation with Hay in Washington "at some length," in order "to explain the project to you, and to learn what might naturally be expected from the diplomatic support of our government and possibly of Great Britain and Japan."[70]

By mid-December and the six weeks following into January 1903, the Mexican and Chinese governments submitted memoranda to Secretary Hay, most likely drafted for them by Conant, officially requesting the cooperation of the US government in reforming the Mexican and Chinese currency systems, and more broadly, in fixing the rate of exchange between the silver-currency and gold-currency countries of the world. The Mexican government of Porfirio Diaz, pressing its modernization program, particularly now under the leadership of *cientifico* Minister of Finance José Yves Limantour, concluded that both the health of Mexico's large silver industry and greater economic development through better terms of trade and an increasing inflow of foreign investment would best be served by converting the Mexican silver currency to a new gold-exchange basis, and working for similar monetary conversions in China and other silver-currency countries of the world. (Mexico's currency conversion would be completed in 1905, at about the same time as that of the Philippines, and with advisory assistance of Conant and Jenks.) The Imperial Government of China, for its part, had a huge international gold debt from the 1895 Japanese Indemnity and the 1901 Boxer Indemnity (the latter, £67.5 million, about US$330 million) and was interested in currency reform as a way of easing the burden of payments, although it remained resistant to free-flowing foreign investment and its modernizing implications. The US

was a principal "Indemnity Power," and it was also in the midst of negotiating with China the new commercial treaty of 1903 that included a
provision for Chinese currency reform.[71]

On January 29, 1903, President Roosevelt sent the Mexican and
Chinese memoranda to Congress, with Secretary Hay's covering letter
to him of the previous day. The president requested "sufficient powers to
lend the support of the United States" to Mexico and China in effecting
"such measures as will tend to restore and maintain a fixed relationship
between the moneys of the gold standard countries and the silver-using
countries." This resulted in the bill passed on March 3, 1903 to establish
the CIE, the day after the passage of the Philippine Coinage Act, followed
in April by Roosevelt and Hay appointing Hanna, Conant, and Jenks to
make up the commission.[72]

It was in this larger international context, developing strongly at the
end of 1902 and the opening weeks of 1903, that Conant's gold-exchange
plan attained adoption as the currency system of the Philippines, and at the
same time as a model for global application by the US in its foreign-policy
initiatives. Almost immediately upon the passage of the Philippine Coinage
and CIE acts, Conant went from New York, on March 5, 1903, to Mexico,
joining Jenks and Edward Brush, an officer (secretary) of the American
Smelting and Refining Company, for consultations with Finance Minister
Limantour and others on the currency reform project. Conant wrote to
Taft before departing that along with the shift of position by the silver
interests, "My active support of the project of Mexico and China for giving
stability to the currency of the silver countries also contributed towards
harmonizing all interests and making it possible to pass the Philippine
bill through the brief period available at the short session [of Congress]."
Along these lines, Conant subsequently wrote to Taft, in August 1903, at
the beginning of the plan's implementation in the Philippines, and as Taft
prepared to return to the US to succeed Root as Roosevelt's secretary of
war. Conant hoped for the same "support in the Cabinet" from Taft as
Root had given him, that is, as "my chief reliance in the plan upon which I
have been engaged for introducing into *China and other silver-using countries* the gold standard system of the Philippines."[73]

CONCLUSION: ORIGINS OF AN "AMERICAN CENTURY"

Secretary Root wrote to President Roosevelt in the summer of 1903, discussing the work of the CIE, which was then in the midst of its European
negotiations. "I think it is much to the interest of the United States," he

told Roosevelt, "to have the result which they are working for accomplished." He judged the project "quite practicable," and although "such things always require time," it would be "greatly to the credit of our country to have taken the lead in it." With China placed on the gold-exchange standard, Root observed, "It is virtually securing the adoption throughout the world of the same plan which we ourselves have already inaugurated in the Philippines."[74]

In US policy planning, the Philippine gold-exchange currency reform proceeded in the larger context of constructing a global system of investment, trade, and modern development, and it became a model for application in the construction work. Its phased installation in the Philippines, from August 1903 to April 1905, provided a learning laboratory for US policy planners in designing a currency-reform model, and in modifying and fine-tuning it in the light of actual experience. After the CIE concluded its negotiations in Europe (England, France, Germany, Holland, and Russia), Root and Roosevelt, with the cooperation of Secretary of State Hay and of Taft and the Philippine government, sent Jenks to China as the CIE's representative to negotiate directly with Chinese officials on the installation of a gold-exchange system in China.[75] En route, Jenks stopped in Manila, from December 23, 1903 to January 16, 1904, to advise and observe with respect to the work then proceeding in installing the gold-exchange system in the Philippines. He informed Taft, who was now in the US preparing to succeed Root as secretary of war, "I have already found enough new information which will have a direct bearing upon any new currency legislation for China to make my visit here of the greatest value in that connection." Similarly, a month later, from Shanghai, China, Jenks filed a fourteen-page report to Secretary Root (with a copy to Secretary Hay) on the Philippine currency situation, and noted, "I find that my observation of the experience in the Philippines in connection with the new monetary system has been of the greatest importance in connection with the work which I am to take up in China."[76]

US leaders applied the Philippine gold-exchange model to helping with currency reform in Mexico (1905),[77] Panama (1905), and Nicaragua (1912), in these years. They made the gold-exchange currency reform program, along with broader and correlated development programs, central to US objectives in China, through the work of the CIE, the terms of the US–China Commercial Treaty of 1903, and sustained programmatic efforts, including the Hukuang Railway, the Indemnity Remission, the Currency Reform and Manchurian Development project, the Four-Power and Six-Power consortiums, and persistent proposals for reforming the Chinese currency, banking, taxation, and fiscal systems, during the Roosevelt, Taft, and Wilson administrations, in pursuit of the broader global objective. The broader objective – with the modernizing development of a nationally unified China as key to it all – sought to replace closed colonial empires and exclusive spheres of interest with an open international system suited to a global network of investment and trade: what McKinley, Hay, Root, Conant, Roosevelt, Taft, Knox, Wilson, and others engaged in US policy planning were referring to in popular parlance as the "Open Door Policy," or, an "Open Door World," where *variable shares* in investment and trade, and in global political-economic competition and development more broadly, would replace *fixed spheres*, with their belligerent national-imperialist rivalries, and their recurrent wars, both small-scale and world-scale. This was the essence of the "Dollar Diplomacy" and "liberal internationalism" (including the "Fourteen Points," and the League of Nations proposal) historians have associated with presidents Taft and Wilson, respectively. Nevertheless, at this historical juncture, it was an "Open Door" policy still entwined with colonial possessions and an older imperialism, including the brutal conflict in the conquest of the Philippines by the US as a means to the end – albeit an imperialism moving, or being pushed and pulled, toward that of a modern corporate-capitalist type, and pointing to a post-imperialism future.

In US policy makers' thinking, moving toward an "Open Door" world would set the stage for worldwide modernizing development, and at the same time, initiate the political-economic basis of a peaceful system of world politics: this would be the progressive-beneficent meaning of an "American Century." It would cohere with a larger pattern of human evolution, not be exceptional to it; it would be *in* history, not utopia. Nevertheless, in replacing the age-old cycles of rising and falling empires with a cumulative process of global human development, although it would be based in past history, it would also be a departure from it, as with other historical turning points in the past: revolution born of evolution – a new yet manifestly destined freedom.

US rule did bring to the Philippines, at length, many aspects of modern development, by 1941 the most prosperous modernizing economy in Asia outside Japan, and effective self-government, and by 1946, in less than a half-century, national independence. The war of conquest, however, with its physical, psychical, and social destructiveness, and years of colonial denial of authentic self-government, distorted and retarded Philippine development in many directions (as may have occurred in similar or other directions with immediate independence and self-government after 1898). As with other countries, great and small, in the twentieth century, US activities and policies, although seeking and promising, and to no insignificant degree enabling and imposing, a worldwide spreading of modern development, could not prevent, and in significant ways contributed to, a century that was also filled with historically unprecedented violence and destruction, marked by two world wars, an epic "Cold War," many smaller wars, countless civil wars, genocidal mass murder and deportations, famine, and recurrent terrorist actions by states, and by nonstate organizations, secular and religious, approaching and feasibly in time reaching cataclysmic proportions even beyond those previously attained. Historical, all too historical.

At the first years of the twenty-first century, as a new age of the Pacific and Indian Oceans emerged, with an increasingly open (not "free" but open and regulated) post-imperialism-global investment and trading system developing strongly, continuously processing the combined characteristics of capitalism and socialism, and becoming institutionalized in the laws and public policies of developed and less developed countries alike, and also in international organizations (however flawed), and with China and India playing major and ever-growing economic and political roles, US long-term foreign-policy planning and objectives, stretching back to 1898, were attaining a fulfillment – with all the monetary, market, political, and military crises consonant with revolutionary change and counterrevolutionary resistance – not with a gold standard but with a surrogate US dollar standard (for the time being), and with what consequences or sustainability it remained to be seen. In this provisional fulfillment, the US–Philippine relationship following upon the US' war with Spain played no small historical role.

Notes

1. Lodge to Henry White (Secretary, US Embassy, London, also for Ambassador John Hay), August 12, 1898, at Allan Nevins, *Henry White: Thirty Years of American Diplomacy* (New York: Harper and Brothers, 1930), p. 137. See also, for discussion of these words and their context, Warren Zimmerman, *The First Great Triumph: How Five Americans Made Their Country a World Power* (New York: Farrar, Straus, and Giroux, 2002), p. 312. Zimmerman inadvertently conveyed Lodge's words incorrectly as "one of the world's great powers," instead of "one of the great world powers." The US had already been a great, but regional, power; now it had become a great world power. Lodge's words were historically precise. For McKinley's words to same effect, see Walter LaFeber, *The American Search for Opportunity, 1865–1913* (New York: Cambridge University Press, 1993), p. 178, also

chs. 7–10, Conclusion. Cf. Robert E. Hannigan, *The New World Power: American Foreign Policy, 1898–1917* (Philadelphia: University of Pennsylvania Press, 2002).

2. President McKinley sent his war message to Congress on April 11, 1898. After a week's debate, Congress passed a Joint Resolution authorizing war (including the Teller Amendment forbidding US annexation of Cuba), on April 19; McKinley signed it on April 20, and the US naval blockade of Cuba began on April 23. Congress formally declared war on April 25, 1898. Land combat in Cuba began after mid-June, the major battles around Santiago (San Juan Hill and others) beginning July 1. See Zimmerman, *First Great Triumph*, pp. 261–265, 277–279.

3. Awareness of this world history context among US policy makers, and across a larger public, may be viewed, e.g., in Hay's Assistant Secretary of State David Jayne Hill's published article in 1899, "The War and the Extension of Civilization," *Forum*, XXVI (February 1899), pp. 650–655 (at p. 651): "Conquered originally by a [Spanish] fleet sent out from Mexico in 1564, they [the Philippines] were a natural adjunct of her [Spain's] American possessions . . . For two hundred years the Philippines were a dependency of Mexico [with Manila as the major transit center between East Asia and Mexico, and thence to Europe]; trade and communication were forbidden except through Acapulco; and their government was administered by the Mexican viceroy and *audiencia*. So thoroughly were these islands identified with America by Spain, that not until 1764 was direct trade commenced between them and Europe by the circumnavigation of Africa. The loss of her continental possessions in America [1820s] left the Philippines in practical isolation from Spain until the opening of the Suez Canal [1869] brought Manila within thirty-two days' steam from Barcelona. [Par.] By another course of development, the feeble colonies planted on the Atlantic coast of North America have spread their civilization to the Pacific, and their institutions over the whole continent. Hawaii, colonized and developed by American enterprise, has become a part of our national territory. California, along whose coasts the Mexican galleons, laden with the treasures of the East on their way to Europe, sailed from the Philippines to Acapulco three hundred years ago, now carries on a great Pacific trade by steam. A submarine cable will soon connect our western shores with Asia; and an interoceanic canal, wedding the Atlantic and the Pacific, will not only shorten the sailing-distance between our coasts by 10,000 miles, but will bring Boston nearer than Liverpool to Polynesia, Japan, and North China."

4. Roosevelt to his sister, Corinne Roosevelt. Likewise, TR's immediate army superior, Gen. Leonard Wood, wrote to his wife: "Hard it is to realize that this is the commencement of a new policy and that this is the first great expedition our country has ever sent overseas [48 vessels carrying about 16,000 troops from Tampa, June 14, 1898] and marks the commencement of a new era in our relations with the world." The Roosevelt and Wood quotes, at Zimmerman, *First Great Triumph*, p. 275. It will be recalled that as assistant secretary of the Navy, TR had issued the official instructions to Adm. Dewey to take Manila; so he attended to the transformation at both ends of the New

World–East Asia connection. Regarding the New World end, cf. Walter Hines Page: "Cuba is the military key to the Gulf [of Mexico] and to the [future] Isthmian canal. Cuba will never be free to permit other governments to obtain a dominant influence there, by purchase, by treaty, or by occupation . . . no student of international, or military, or even financial affairs is likely to reach any different conclusion." W. H. Page, "The Future of Cuba," *The World's Work*, I: February 4, 1901, p. 362.

5. Hay to McKinley, July, 6 1898, at David Trask, *The War with Spain in 1898* (New York: Macmillan, 1981), p. 427. Cf. Zimmerman, *First Great Triumph*, p. 312. By September 1898, Hay had succeeded William R. Day as secretary of state. Day went to the Supreme Court, his own preference, upon appointment by McKinley.

6. Cf. Assistant Secretary of State David J. Hill, in December 1898: "The possession of the Philippine Islands brings the Government of the United States face to face with the political changes now taking place in the Chinese Empire. In addition to the French and English spheres of influence which have been long established, the territorial encroachments of Russia and the ambitions of Germany are conspicuous elements in the Eastern Question. The territory of the Chinese Empire is threatened with partition by the leading powers of Europe in a manner which promises a transformation of the map of Asia as complete as that which has taken place in Africa . . . the Government and people of the United States have important interests to maintain in the Chinese Empire, and cannot be indifferent to the destiny of its territorial control . . . The situation suggests the following questions: . . . Would our new possessions in the Pacific as well as our Asiatic trade be exposed to ultimate menace by the dismemberment of the Chinese Empire?" D. J. Hill, "Notes Relating to China," [s.] "D. J. H. December 1898," internal memorandum, Department of State, Hill Collection, "Boxer Rebellion," Box 1, Bucknell University Archives, Ellen Clarke Bertrand Library (hereafter cited as Hill Papers). At about the same time, Charles Denby, US minister to China under Presidents Cleveland and McKinley (recently succeeded by Edwin Conger), stated publicly, in supporting the Treaty with Spain, with the annexation of the Philippines: "By holding them we gain 8,000,000 of people who are ripe for the opening . . . We open up new markets for our manufactured goods . . . We become an Asiatic Power; and we shall have something to say about the dismemberment of China." Denby, "Why the Treaty Should Be Ratified," *Forum*, XXVI, February 1899, pp. 641–649, at p. 648. And, about two years later, in November 1900, Walter Hines Page (referring to the US projection of power in the Philippines and eastern Pacific, its participation in the anti-Boxer intervention in China, and the US "Open Door" notes): "What the United States desires has been made plain enough. To change the map of the world is commonly considered to be a demonstration of great power, but it will be an exhibition of greater strength to prevent it from being changed." W. H. Page, "Our Place among the Nations" (editor's essay), *World's Work* (I: 1), November 1900, p. 54.

7. Cf. the formulation in an official US military history: "One important argument advanced for retaining the Philippines was that they would serve as

a convenient way station in carrying on trade and protecting American interests in the Manchu empire [China] . . . Although General MacArthur . . . was somewhat reluctant to weaken his already overextended forces, he agreed to dispatch to China immediately the 9th Infantry and later the 14th Infantry and some artillery units. Other units, including the 6th Cavalry, came directly from the United States. Using Manila as a base and Nagasaki, Japan, as an advance port, the United States eventually assembled some 2,500 soldiers and marines under command of Maj. Gen. Adna R. Chaffee." (Chaffee subsequently succeeded MacArthur as commanding general in the Philippines.) Vincent C. Jones, "Emergence to World Power, 1898–1902," ch. 15 in Maurice Matloff, ed., *American Military History*, Office of the Chief of Military History, United States Army (Washington: Government Printing Office, 1969, 1973 revised ed.), pp. 318–342, at pp. 339, 341. On US naval action and troops sent from Manila to China: Assistant Secretary of State David J. Hill, "The Chinese Question: Statement of Policy and Action of US Government in Chinese Trouble," internal memo, DS, nd, *c.* September 1900, Hill giving details, and noting: "The recent events growing out of the anti-foreign insurrections in China . . . illustrate the necessity of a naval and military base . . . in the Far East and the value and availability of the Philippine islands in that respect." Hill Papers, "Boxer Rebellion," Box 1. See also, Max Boot, *The Savage Wars of Peace: Small Wars and the Rise of American Power* (New York: Basic Books, 2002), pp. 86–98, 114–115. Boot's main title is a line from Rudyard Kipling's "The White Man's Burden," first published in the US magazine *McClure's*, February 1899, not, as often assumed, in praise of Western imperialism, but as something of a rebuke and a warning against US imperialist ventures. Zimmerman reproduces the entire Kipling poem at *First Great Triumph*, pp. 364–365. On Manila, annexation of the Philippines, US in Asia, and the US–British alignment, see, e.g., Nevins, *Henry White*, ch. IX, pp. 136–160, and esp. pp. 136–137; and R. G. Neale, *Great Britain and United States Expansion: 1898–1900* (E. Lansing: Michigan State University Press, 1966), chs. 3, 4, and esp. p. 133.

8. "American Century" roots in the Spanish–American War has become a common historical theme: e.g., David Traxel, *1898: The Birth of the American Century* (New York: Knopf, 1998); Ivan Musicant, *Empire by Default: The Spanish–American War and the Dawn of the American Century* (New York: Henry Holt, 1998). On the larger global framework, note, e.g., contemporary commentary (1898–1901) of policy-engaged persons such as the following by Charles A. Conant, Brooks Adams, and Paul S. Reinsch.
Conant: "If commercial freedom were the rule among nations, so that there could be no discrimination against the most efficient producer, the industries of the United States would need no political support in the contest for commercial supremacy. But, by reason of the conditions which have prevailed in the world from the beginning, under which diplomatic finesse and military force have been brought to the support of national commerce, it is essential that those peoples who can produce under the best conditions should not be deprived of the opportunity to sell in the world's markets. This is the significance of the economic and political problem which confronts the American

people, and which makes important their foothold in the Philippines as a lever for keeping open the door of China and for sharing in the development of Asia." Conant, "The United States as a World Power: I. The Nature of the Economic and Political Problem," *Forum*, XXIX (July 1900), pp. 608–622, at p. 609.

B. Adams: "The United States stands face to face with the gravest conjuncture that can confront a people. She must protect the outlets of her trade, or run the risk of suffocation. These outlets are maritime, and are threatened by the same coalition that threatens England [France, Germany, Russia]. The policy of Continental Europe is not new . . . the moment seems at hand when two great competing systems [the continental and the maritime] will be left pitted against each other . . . The Philippine Islands, rich, coal-bearing, and with fine harbors, seem a predestined base for the United States in a conflict which probably is as inevitable as that with Spain . . . Should an Anglo-Saxon [UK–US] coalition be made, and succeed, it would alter profoundly the equilibrium of the world. Exchanges would then move strongly westward [i.e., toward London and New York] . . . By 1870, the most tempting regions of the earth had been occupied, for the Anglo-Saxons had reached the Pacific . . . The last step of the advance was taken in the war with Spain. Then the Americans crossed the Pacific, and the two great branches of the Anglo-Saxon race met on the coast of China, having girdled the earth . . . Eastern Asia now appears, without much doubt, to be the only district likely soon to be able to absorb any great increase of manufactures, and accordingly Eastern Asia is the prize for which all the energetic nations are grasping. If the Continental coalition wins, that coveted region will be closed to its rivals . . . and the pressure caused by the stoppage of the current which has so long run westward might shake American society to its foundations, and would probably make the scale of life to which our people are habituated impossible." "Whether we like it or not, we are forced to compete for the seat of international exchanges, or, in other words, for the seat of empire . . . Probably, within two generations, the United States will have faced about, and its great interests will cover the Pacific, which it will hold like an inland sea. The natural focus of such a Pacific system would be Manila. Lying where all the paths of trade converge, from north and south, east and west, it is the military and commercial key to Eastern Asia. Entrenched there, and backing on Europe, with force enough to prevent our competitors from closing the Chinese mainland against us by discrimination, there is no reason why the United States should not become a greater seat of wealth and power than ever was England, Rome, or Constantinople." Adams, "The Spanish War and the Equilibrium of the World," *Forum* (Aug. 1898), pp. 1–25, and "The New Struggle for Life Among Nations," *McClure's Magazine* (April 1899), pp. 26–53, reprinted as Chapter I and II, respectively, in Adams, *America's Economic Supremacy* (New York: Macmillan, 1900), quotations at book pp. 19, 22, 25, 42, 43, 50, 51.

Paul S. Reinsch (later, President Wilson's minister to China): "the general conclusion reached by all who have investigated the matter [is that] . . . the coal and general mineral wealth of China, taken in connection with the vast

and highly trained, frugal, and capable population, will, during the coming century, make China the industrial centre of the world, and the Pacific
the chief theatre of commerce." Reinsch, *World Politics at the End of the
Nineteenth Century, As Influenced by the Oriental Situation* (New York:
Macmillan, 1900; 1904 edn.), p. 111. "Uninterrupted and rapid communication with the regions to be opened to modern trade and industry is the
principal need of contemporary [international economic] expansion . . .
The occupation of Malta, Cyprus, Aden, and even of lower Egypt by Great
Britain was due to the desire to control the Suez Canal route to India. The
possession of the Philippines [by the US] is valued chiefly on account of the
facility of access to China which they afford, while Cuba and Porto Rico are
the keys to the Isthmian canal. These are only a few of the many examples
illustrating the importance of communications in modern [world] politics."
Reinsch, "The New Conquest of the World," *World's Work*, I: February 4,
1901, pp. 425–431, at p. 427.

9. The "neoimperialism," "neocolonialism," or "post-territorial empire," that
some scholars ascribe to the later twentieth century was central to US policy
planning beginning over 100 years ago. For my treatment of the meaning of
"corporate-administered stage of development," and its relation to imperialism and post-imperialism, see M. J. Sklar, *The Corporate Reconstruction of
American Capitalism, 1890–1916* (New York: Cambridge University Press,
1988), ch. 2; and M. J. Sklar, *United States as a Developing Country*, chs. 1,
3, 4; and M. J. Sklar, "The Open Door, Imperialism, and Postimperialism:
Origins of US Twentieth-Century Foreign Relations, Circa 1900," ch. 11
in David G. Becker and Richard L. Sklar, eds., *Postimperialism and World
Politics*, pp. 317–336. On postimperialism, see also ibid., esp. Introduction
by Becker and R. L. Sklar, and ch. 1 by R. L. Sklar, chs. 2, 12 by Becker, ch. 3
by Scott Bowman, ch. 9 by Arturo Grunstein, ch. 10 by Keith A. Haynes, and
also by Haynes, "Dependency, Postimperialism, and the Mexican Revolution:
An Historiographical Review," *Mexican Studies/Estudios Mexicanos*, 7: 2,
Summer 1991, pp. 225–251.

10. In seeking Taft's acceptance of the appointment as commission head, President
McKinley told Taft: "We must establish a government there and I would like
you to help." Taft demurred: "But, Mr President, I am sorry we have got the
Philippines, I don't want them and I think you ought to have some man who
is more in sympathy with the situation." McKinley replied: "You don't want
them any less than I do, but we have got them and in dealing with them I
think I can trust the man who didn't want them better than I can the man who
did." Margaret Leech, *In the Days of McKinley* (New York: Harper Brothers,
1959), p. 484; also at Zimmerman, *First Great Triumph*, p. 390.

11. "The President's Instructions to the Commission," McKinley to Root, and Root
to Taft, both April 7, 1900, in War Department, *Annual Reports of the War
Department*, for fiscal year ended June 30, 1901 (Washington: Government
Printing Office, 1901), pp. 5–10. Hereafter cited as "President's Instructions."
Cf. Peter W. Stanley, *A Nation in the Making: The Philippines and the United
States, 1899–1921* (Cambridge: Harvard University Press, 1974), p. 60. For
some comparative perspectives on US colonial government in the Philippines,

see e.g., Anne L. Foster and Julian Go *et al.*, *The American Colonial State in the Philippines: Global Perspectives* (Cambridge: Harvard University Press, 2003). Root also crafted the Platt Amendment applying to Cuba, and the Spooner Amendment giving the president military, civil, and judicial powers in the Philippines, both included in the Army Appropriations Act of March 2, 1901. What may be called the "Root Doctrine," in US colonial affairs, was that the Constitution followed the flag, but, as he said, it "doesn't quite catch up with it," and that Congress and the president had a very large discretion in these matters beyond that traditionally applying to US territories. Cf. Zimmerman, *First Great Triumph*, pp. 390–395. This doctrine was embodied and constitutionally validated in the Supreme Court's decisions in the Insular Cases of 1901, argued by Root's "law partner," Attorney-General John W. Griggs. (See James E. Kerr, *The Insular Cases*, Port Washington, New York: Kennikat Press, 1982; and Root, *The Military and Colonial Policy of the United States*, ed., Robert Bacon and James B. Scott, Cambridge: Harvard University Press, 1916.) The Insular Cases may have a bearing, apparently neglected (or deliberately excluded), on recent controversies, legislation, and judicial decisions respecting war-combat prisoners or "detainees" at Guantánamo and elsewhere. The Root Doctrine, its implementation by Congress and the Executive, and its affirmation by the Supreme Court, in effect inaugurated, without formal amendment, a Third Constitutional Order (1900–1933). Here not including the Continental-Congress Order (1774–1781), and the Articles-of-Confederation Order (1781–1788), the First Constitutional Order was that of 1788–1860, the Second, that which emerged from the Civil War and the 13th and 14th Amendments, 1860s–1890s, and the Third representing an overlapping of the Second with the colonial dispensation codifying the Root doctrine in law and jurisprudence, without formal constitutional amendment. It may be said that, again without formal amendment, but with laws and Supreme Court validation, the "New Deal" inaugurated a Fourth Constitutional Order, deepened and consolidated by World War II and "Fair Deal" measures, 1933–1965; and that the "Great Society" programs and cor-related Civil Rights–Human Rights Revolution (in race relations, sex relations, and entitlements) brought with it a Fifth Constitutional Order, again via laws and jurisprudence, without formal amendment, 1960s–2000s. It may be considered that the American people have been struggling, since the 1990s, over whether to bring into being a Sixth Constitutional Order, and just what it should be.

12. "President's Instructions," p. 6.

13. Cf. *World's Work*, I: November 1, 1900, p. 14: "One of the first acts of the [Philippine] Commission was the establishment of a stringent civil service law, giving preference to such Filipinos as showed qualifications equal to American applicants . . . Judge Taft was for many years the president of the civil-service-reform organization in Cincinnati and one of the reform's most earnest advocates in the whole country. The National Civil Service Reform Commission detailed a man to establish a bureau in the islands." "Our Progress in the Philippines," Editor's column, "The March of Events," by Walter Hines Page.

14. "President's Instructions," pp. 7–8. The Civil War–Republican experience of senior US policy makers may be noted here. McKinley served with distinction as an officer (Major) in the Union Army during the Civil War and (like Civil War Senator Benjamin Franklin Wade – of Wade-Davis Bill fame) was a staunch Ohio Republican. Root was a 15-year-old at the outbreak of the war, and during it, he tried to enlist in the Union Army, but was rejected, and he remained a student at Hamilton College in upstate New York (where his father was a professor), and like McKinley, he was a strong Republican. Hay, of course, had served, along with John G. Nicolay, as President Lincoln's secretary in the White House. As with the Second Constitutional Order emerging from the Civil War (in addition to McKinley, think also of Generals William T. Sherman and Philip H. Sheridan, political leaders Wade, Salmon P. Chase, John Sherman, James A. Garfield, Rutherford B. Hayes, and Ohio-born Ulysses S. Grant and Jay Cooke), so with the Third (McKinley, secretaries of state John Sherman and William R. Day, Taft, Sen. Joseph B. Foraker, and Sen. Mark Hanna), Ohioans played major founding roles; and Ohioans may be regarded as playing a major role in the struggle over the Sixth, in the reelection of President George W. Bush in 2004. Also, it may be recalled that Ohio's centrality to US national and international history can be regarded as going back to the French and Indian War and George Washington's emergence as a frontline American leader. Those who have thought of President George W. Bush as a "cowboy" may be missing the strong Ohio (via Connecticut) Yankeedom in him, as with his father and paternal grandfather (remember: the Ohio Western Reserve).

15. "President's Instructions," p. 8. For specific reference to US–Indian relations as bearing upon policy in the Philippines, see ibid., pp. 9–10.

16. Ibid., pp. 8–9.

17. Ibid., p. 9. Note that such eminent American Republicans as McKinley, Root, and Taft, firm also in their Christian faith, had no problem with, indeed insisted upon, a "real, entire, and absolute" separation between state and church, and universal free public education. These, along with the provisions for rights and liberties, economic development, and modern government, may help to understand as essentially genuine the statement to Root by Taft, a man not given to rhetorical exuberance or ingratiating flattery, that "we of the Commission," regarded the Instructions "as one of the greatest state papers ever issued." Taft to Root, November 30, 1900, Root Papers, Library of Congress, Special Correspondence, Container 167. (Hereafter cited as Root Papers.) Also, interesting discussion by Taft of religious affairs in the Philippines, including American Catholic and Vatican dispositions, and separation of church and state, is at Taft to Mrs. Bellamy Storer, October 26, 1903, William Howard Taft Papers, Library of Congress, Series 3, Reel 4. (Hereafter cited as WHT.)

18. Cf. *World's Work*, I: November 1, 1900 (W. H. Page, "Our Progress in the Philippines"), p. 15: "The Commission is establishing schools with English teachers and high schools for teaching English to adults. The educational work is in the hands of Dr. W. F. Atkinson, of Springfield, Mass., who is Superintendent of Public Instruction in the islands." For Taft's and Conant's

testimony: Taft, February 17, 1902, US Senate Committee on the Philippines, *Hearings: Affairs in the Philippine Islands,* Doc. No. 331, Part I, 57th Congress, 1st Session (Washington: GPO, 1902), pp. 332–333. Hereafter cited as Sen. Comm., *Hearings.* Conant, January 16, 1902, US House of Representatives, Committee on Insular Affairs, *Hearings,* "Coinage System in the Philippines," 57th Cong., 1st and 2nd Sess., 1901–1903 (Washington: GPO, 1903), p. 537. Hereafter cited as House Comm., *Hearings.* Regarding Taft's strong espousal of Philippine self-government and his conflicts over this with members of the press, publicists, and US military officers, including Gen. Chaffee, of particular interest is Taft's personal letter to Mrs. E. B. McCagg, October 21, 1901, WHT, S. 3, R.37. It was not until September 1907 that the Philippine National Assembly was first popularly elected and convened. See the interesting discussion in Paul S. Reinsch, "Can the United States Americanize Her Colonies," *The World Today,* XV: September 3, 1908, pp. 950–953. Reinsch noted (pp. 952–953), "The Philippine Assembly, convoked for the first time last September, is the only colonial assembly in existence elected by practical manhood suffrage, outside of two or three unimportant French colonies. This Assembly, however, while resting upon a popular electorate, has only limited legislative powers. All legislation must be introduced by the Commission, of which American members form the majority, and which acts as an upper house. The Assembly also has no control over the budget. Should it refuse to vote the budget proposed by the Commission, the financial legislation of the preceding year would remain in force. This arrangement is, of course, only a very moderate installment of self-government. It is plainly an experimental and transitional stage in our colonial policy."

19. "President's Instructions," pp. 9–10.

20. Root to McKinley, January 24, 1901 (endorsed by McKinley in his Message to Congress), Philippine Commission, *Annual Reports,* 1901 (Washington: GPO, 1901), p. 7.

21. US internationalism at the time, even including such commitments as the Boxer intervention, the China-indemnity condominium, the Hague conferences, conventions, and tribunal, the more than forty US arbitration treaties with other countries, the Algeciras Conference on North Africa, and government-private activity related to multinational banking consortiums, was more unilateral than multilateral, as those terms are commonly used today, and Wilson's no less so, and perhaps more so, than that of his predecessors: think of Wilson's unilateral policies, for example, in the Caribbean, Mexico, and China (withdrawal from the Six-Power Consortium in order to pursue a more active unilateral engagement there), and also in World War I, the US entering late, as an "associated" power separate from the other Allies, at first (April 1917) declaring war only against Germany, later (December 1917) against Austria-Hungary, not at all against Ottoman Turkey, and promulgating peace-settlement policies independently of the Allies and without mutually consulting with them. It may be kept in mind also that Wilson was a latecomer to the advocacy of a league of nations. The idea had been under widespread discussion both in Europe and the US for some years. Theodore Roosevelt, Senator Lodge, and Wisconsin Senator Robert M. LaFollette, e.g., had advocated a

league of nations well before Wilson. In 1916, Wilson did endorse the idea, proposed by others, of a great-power League to Enforce Peace. But as late as February 1917, Wilson still had not come to favor officially adopting a policy of establishing a league of nations. See, e.g., Wilson's "Bases of Peace," February 7, 9, 1917 (internal memorandum, with Secretary of State Robert Lansing's comments), where Wilson wrote: "It would in all likelihood be best, in this matter of executive organization, to await the developments and lessons of experience before attempting to set up any common instrumentality of international action." Department of State, National Archives, Record Group 59, File No. 763.72/3261½ (hereafter, DS NA RG 59, File no.). Further discussion of Wilson in Part Three, chapter 6, below.

22. Leech, *In the Days of McKinley*, pp. 379–386. See, also, Russell F. Weigley, *History of the United States Army* (Bloomington: University of Indiana Press, 1984 edn.), pp. 313–315, 654n2; Stanley, *A Nation in the Making*, p. 60; Zimmerman, *First Great Triumph*, pp. 146–148. As it turned out, Root came to learn very much about the Army, and in his command restructurings became the founder of the modern US army, until restructuring on a comparable or greater scale of magnitude under George C. Marshall during World War II and then after the war with the establishment of the Defense Department (in place of the War Department), and the restructuring under Secretary of Defense Donald H. Rumsfeld during President George W. Bush's administrations.

23. Stanley Karnow, *In Our Image: America's Empire in the Philippines* (New York: Ballantine Books, 1989), pp. 119–125, 185, 194. Boot, *Savage Wars of Peace*, p. 125, reports: "Between 1898 and 1902, a total of 126,468 American soldiers served there [in the Philippines] (though never more than 69,000 at one time) and fought in 2,811 engagements. By July 4, 1902, [when President Roosevelt officially declared the war ended] the US had lost 4,234 dead and suffered 2,818 wounded. By comparison, only 379 Americans were lost in combat in the Spanish–American War [i.e., in combat against Spanish forces in the Caribbean and East Asia]. By their own count, US forces killed 16,000 Filipinos in battle." See also, Brian M. Linn, *Guardians of Empire: The United States Army and the Pacific, 1902–1940* (Chapel Hill: University of North Carolina Press, 1997), esp. chs. 1, 2 (Linn also uses Kipling's words, "Savage Wars of Peace," as a chapter heading); Linn, *The US Army and Counter-Insurgency in the Philippine War, 1899–1902* (Chapel Hill: University of North Carolina Press, 1989), and Linn, *The Philippine War, 1899–1902* (Lawrence: University Press of Kansas, 2000), for detailed accounts of battles and campaigns. Of interest here are the editorial words of Walter Hines Page, well into the second year of the Philippine war, and in the midst of the second McKinley-vs.-Bryan presidential contest, with Bryan running on a strong antiwar, anti-imperialist platform: "The [Taft-headed Philippine] Commission [appointed March 1900] made its first report . . . on August 31 [1900], and the most important news in it was that the activity of the insurgents . . . was kept alive by the hope that the presidential election would cause the withdrawal of American troops . . . [Par.] Since the Commission's report was made, the hostility of the insurgents has

continued; and the total losses of American troops since our occupation of the islands by death in battle and by disease has been great. But the necessity of a large military force unfortunately continues [Par.] . . . The complete pacification of the islands – an achievement yet unaccomplished since the Spanish occupancy [nearly 350 years] – will require time. The pity of it is that it may require a long time. But the building of roads and railroads and the establishment of schools are weapons that the Spaniards never used in their warfare against the insular ignorance and turbulence. The best weapon of all is – time." *World's Work*, I:1 (November 1900), p. 15.

24. Some contemporary estimates of war-related deaths of Filipinos were much higher. For example, US Brig. Gen. J. Franklin Bell, known for his ruthless military and relocation operations, estimated in 1902 that one-sixth of the residents of Luzon island perished as a direct or indirect result of hostilities, a figure which would mean, H. Parker Willis noted in 1905, "a total death-toll of at least 600,000 persons." Willis, *Our Philippine Problem* (New York: Macmillan, 1905), p. 23. Cf. Leon Wolff, *Little Brown Brother* (New York: Harper Brothers, 1965), p. 360; Boot, *Savage Wars*, p. 125; Zimmerman, *First Great Triumph*, p. 408. On agricultural and economic conditions, Governor Taft reported in late 1902, for example, that "the agricultural depression here induced by the loss of 90 percent of the carabaos, presents a condition that is almost appalling."; and that "Economic conditions are very discouraging and it will take several years to recover from them"; and again in late 1903, that "The agricultural conditions have been very bad." Taft to Conant, and Taft to Jacob G. Schmidlapp, November 23, 1902, Taft to S. M. Felton, and Taft to Mrs. Bellamy Storer, October 26, 1903, WHT, S. 3, R. 37, 41. See also, Stanley, *A Nation in the Making*, pp. 96–97; Boot, *Savage Wars*, pp. 123–124; Edwin W. Kemmerer, *Modern Currency Reforms* (New York: Macmillan, 1916), p. 256. Regarding the continuing impact of the war-related and natural damages, Jeremiah W. Jenks's observations as late as 1907 are indicative: "the business conditions in the islands are not good [and] . . . while better than they were, are in many places worse than under the Spanish occupation . . . [and] agricultural conditions have not been good of late years." Jenks, "The Agricultural Bank for the Philippines," *Annals*, XXX (July 1907), pp. 38–44, at pp. 38–39. This was a paper delivered at the Special Annual Meeting of the American Academy of Political and Social Science (1907) on "American Colonial Policy and Administration."

25. Governor Taft, in 1902, estimated that Filipino landowners accounted for about 5 million acres; the friars owned about 403,000 acres, of which about 250,000 "are among the best lands in the Philippines and in the populous provinces." Taft, February 5, 1902, Sen. Comm. *Hearings*, p. 100; also, Taft, February 6, 8, 1902, at ibid., pp. 178–187, 229–233. Five years later, June 8, 1907, Conant, Taft (now secretary of war), and other US representatives, in meeting with Vatican representatives, settled the Catholic Church's loss of land titles in return for the Church-owned Spanish-Filipino Bank getting charter extension and note-issue rights. Charles A. Conant, *A History of Modern Banks of Issue* (6th edn., New York and London: G. P. Putnam's Sons, 1927), p. 590n1.

26. Cf. Stanley, *A Nation in the Making*, pp. 81–98. Cf. subsequent comment in *World's Work* (I:1, p. 15), November 1900: "[The Philippine Commission reports that it has] a surplus fund of $6,000,000 Mexican, which should be expended in much needed public works, notably improvement of Manila harbor." "The Commission has appropriated $1,000,000 for the construction of highways and bridges . . . It will give work to many and be an education in the arts of modern construction and modern sanitation. Forty-five miles of railroad extension are also under way, giving further employment and opening a province rich in minerals . . . This practical work itself gives hope of a new era."

27. See, e.g., Charles A. Conant, "The Way to Attain and Maintain Monetary Reform in Latin America," *Annals*, XXXIV (1911), pp. 40–49, at p. 40: "The reform of fiscal affairs of a government which has been in difficulties is perhaps a wise preliminary to reform in the monetary system, but in a sense the monetary reform transcends in importance the fiscal reform." Whereas fiscal reform centers upon "the restoration of a favorable balance to the budget and the prompt payment of interest on public obligations," monetary reform "reaches deeper in the heart of commercial affairs, because it alone makes possible the free interchange of products and the investment of foreign capital upon a basis which ensures permanency in gold value."

28. Gage had been a member of the IMC executive committee, but withdrew upon his appointment by President McKinley as secretary of the treasury.

29. On Conant's thinking and activities, see David Healy, *United States Expansionism* (Madison: University of Wisconsin Press, 1970), pp. 194–209; Carl P. Parrini and Martin J. Sklar, "New Thinking about the Market, 1896–1904: Some American Economists on Investment and the Theory of Surplus Capital," *Journal of Economic History*, XLIII: 3 (September 1983), pp. 559–578; M. J. Sklar, *Corporate Reconstruction*, pp. 62–85; Parrini, "Theories of Imperialism," in Lloyd C. Gardner, ed., *Redefining the Past* (Corvallis: Oregon State University Press, 1986), pp. 65–83; Parrini, "Charles A. Conant, Economic Crises and Foreign Policy, 1896–1903," ch. 2 in Thomas J. McCormick and Walter LaFeber, eds., *Behind the Throne: Servants of Power to Imperial Presidents, 1898–1968* (Madison: University of Wisconsin Press, 1993), pp. 35–66; James Livingston, *Origins of the Federal Reserve System: Money, Class, and Corporate Capitalism, 1890–1913* (Ithaca: Cornell University Press, 1986), chs. 3-6; Emily S. Rosenberg, "Foundations of United States International Financial Power: Gold Standard Diplomacy, 1900–1905," *Business History Review*, 59: 2 (Summer 1985), pp. 169–202; Rosenberg, *Financial Missionaries to the World: The Politics and Culture of Dollar Diplomacy, 1900–1930* (Cambridge: Harvard University Press, 2002), chs. 1–3.

30. Gage to Root, November 8, 1900, covering Conant to Gage, October 16, 1900, Root to Taft, July 23, 1901, War Department, National Archives, Record Group 350, File 808, pp. 59, 60, and File 3197, p. 4; hereafter cited as WD NA RG 350.

31. Root to Taft, July 23, 1901, WD NA RG 350/3197-4. The full title of Conant's book of essays was *The United States in the Orient: The Nature of*

the Economic Problem (Boston: Houghton, Mifflin and Co., 1900, reissued by Kennikat Press, Port Washington, New York, 1971). It was a collection of some of his recently published essays, and included "The Economic Basis of Imperialism" (*North American Review*, September 1898), "Russia as a World Power" (ibid., February 1899), "The Struggle for Commercial Supremacy" (*Forum*, June 1899), "Can New Openings Be Found for Capital?" (*Atlantic Monthly*, November 1899), "The New Economic Problems" (printed as "Recent Economic Tendencies" in ibid., June 1900), "The United States as a World Power – The Nature of the Economic and Political Problem" (*Forum*, July 1900), and "The United States as a World Power – Their Advantages in the Competition for Commercial Empire" (ibid., August 1900). Regarding the historical importance of the Gold Standard Act of 1900 (also known as the Currency Act of 1900): aside from officially placing the US dollar on the gold standard, the act restructured the US Treasury to separate the gold reserve from general revenues, and authorized the Treasury Department to issue bonds as necessary to replenish the gold fund. This made it possible to run federal fiscal deficits (whether it be from economic contraction, war, or rising public expenditures) without the dollar falling off the gold standard from want of sufficient reserve to back it. It marked a major turning point, indeed a decisive enabling breakthrough, toward the "bigger government" and internationalism associated with modern "liberalism" or "progressivism." In this respect, the Gold Standard Act may be considered as on a par in significance with the federal income tax (16th Amendment, Underwood Revenue Act) and the Federal Reserve Act, both of 1913, and Conant had a strong hand in both the earlier and later reforms. A further implication, not often observed, is that coming almost two years before the Gold Standard Act, the Spanish–American War, if too big and costly a conflict, might have thrown the dollar off gold and onto silver – something many "Cuba-Libra" populists and silverites were hoping for; hence, this was one of the stronger ingredients (military capacity another) in McKinley's delay in deciding for war, until he felt assured by British diplomatic advices and other indications that Germany would not intervene on Spain's side, that British naval power would be favorably deployed (a guarantee of German quiescence), and that it would indeed be "a splendid little war," in Hay's retrospectively felicitous words. (Hay's well-known words may be found at Zimmerman, *First Great Triumph*, p. 310, among many other places.) Cf. Brooks Adams's informed observation in 1899 concerning Germany as "the centre of an entirely new economic system," and major rival of Anglo–US power: "Our adversary is deadly and determined. Such are his jealousy of our power and his fear of our expansion, that to cripple us he would have gladly joined with Spain. But for the victory of Manila and the attitude of England, his fleets would last spring have been off our coasts. If we yield before him [in China], he will stifle us." "The New Struggle for Life Among Nations," *McClure's*, April 1899, at *AES*, pp. 26–27, 52. Also, Adams's statement in 1900: "no one can fail to appreciate the part played by England [in shaping] . . . the modern world . . . [since] Trafalgar and Waterloo: . . . it was she who bridled the ambitions of Germany; it was she who rendered abortive the coalition forming against the

United States at the outbreak of the war with Spain." *AES*, ch. 5, "The Decay of England," pp. 142–192, at p. 190.

32. Conant, "The Currency of the Philippine Islands," *Annals*, XX (Dec. 1902), pp. 44–59, at pp. 45–46; Kemmerer, *Modern Currency Reforms*, pp. 249–253, 269–270; A. Piatt Andrew, "The End of the Mexican Dollar," *Quarterly Journal of Economics*, XVIII (May 1904), pp. 321–356, at pp. 332–333; Conant to Clarence R. Edwards, May 7, 1903, WD NA RG 350/808–159; Conant, *A Special Report on Coinage and Banking in the Philippine Islands*, Made to the Secretary of War by Charles A. Conant of Boston, November 25, 1901, Appendix G in *Annual Report of the Secretary of War*, 1901 (Washington: GPO, 1901), pp. 9–10 (hereafter cited as Conant, *Special Report*).

33. Conant to Gage, October 16, 1900, WD NA RG 350/808–60; Taft to Root, December 14, 1900, Root Papers, Library of Congress, Spl. Corr., Contnr 164; Kemmerer, *Modern Currency Reforms*, pp. 270–275, 383–385. Subsequently, in 1903, when the Manila banks offered to assist the Philippine government in a way that would have yielded them large arbitrage profit and disrupted or wrecked the currency reform program about to be implemented, Root, who counted bankers among his close friends and professional associates, instructed Gov. Taft to reject the bankers' offer, and commented, with a Virgilian realism, "Timeo bankers dona ferentes" [*sic*]. ("I fear bankers bearing gifts"; derived from Virgil, *The Aeneid*, Book II, Line 49, the warning to Troy's King Priam about the Greeks' wooden-horse gift, by Laocoön, priest of Neptune: "*Quidquid id est, timeo Danaos* [Greeks] *et dona ferentis.*") Root to Taft (War Dept. telegram), August 11, 1903, Root Papers (LC), Letterbooks, Letters Semi-Official, Contnr 177.

34. Conant to Gage, October 16, 1900, WD NA RF 350/808–60.

35. Taft to Root, December 14, 1900, Root Papers (LC), Spl. Corr., Contnr 164; Conant, "The Currency of the Philippine Islands," p. 47; Conant, *Special Report*, p. 6.

36. Conant to Edwards, July 9, 1901, WD NA RG 350/3197–1.

37. Ibid. In his letter of introduction of Conant to Taft, Root noted "the necessity of an expert report being made by some one who has become familiar with local conditions, and who returning to this country can support the conclusions reached . . . by answering questions and meeting objections before the committees of Congress." Root to Taft, July 23, 1901, WD NA RG 350/3197–4. At the House hearings, Insular Affairs Committee Chair Henry A. Cooper (Repub.-IL) asked Conant, "You received your instructions from the War Department – [and] from Secretary Gage – and went?" Conant replied: "Yes, I do not know that I received any specific instructions." He had had "several talks with Col. Edwards," and he "had written a letter to Secretary Gage . . . after a conversation which he asked me to put in writing stating what I thought ought to be done there . . . But Mr. Root was aware of my knowledge and experience in the matter, and he asked me if I would go out and investigate the subject." This is indicative of Conant's peer-standing as a policy maker. House Comm., *Hearings*, January 14, 1902, p. 491.

38. For Conant's itinerary and the information and quotations in this and the following four paragraphs: House Comm., *Hearings*, pp. 491–492; Conant, *Special Report*, p. 5; and ibid., pp. 116–119, for Exhibit No. VII, a transcript of Conant's interview with Takahashi, October 29, 1901; also, Conant to Edwards, September 28, October 7, 15, 1901, WD NA RG 350/3197–4, 5, 7.

39. Taft to Root, October 14, 1901, Root Papers (LC), Spl. Corr., Contnr 164.

40. Conant, *Special Report* (note 32). For Conant's advocacy of the new imperialism, centered on investment expansion, not simply trade, and these broader implications, see his essays as cited in note 31. See also, Reinsch, "The New Conquest of the World." The reader may note that this American view of modern capitalist imperialism differs from Schumpeter's later view that modern Western imperialism was something atavistic or inconsistent with modern capitalism. The American view preceded both John A. Hobson's and Lenin's treatments, which themselves drew upon Conant and other American authors. See my discussion of this and related matters, at *Corporate Reconstruction*, pp. 78–85, and esp. pp. 79–80n52, n53; and at "The Open Door, Imperialism, and Postimperialism," pp. 328–329, and esp. p. 328n6; and Part Two, chapters 3–5, below.

41. Regarding lines of continuity from early twentieth-century to later twentieth/twenty-first-century thinking about the interrelation of modern markets and political-legal institutions, or, the rule of law, a good latter-day example may be seen in the essay in the *Wall Street Journal*, Op-Ed, July 30, 2003, by Stephen Haber, Douglass C. North, and Barry R. Weinglass: "The efficient functioning of markets requires that some organizations enforce contracts and property rights . . . [And] the enforcer is the government. History offers us no case of a well-developed market system that was not embedded in a well-developed political system . . . Without attention to their political foundations, markets cannot flourish. Donor governments and agencies must . . . attend to the political security of markets as well as to the economic policies creating them." (Headlined: "If Economists Are So Smart, Why Is Africa So Poor?") See also, M. J. Sklar, *United States as a Developing Country*, chs. 1, 7. It might also be noted that such early twentieth-century arrangements as international interbank consortiums, customs receiverships, and parallel intergovernmental diplomacy, did the work, or were in effect forerunners of the work, that the Bretton Woods and other post-World War II international arrangements institutionalized, systematized, and routinized.

42. Regarding Conant's authority, consider, e.g. Edmund Brumaud, French Consul-General, New York City, to Théophile Delcassé, French Foreign Minister, Paris, reporting on and enclosing dispatches from Conant printed in November 1899 in the *Journal of Commerce* ("From Our Own Correspondent"), on responses of "les Puissances" to Hay's Open Door Notes, and on "la politique suivie en ce moment par le Départment d'Etat dans la question chinoise": "Le correspondent de Washington du 'Journal du Commerce de New-York', M. Charles A. Conant, a ses grandes entrées dans les bureaux de l'Administration et il est bien rare qu'il ne soit pas mis au courant des desseins des hautes fonctionnaires, lorsque ceux-ci ont intérêt à les faire connaitre au public par la voie officieuse de la presse . . . [Par.]

D'après M. Conant, qui se fait évidemment l'echo de confidences recues, M. John Hay ne se propose pas de demander à Pekin une sphere d'influence." (Consulate Générale de France, New York, No. 596, November 9, 1899). And: "J'ai l'honneur de vous transmettre ci-joint, le texte de cette letter qui sort d'une plume généralement fort bien inspirée et guidée." (No. 603, November 27, 1899). My thanks to William Burr, now senior analyst at the National Security Archive, for ferreting out these documents for me some time ago. See Burr, ed., *The Kissinger Transcripts: The Top Secret Talks with Beijing and Moscow* (New York: The New Press, 1998), which among many other matters, reveals to the knowledgeable reader significant lines of continuity from McKinley, Hay, and Conant, to Nixon and Kissinger, concerning US–China relations, and US–China–Russia relations; also, Burr, "The Complexities of Rapprochement," in *The Harmony and Prosperity of Civilizations: Selected Papers of Beijing Forum (2004)* (Beijing: Peking University Press, 2004), pp. 190–219.

43. Cf. Parrini's assessment at "Conant, Economic Crises and Foreign Policy," p. 59, that Conant was not simply "an 'economist' or 'economic adviser,' . . . [which] gives the innocent reader the impression that he operated largely at a technical, hence secondary, level of policy-making," but rather that Conant was "a theoretician of the domestic corporate reorganization" of the US political economy, and "a theoretician and formulator" of policies "appropriate to the crafting of the nation's foreign policy in the epoch of the new imperialism." On neglect of Conant's policy-making importance, see in particular, Parrini and Sklar, "New Thinking about the Market," p. 563n9, and M. J. Sklar, *Corporate Reconstruction*, pp. 63nn26–27, 64n28, 84–85, 84–85n59, 85n60. Emily S. Rosenberg, "Foundations of United States International Financial Power," also notes neglect of Conant, but has a different, more minimalist, assessment of his thinking and policy-making role, which the reader may compare with that offered here.

44. Cf. Conant, B. Adams, Reinsch, note 8; "Alfred Thayer Mahan on the Problem of Asia, 1900," (excerpt from Mahan's *The Problem of Asia*, Boston, 1900), in Norman A. Graebner, ed., *Ideas and Diplomacy: Readings in the Intellectual Tradition of American Foreign Policy* (New York: Oxford University Press, 1964), pp. 378–383; see also, Walter LaFeber, *The New Empire: An Interpretation of American Expansion, 1860–1898* (Ithaca: Cornell University Press, 1963, new edn., 1998), pp. 85–95; Zimmerman, *First Great Triumph*, chs. 3, 9. For an authoritative "missionary" view of the US in the Philippines, not at all lacking in historical realism, see, e.g., Arthur Judson Brown (secretary of the Board of Foreign Missions of the Presbyterian Church in the US), *The New Era in the Philippines* (New York: Fleming H. Revell Co., 1903).

45. "President's Instructions," ending with the following words, p. 10: "[A] high and sacred obligation rests upon the Government of the United States to give protection for property and life, civil and religious freedom, and wise, firm, and unselfish guidance in the paths of peace and prosperity to all the people of the Philippine Islands. I charge this commission to labor for the full performance of this obligation, which concerns the honor and conscience of

their country, in the firm hope that through their labors all the inhabitants of the Philippine Islands may come to look back with gratitude to the day when God gave victory to American arms at Manila and set their land under the sovereignty and protection of the people of the United States."

46. Conant, *Special Report*, p. 66. Emphasis added.
47. Ibid., pp. 7, 16–17.
48. Ibid., pp. 15, 16, 64–65.
49. In addition to the essays by Conant cited above, the following works, all by Conant, are notable (in chronological order): *A History of Modern Banks of Issue: With an Account of the Economic Crises of the Present Century* (New York and London: G. P. Putnam's Sons, 1896), chs. 19–22 (pp. 453–553) deal specifically with crises; "Securities as a Means of Payment," *Annals*, 14 (September 1899), pp. 25–47; "The Law of the Value of Money," *Annals*, 16 (September 1900), pp. 13–35; "The Growth of Public Expenditures," *Atlantic Monthly* 86 (January 1901), pp. 45–47; "Crises and Their Management," *Yale Review*, 9 (February 1901), pp. 374–398 (Yale President Arthur T. Hadley and Professor Irving Fisher were among *Yale Review*'s six editors at the time); "The Future of Political Parties," *Atlantic Monthly*, 86 (September 1901), pp. 365–373 (this appeared during Conant's mission to the Philippines); *Wall Street and the Country: A Study of Recent Financial Tendencies* (1904; Westport, CT: Greenwood, 1968) (this appeared during Conant's work with the US Commission on International Exchange; see related text, below); *The Principles of Money and Banking* (New York: Harper Bros., 1905), 2 vols.; "The Influence of Friction in Economics," *Science*, N.S. XXVII: 681 (January 17, 1908), pp. 99–104 (this was Conant's "Address of the vice-president and chairman of Section 1 – Economics and Social Science – American Association for the Advancement of Science, Chicago meeting, 1907–1908"); "The Functions of Centralized Banking," *Bankers Magazine* (NY), 89 (October 1914), pp. 388–398. Conant also wrote the volumes for the National Monetary (Aldrich) Commission on the banking system of Mexico and the National Bank of Belgium, both published in 1910 by GPO. On 1890s Chicago civic and political activity of Gage (McKinley's secretary of the treasury) and MacVeagh (Taft's secretary of the treasury), see Richard Schneirov, *Labor and Urban Politics: Class Conflict and the Origins of Modern Liberalism in Chicago, 1864–1897* (Urbana: University of Illinois Press, 1998), various pages, consult its index.
50. On currency convertibility as key to long-term investment and sustained development, and its relation to banking reform, Russian policy over a century later is indicative. See, e.g., Erin E. Arvedlund, "Putin Calls for Convertible Currency," *New York Times*, May 27, 2004, pp. W1,7: "Russian President, Vladimir V. Putin, said, in his state of the nation address on Wednesday [May 26, 2004] that he wanted to make the Russian ruble fully convertible by 2006, moving up the target date from 2007." [Par.] "Ruble convertibility is an issue close to Mr. Putin's heart, as a major step in making the country a global economic presence. 'He sees it as one of the prerequisites for Russia moving towards a more developed economy,' said Paul Timmons, an economist with Moscow Narodny Bank, which is owned by Russia's

central bank." [Par.] "Rubles are convertible into [US] dollars inside Russia at a floating rate [that stood at US$1=R28.98 on May 26, 2004] . . . Rubles are not convertible outside the country." [Par.] "But Russia needs changes in its financial system, particularly steps that would strengthen its banking sector, before ruble convertibility becomes a reality, economists said." Also, with respect to present-day China (yuan convertibility and banking reform), see e.g., *Wall Street Journal* ("News Roundup"), "China Plans Gradual Opening of Capital Account," February 28, 2005, p. A14; Victoria Ruan, "China Think Tank Predicts Yuan Will Rise," *WSJ*, March 1, 2005, p. A16.

51. On market-determined (instead of metal-determined) convertibility, see, e.g., P. Chidambaram (finance minister of India), "A Passage to Prosperity," *Wall Street Journal*, Op-Ed, March 4, 2005, p. A14: "India now has over a decade of experience of conducting macropolicy in a setting where foreign portfolio investors have full convertibility, and the exchange rate is determined in the currency market." Also, Leo Melamed (chairman emeritus of the Chicago Mercantile Exchange), "The American Century," *WSJ*, Op-Ed, May 3, 2007, p. A17. On dollar equivalency and a market-currency basket in China's present-day policy, see, e.g., Charles Hutzler, "China Rethinks the Peg Tying Yuan and Dollar," *WSJ*, February 13, 2004, pp. A1,10: "Pressures . . . are driving Beijing to re-examine the Chinese currency's iron-like tether to the US dollar [Par.] . . . Premier Wen Jia-bao told a high-level meeting of economic officials in Beijing this week that the government will 'maintain the basic stability of the yuan' . . . Mr. Wen also said the government intended 'to gradually perfect' the exchange-rate mechanism." [Par.] "A change in the yuan's value [fixed at Yuan 8.277=US$1 since 1994] would be the biggest shift in monetary policy in a decade. In the most recent major change, China abolished a two-track system – with different exchange rates for foreigners with hard currency and Chinese – while placing the yuan in a narrow trading band, or desirable range of values in relation to the dollar." [Par.] "The peg has served China well, providing stability for an economy well enmeshed with the global-trading system. For similar reasons, many multinational companies and investors – an important constituency for China – favor the peg. [Par.] If China did move toward loosening the peg, however, any alteration . . . would likely be followed by other Asian economies adjusting the value of their currencies against the dollar in step with China." [Par.] "Among the options under consideration . . . are widening the trading band or revaluing the yuan, not just against the dollar but against *a basket of the currencies* of major trading partners and investors." [Par.] "A basket, proponents argue, would give China more flexibility, allowing it to alter the mix and stabilize the yuan's value. Singapore and India, for example, manage their exchange rates with baskets, though their models differ." (Emphasis added.) See also Christopher Wood, "Currency on a Collision Course," *WSJ*, Op-Ed, November 29, 2004, p. A14; and "Malaysia Vows to Keep Ringgit Pegged to Dollar," *WSJ* ("Dow Jones Newswires"), February 4, 2005, p. A7.

52. Conant, *Special Report*, p. 66; Conant, *History of Modern Banks of Issue*, p. 3n1.

53. Conant, *Special Report*, pp. 50–51. Conant elsewhere applied the same reasoning to agriculture in the US South, arguing that giving the national banks an elastic note-issue power based on assets (bills of exchange), instead of the inelastic post-Civil War bond-based system, would help free Southern farmers from their debt-peonage under the share-crop system, and pave the way for more modern agricultural market relations with greater general prosperity in the region. As this implied a transformation of the South's racist sociopolitical system, it was a potent reason for Southern congressional opposition to such banking reform within the US, aside from, and along with, the resistance to centralized banking power in general in all sections of the US. See Conant's testimony, February 16, 1901, on behalf of an assets bank-note currency, at US House Committee on Banking and Currency, "Currency Responsive to the Needs of Business," *Hearings and Arguments*, Lovering Bill, HR 13303, 56th, 2nd (Washington: GPO, 1901), pp. 87–88. Conant had also made this same point in an earlier published article: "This stifling of production, by the lack of the tools of exchange or an excessive price for them, may throw its pall over whole communities, as is the case in the South to-day, from the absence of an elastic banking currency." "Recent Economic Tendencies," *Atlantic Monthly*, Vol. 85, June 1900, pp. 737ff, reprinted as Chapter 5; "The New Economic Problems," in *United States in the Orient*, pp. 121–155, at p. 145.
54. Conant, *Special Report*, pp. 56, 57.
55. Ibid., pp. 57, 58, 62.
56. Ibid., pp. 65–66.
57. Ibid., pp. 65–66. Another way of putting some of this is that capital inflow would finance both development and the trade deficit, pending fuller development and surplus production. An analogy may be made with the position of the US in the 1980s–2000s, where (to paraphrase Conant) foreign investors and producers "steadily send more to the US than they take away." Note the variance, implied in Conant's *Report*, from the usual "Imperialism" or "Dependency" model, and note also the inversion in the later US position. In the model, the imperialist country exports extractive capital, finished goods, and high-end services to the colony (or dependency), imports cheap raw materials, less-finished, low-end, and exotic goods from the colony, and maintains a sustained current account and long-term surplus against the colony, which itself suffers sustained deficits, indebtedness, capital flight, currency weakness, and underdevelopment. In the gold-exchange currency reform plan, the US was seeking to strengthen the less developed country's currency to promote export of developmental capital and goods to the LDC, and at the same time, to raise the LDC's real income earned on its own exports and investments, lessen the cost of incurring and paying gold-denominated foreign debt, and thereby spur the LDC's development. Regarding the US in the 1980s–2000s, sustained trade and current account deficits, plus net import, instead of export, of capital, finished goods, and some high-end services, along with strong growth-rates and continuing development, with foreign investors content to "take away" US securities, are indicative of "post-imperialism" in the current stage of world history, often also referred to

as "globalization," but not necessarily with an awareness or acknowledgment of this inversion and its implications. It is possible, though, to argue that China (like India and such other "emergent" nations) is the looming imperialist country (and "Hegemon"), and the US (like such other presently "advanced" nations) the prospective colony – reversal of fortune in the endless cycles of history. On fears about the US losing capital-inflow financing its deficits and development, and hence itself on the road to becoming a less developed, or no longer the "hegemonic," country, see e.g., Christopher Wood, "Currency on a Collision Course" (note 51) and "The Insourcing Problem," Editorial, *Wall Street Journal*, December 1, 2004, p. A10; Mark Whitehouse, "Rate Rises Expose US Foreign Debt as a Clear Burden," *WSJ*, September 25, 2006, p. A1, 9; Michael M. Phillips, "The Outlook: Capital Flow from Emerging Nations to US Poses Some Risks," *WSJ*, June 23, 2008, p. A2. Another model – still rather inchoate – is imperialism (not post-imperialism) as *supranational*, a function of multinational (or transnational) corporations tied definitively to no particular state or country; in which case, every country may become a colony, and the imperialist power is multicentered, with perhaps a transnational class and political base, but no country is imperialist or is "The Imperialist." A political system in past history close or analogous to this supranational model may be the Ottoman Empire, or the Holy Roman Empire, and prospectively, in present-day history, a pan-Islamist Empire, economically oil-gas fueled and sovereign-wealth-fund managed, whether Arab- or Iran-led, or in combination.

58. Conant, January 14, 1902, at House Comm., *Hearings* (1902), pp. 492–495; Taft, February 8, 1902, at Sen. Comm., *Hearings* (1902), pp. 232, 238–239, 241, 243; Conant to Lt. Col. Clarence R. Edwards (War Dept.), March 26, 1902, and Conant to Taft, August 8, 1902, WD NA RG 350/3197–27, 35; and Conant, "The Currency of the Philippine Islands," p. 51.

59. Sen. Comm., *Hearings* (1902): among the committee's members were Republicans William B. Allison of Iowa, Albert J. Beveridge of Indiana, Julius Caesar Burrows of Michigan, Charles H. Dietrich of Nebraska, Eugene Hale of Maine, Louis E. McComas of Maryland, and Redfield Proctor of Vermont; and Democrats Edward W. Carmack of Tennessee, Charles A. Culberson of Texas, Fred T. Dubois of Idaho (elected in 1901 as a Silver Republican, and then switching parties), Thomas M. Patterson of Colorado (also a Populist and supported by Silver Republicans), and Joseph L. Rawlins of Utah. See Henry F. Graff, ed., *American Imperialism and the Philippine Insurrection* (Boston: Little, Brown, 1969), pp. xvi–xx.

60. Taft, February 8, 1902, Sen. Comm., *Hearings*, p. 232, 241; also Taft on the currency, mortgage banking, and agricultural development, relying on Conant, ibid., 238–239, 241, 243. Also, e.g., House Comm., *Hearings* (January 14, 1902), p. 492: Henry A. Cooper (chairman): "Now, in the bill which is before the committee (H. R. 7925), you drew practically the provisions regulating coinage in the Philippines and the banking law for the Philippines." Conant: "Yes, sir."

61. Culberson and Taft, February 17, 1902, Sen. Comm., *Hearings*, p. 408. Taft was here referring to Conant's book of essays, *United States in the Orient* (1900).

For similar emphasis on investment as central to the new imperialism, see also Reinsch, "The New Conquest of the World." Also, Taft, in response to questions by Sen. McComas, February 17, 1902, Sen. Comm., *Hearings*, p. 409. For congressional testimony by Conant in Jan. 1902, see, e.g., House Comm., *Hearings*, pp. 491–555. Elected to the Senate in 1898, Culberson had been governor of Texas, 1894–1898. Col. Edward M. House had served as his campaign manager, as House had done also with Culberson's gubernatorial predecessor, populist Democrat James Hogg. Graff, *American Imperialism*, p. xviii; Philip Bobbitt, *The Shield of Achilles* (New York: Alfred A. Knopf, 2002), pp. 367–371.

62. Lodge, McComas, and Taft, February 15, 1902, Sen. Comm., *Hearings*, pp. 327–328. Taft added (p. 328) that "constant agitation" about independence "would at once discourage the sincere efforts of the educated Filipinos who are with us to-day in building up a stable government." See also, Leo S. Rowe, "The Establishment of Civil Government in the Philippines," *Annals*, XX (October 1902), pp. 9–23, at p. 21: "The successful administration of the islands is so intimately bound up with the exploitation of their resources by American and foreign capital that any discouragement to the latter is bound to increase the difficulties of the civil government." Rowe was a professor of public administration at the University of Pennsylvania, and adviser to the US government on Asian and Latin American affairs; in 1906, for example, he served as one of the six US delegates (along with Paul S. Reinsch) to the Third International Conference of American States in Rio de Janeiro, Brazil, under instructions of Secretary of State Root.

63. On the automaticity of the gold-exchange system, see, e.g., Kemmerer, *Modern Currency Reforms*, pp. 320–322; Conant, "The Gold-Exchange Standard in Light of Experience," *Economic Journal* (London, June 1909), pp. 190–200, at pp. 191–192. (John Maynard Keynes became editor of this journal in 1911; on Conant–Keynes intellectual relations, see M. J. Sklar, *Corporate Reconstruction*, pp. 73–74, 74n45; and Parrini and Sklar, "New Thinking about the Market," pp. 566–571, 573, 576–577.) This gold-exchange system is similar to the present-day currency board system of Hong Kong, and to the currency board system proposed in the advisories of Professor Steve H. Hanke both for Indonesia and subsequently for Iraq. Compare, for example, this explanation of the currency board system by the editors of the *Wall Street Journal* (Editorial, February 11, 1998): "Currency boards, like a gold standard, belong to the fixed group [of "exchange rate regimes," as against the looser "pegged" and "free-floating" regimes], and function with foreign reserves backing the monetary base. Financial authorities working under their constraints can target the exchange rate, but can do nothing to set or move interest rates. As private actors buy foreign currencies (or gold), they extinguish local currency, thereby diminishing the monetary base. With a falling supply of the local currency, its price will stabilize. The point is that the system is automatic, with no central bank discretion; foreign currency transactions themselves change the local money supply." See also, regarding Iraq, Steve H. Hanke, "Dinar Plans," *WSJ*, Op-Ed, July 21, 2003.

64. Conant to Edwards, January 16 and March 26, 1902, Conant to Taft, August 8, 1902, WD NA RG 350/3197–18, 27, 35; Conant to Taft, March 28,

1902, WHT, S. 3, R. 35. The following exchange between Taft and Tennessee Senator Edward W. Carmack, a Bryan-Democrat, is indicative of the charged atmosphere regarding imperialism. Carmack: "Do you think we ought to be looking about the earth to find places on the other side of the sea in which to invest capital? Have we not a comparatively undeveloped country of our own here?" Taft: "I think we have a large country." Carmack: "Do we not have to borrow capital constantly from abroad?" Taft: "Senator, I have not made any expansion speeches. (Laughter)." Carmack: "I want to check you before you get to doing it. (Laughter)." Sen. Comm., *Hearings* (February 17, 1902), p. 408. The exchange occurred just after Taft's discussion of colonies and investment of surplus capital, citing Conant.

65. For Conant's recommendation that the bill go in as the Lodge–Cooper bill, see Conant to Root, December 11, 1901, and Conant to Taft, August 8, 1902, WD NA RG 350/3197–13, 35.

66. The state-chartered Guaranty Trust Company of New York (close ties with J. P. Morgan & Co) established a branch in Manila, but with insufficient business growth it soon withdrew, selling its assets to the IBC. After passage of the Federal Reserve Act, the National City Bank of New York, under the leadership of Frank A. Vanderlip, became the major US international commercial banking institution (while remaining preeminent in domestic banking as well), establishing branches worldwide. Regarding congressional action on Philippine banking and its effects: Conant to Edwards, January 16 and March 26, 1902, Conant to Taft, August 8, 1902, WD NA RG 350/3197–18, 27, 35; Conant to Taft, February 21 and March 28, 1902, WHT, S. 3, R. 35; Sen. William B. Allison (chairman, Sen. Comm. on Appropriations) to Taft, August 23, 1902, WHT, S. 3, R. 37. On the bond-based instead of assets-based bank-note issue in the banking part of the bill: Conant, January 25, 1902, at House Comm., *Hearings*, pp. 616–617; and Conant to Edwards, January 25, 1902, WD NA RG 350/3197–19, 21. Also on banking in the Philippines, see Henry C. Ide, "Banking, Currency and Finance in the Philippine Islands," *Annals*, XXX: 1 (July 1907), pp. 27–37; Jeremiah W. Jenks, "The Agricultural Bank for the Philippine Islands," ibid., pp. 38–44; Taft to J. Hudson McKnight, April 16, 1903, WHT, S. 3, R. 39; "Agricultural Bank of Egypt, Report to the Secretary of War and the Philippine Commission by Edwin W. Kemmerer," July 1, 1906, and e.g., Charles P. Scott (IBC, Hong Kong) to Kemmerer (Manila), July 3, 1905 (Letterhead listing branches), in Edwin W. Kemmerer Papers, Seeley G. Mudd Manuscript Library, Princeton University, Boxes 184, 242; hereinafter cited as EWK. For Conant's role in the establishment of the Federal Reserve System, going back to the 1890s before and during his work with the Indianapolis Monetary Commission and continuing in steady activity thereafter, see Parrini, "Charles A. Conant, Economic Crises and Foreign Policy," pp. 35–36, 40, 59, 61n9; Livingston, *Origins of the Federal Reserve System*, chs. 3–6; Parrini and Sklar, "New Thinking about the Market," p. 571, 571n27; M. J. Sklar, *Corporate Reconstruction*, p. 75, 75n46.

67. This time, it went in as the Lodge bill, and Lodge and Rhode Island Senator Nelson W. Aldrich, the powerful Republican leader (and Nelson A. Rockefeller's grandfather), together managed the bill and its passage on the

Senate floor. Conant to Taft, March 2, 1903, WHT, S. 3, R. 38; Lodge to
T. Roosevelt, February 17, 1903, Theodore Roosevelt Papers (Lib. of Cong.),
Series 1, Reel 33. In his letter, Lodge told Roosevelt: "I did a good piece of
work yesterday in getting through the Philippine Currency Bill. Aldrich and
I managed it, and I think it did credit to our heads and hearts. Aldrich's
power of psychic suggestion was very much in evidence in the means by
which we brought the Colorado Senators into line [Thomas M. Patterson
and Henry M. Teller]." Regarding the fractional coins matter: Taft to
Conant, September 1, 1902, WD NA RG 350/3197-38. Passage of the act:
Congressional Record, 57th, 2nd, Vol. 36, Part 2, pp. 2249–2251, 2570–2581.
This act and its implementation by the Philippine Commission in the
Philippine Gold Standard Act of October 10, 1903, became the fundamental law of the Philippine currency system. So closely and prominently was
Conant associated with the new system that in the Philippine press, in pop-
ular parlance, and in terms used by scholars and policy makers, at the time,
the new Philippine pesos were commonly called "Conants" or "Conant dol-
lars," and the currency in general "Conant money." See Kemmerer, *Modern
Currency Reforms*, pp. 331–332, 331n2, 335–336n2; Kemmerer, "Copy of
Rough Memorandum Notes Used by Mr. E. W. Kemmerer in Making His
Recommendations to the Philippine Commission Relative to the Currency
Question, Made August 11, 1903" (8 typescript pages, esp. pp. 6, 7, 8), WD
NA RG 350/808-206; Conant to Edwards, April 25, 27, 29, May 3, 1903,
WD NA RG 350/3197-48–51; Conant, *Principles of Money and Banking*,
Vol. I, p. 139n4.

68. For establishment of the CIE, *Cong. Rec.*, 52nd, 2nd, Vol. 36, pp. 1408–1410,
     1446, 2542. For appointment of CIE members: Hay to Hanna, Jenks,
     Conant, April 21, 1903, DS NA RG 59, Domestic Letters, M 40, R. 158;
     Conant to Hay, April 22, 1903, accepting the appointment, DS NA RG 59,
     M179, R. 1168. Hay's instructions to the CIE were based on a draft written
     by Conant at Hay's request: Hay to Conant, April 21, 1903, DS NA RG 59,
     M 40, R. 158, and Secretary of the Treasury Shaw to Hay, April 20, 1903,
     Hay Papers (LC), General Correspondence, Box 25. Concerning Jenks's
     mission: *Report on Certain Economic Questions in the English and Dutch
     Colonies in the Orient*, by Jeremiah W. Jenks, Special Commissioner, Bureau
     of Insular Affairs, War Department, September 1902 (Washington: GPO,
     1902); ch. II of this report (pp. 11–30) is devoted to "Currency Systems"
     of India, Burma, Ceylon, Netherlands Indies, Straits Settlements, Federated
     Malay States, and French Indo-China. See also, Parrini and Sklar, "New
     Thinking about the Market," pp. 573–577.

69. Conant to Taft, July 21, 1902, WD NA RG 350/3197-36; Conant to
     Taft, February 21, 1902, March 2, 1903, WHT, S. 3, R. 35, 38; Conant
     to J. G. Jester, February 27, 1902, WD NA RG 350/3197-24; Kemmerer,
     Modern Currency Reforms, p. 315; Conant, "The Gold Exchange Standard
     in the Light of Experience," p. 192; Conant, "Putting China on the Gold
     Standard," *North American Review*, November 1903, at CIE, *Stability of
     International Exchange: Report on the Introduction of the Gold Exchange
     Standard into China and Other Silver-Using Countries*, House Doc. No. 144,
     58th, 2nd (Washington: GPO, 1903), p. 269; A. Piatt Andrew, "The End of

the Mexican Dollar," *Quarterly Journal of Economics*, XVIII (May 1904), pp. 332, 334–336. The Straits Settlements (including Singapore) converted to the gold-exchange standard in 1903–1905, paralleling the conversion period of both the Philippines and Mexico; see Kemmerer, "Gold Standard for the Straits Settlements," *Political Science Quarterly*, XXI (December 1906), pp. 663–698; also Kemmerer, "The Establishment of the Gold Exchange Standard in the Philippines," *QJE*, XIX (August 1905), pp. 585–609; and Kemmerer, "Two Years of the Gold Exchange Standard," August 10, 1905, and "The Recent Currency Reform in the Philippines" (Rio Conference, 1906), at EWK, Box 243.

70. Conant to Hay, November 13, 1902, Hay Papers (LC), General Correspondence, Box 24, File: November 1–13, 1902. This may suggest putting to rest the old saw of whether, in US-China policy, government was "using" capitalists for political-diplomatic ends, or capitalists were "using" government for economic ends. Rather, a broad framework was at work, embracing both conceptual perspectives and property-production-market activity and interests, across government–society lines. Note that with foreign governments directly in play, the Department of State now assumed a leading role, along with, and in some basic respects superseding, the War Department – hence Conant's addressing this letter to Hay; it was on Morton Trust Company letterhead (38 Nassau Street, New York) and sent to Hay, not at the State Department, but at his DC residence, H and 16th Sts., NW, opening with a more personal "My Dear Mr. Hay."

71. On the US and the Boxer Indemnity, the US–China Commercial Treaty of 1903, and their relation to long-term US-foreign-policy objectives, the best studies are Carl P. Parrini, "United States, China, and the Boxer Indemnity," and "Framing the Commercial Treaties: Punishment by Reform" (unpublished papers); see also, Parrini, "Charles A. Conant, Economic Crises and Foreign Policy, 1896–1903," in *Behind the Throne*, and Parrini and Sklar, "New Thinking about the Market," pp. 573–574. Regarding the Mexican and Chinese government memoranda: Mexican Minister of Foreign Affairs Mariscal to Mexican Ambassador to the United States M. de Azpiroz, December 16, 1902, and M. de Azpiroz to Secretary of State John Hay, January 15, 1903, with Memorandum on the subject from Mexican Foreign Minister, of same date, DS NA RG 59, M. 54, R. 36, 37; Shen Tung (First Secretary and Chargé d'Affaires *ad interim*, Chinese Legation, Washington, DC) to Secretary of State Hay, January 19, 1903 and January 22, 1903, with Memorandum of same date, DS NA RG 59, M. 98, R. 5; Hay to Azpiroz, February 5, 1903; Azpiroz to Hay, April 4, 1903, enclosing long memorandum by Mexican Minister of Finance Limantour to Mexican Minister of Foreign Affairs Mariscal, March 26, 1903, DS NA RG 59, M. 54, R. 37. The Mexican and Chinese memoranda to the US were essentially identical, except for the parts dealing with particular circumstances of the respective countries. From the identical content, the style of writing, and the subject matter emphasized, it may be conjectured that Conant drafted them. On Limantour and the *cientificos*, see Arturo Grunstein, "From Imperialism to Postimperialism: An Early Mexican Response to Transnational Capitalism,"

ch. 9 in Becker and Sklar, eds., *Postimperialism and World Politics*, pp. 253–282, esp. pp. 270–271.

72. Roosevelt to the Senate and House, January 29, 1903, enclosing Hay to Roosevelt, January 28, 1903, in turn enclosing Azpiroz to Hay, January 15, 1903, with Memorandum, and Shen Tung to Hay, January 19, 1903, with Memorandum, at *Cong. Rec.*, January 29, 1903, 57th, 2nd, Vol. 36, Pt. 2, pp. 1408–1410 (Senate), and p. 1446 (House).

73. Conant to Taft, March 2, 1903 and August 27, 1903, WHT, S. 3, R. 38, 40; emphasis added. Conant wrote the August letter from London, where the CIE and the Mexican commission were negotiating with the British about Chinese currency reform. Relating to the earlier mission to Mexico, see, e.g., "The Influence of Falling Exchange Upon the Return Received for National Products (Arguments submitted to the monetary commission of the Republic of Mexico, April 18, 1903, by Messrs. Charles A. Conant, Jeremiah W. Jenks, and Edward Brush)," Appendix L, No. 1, in CIE, *Stability of International Exchange*, pp. 431–439. Here, the Americans argued that with a falling silver currency, Mexico in its trade with gold countries lost wealth in real terms, receiving less for its exports and paying more for its imports. Brush was initially slated to serve with Conant and Jenks on the CIE, but his being a director and an executive (secretary) of the American Smelting and Refining Company made the appointment untenable. Hanna replaced him and served as CIE chair. Brush served, instead, as "Technical Counsellor" to the Mexican commission negotiating in tandem with the CIE in England and Europe. "The International Exchange Commission," *Sound Currency*, Vol. 10 (1904), pp. 60–72, at pp. 60–61; also, attachments with Hanna (London) to Hay (Washington), June 6, 1903 ("Conference between Delegations from the United States, China, Mexico, and Representatives of Great Britain. Memoranda presented by the Comisión de Cambios Internacionales de la Republica Mexicana"), DS NA, *Miscellaneous Letters*, M. 179, R. 1174.

74. Root to Roosevelt, August 10, 1903, Root Papers (LC), Letterbooks, Letters Semi-Official, Container 177, Part 1, p. 34. Valuable studies of US currency reform programs for the Philippines, China, Mexico, and elsewhere, their interrelatedness, and the activity and thinking of Conant, Jenks, and others in the work, are: Carl Parrini, "Charles A. Conant, Economic Crises and Foreign Policy, 1896–1903," Emily S. Rosenberg, "Foundations of United States International Financial Power: Gold Standard Diplomacy, 1900–1905" and Rosenberg, *Financial Missionaries to the World*, chs. 1–3. See also, Parrini and Sklar, "New Thinking about the Market," and M. J. Sklar, *Corporate Reconstruction*, pp. 73–75, 74n45, 75n46.

75. Root to Roosevelt, August 10, 1903, with enclosures of cables and telegrams between the CIE (in Europe) and Hay, and between Root and Taft, regarding immediately sending Jenks to China, Root Papers (LC), Letterbooks, Letters Semi-Official, Container 177, Part 1, pp. 34–35.

76. Jenks to Taft, December 23, 1903, Jenks to Root, January 23, 1904, WD NA RG 350/808–205, 206. Also, Conant printed the Philippine Gold Standard Act of October 10, 1903, in the appendix of the CIE's report on stability of international exchange and installing the gold-exchange system in China

as, in his words, "an illustration of the proper method of doing the thing." Conant to Edwards, October 21, 1903, WD NA RG 350/3197–52. It is of interest to note here that Edwin W. Kemmerer, who by the 1920s was one of the world's leading international currency reform experts, and frequent adviser on, and implementer of, US government policy, started on that career in the summer of 1903 as 28-year-old Director of the Currency of the Philippine Treasury, in charge of installing and administering, in 1903–1906, the new Philippine gold-exchange currency system, under the detailed preparation by, and the continuous close guidance of, Conant and Jenks, who had jointly recommended his appointment. Kemmerer had been Jenks's prize graduate student at Cornell, completing his dissertation, on currency reform, under Jenks's supervision, in 1903, while Kemmerer was employed as an assistant professor of political economy at Purdue University. Kemmerer had also served as Jenks's assistant in 1901 in Jenks's work with the US Industrial Commission on Trusts and Industrial Combinations. After his service in the Philippines, Kemmerer returned to the US to become, with Jenks's decisive support, an assistant professor of political economy at Cornell, 1906–1912 (instead of Robert Hoxie who departed Cornell feeling Jenks had wronged him), and he then went on to his long-held professorship at Princeton, 1912–1943. Kemmerer dedicated his book, *Modern Currency Reforms*, "To my former teacher and colleague Jeremiah Whipple Jenks who first directed my interest to the field of modern currency reform." Regarding Kemmerer's appointment to the Philippine post: Conant and Jenks to Edwards, May 14, 1903, Ide to Edwards, May 28, 1903, WD NA RG 350/808–164, 165; Kemmerer to Jenks, April 6, May 18, 27, 31, August 27, 1903, EWK, Box 242 (also Box 242 for correspondence relating to the Cornell appointment). See also Emily S. Rosenberg and Norman L. Rosenberg, "From Colonialism to Professionalism: The Public–Private Dynamic in United States Foreign Financial Advising, 1898–1927," *Journal of American History*, 74: 1 (June 1987), pp. 59–82; M. J. Sklar, *Corporate Reconstruction*, pp. 73–74, 74n45.

77. The new Mexican gold-exchange currency system disintegrated under the impact of the events of the Mexican Revolution and the demise of the Diaz government, 1910–1911.

CHAPTER 2

A Panel at the AEA

The further backward you look, the further forward you can see.

Winston Churchill

On the morning of Saturday, December 28, 1901, a panel convened in Washington, DC, at the Fourteenth Annual Meeting of the American Economic Association (AEA). Brooks Adams delivered the panel paper on "Meaning of the Recent Expansion of the Foreign Trade of the United States." The two assigned discussants were George E. Roberts, director of the US Mint, Treasury Department (previously in private life, a prominent Iowa newspaper publisher), and Charles A. Conant, just returned to the US from East Asia on his Philippine mission. Among those adding extended discussion from the floor were Henry P. Willis (also known as H. Parker Willis), professor of economics and politics at Washington and Lee University, successor to Conant as correspondent at the *Journal of Commerce* (later the *Journal's* associate editor); Henry B. Gardner, professor of Political Economy of Brown University (specializing in money and banking, and public finance); John F. Crowell, head of the Bureau of Statistics, Treasury Department; and Edwin R. A. Seligman, eminent professor of Political Economy and Finance at Columbia University, scion of the J. & W. Seligman investment banking family, and the AEA's current president-elect.

Indicative of the historical orientation of the thought at work, the AEA, as several times previously, was once again meeting simultaneously with the American Historical Association, this time in 1901, at the Columbian University (today's George Washington University). In addition to mixed and collateral informal gatherings, the two associations

65

held their opening and closing sessions jointly. Seligman presented his notable essay, "Historical Materialism and the Economic Interpretation of History," at the closing joint session. At the opening joint session, the Friday night before the Brooks Adams panel that headed the AEA's regular sessions, addresses were delivered by AEA President Richard T. Ely, social-Christian reform advocate and professor of Political Economy at the University of Wisconsin (faculty colleague of Frederick Jackson Turner, John R. Commons, and Paul S. Reinsch), and by AHA President Charles Francis Adams, brother of Henry and Brooks. Historical consciousness intricately interwoven with a primordial American national identity was here strongly manifested in venue, personification, and thematic selection.[1]

Brooks Adams and his co-panelists could assume that the scholars in attendance knew well the character and dimensions of the "recent expansion of the foreign trade of the United States." Over the previous several years, the subject had been laid out in qualitative and statistical detail, discussed, analyzed, and placed in international economic context along with geopolitical implications, time and again, in many instances by panelists and audience members themselves, in government reports, scholarly and policy-oriented periodicals, trade journals, newspapers, and popular magazines. The panelists could therefore largely skip over the details, to focus on "Meaning." But a brief indication of these details as they were widely known and circulating at the time will serve to give the reader a more informed engagement with the panel discussion and its immediate historical context.[2]

A year earlier, for example, in the premier issue (November 1900) of Walter Hines Page's magazine, *The World's Work*,[3] Frederic Emory, the chief of the Department of State's Bureau of Foreign Commerce, reprised statistics and information that the bureau, since the mid-1890s, had been regularly dispensing in its annual reports, here (as also in the reports) with interpretive commentary, and under the title, "Our Growth as a World Power," with a subtitle, "Economic Reasons for Political Expansion – The Increase by Leaps of Our Foreign Trade." The trade increase centered in exports, and particularly a strong steady rise in the exports of manufactured goods: "The United States has long been a great exporter, but it was not until a few years ago that this country began to show a steady advance in the sale [abroad] of manufactured goods." At the same time, in addition to "the large excess over any preceding year," US manufactures exports "show also a great gain in the extent of territory covered in the markets of the world."[4]

By the late 1890s, the State Department's Bureau of Foreign Commerce had already been reporting on what it called, in a phrase that became quite common thereafter, "an American invasion of the markets of the world," in which "the commercial relations of the United States are undergoing a marked and significant change" that was proceeding "at an accelerated pace." The US was no longer "the 'granary of the world' merely." US manufactures exports had "continued to extend with a facility and promptitude of results which have excited the serious concern of countries that, for generations, had not only controlled their home markets, but had practically monopolized certain lines of trade in other lands." These "certain lines" of US manufactures that were now penetrating markets "throughout the world" included high-value capital goods and consumer durables, and ranged the gamut of "iron and steel, labor-saving machinery and tools, boots and shoes, leather, furniture, bicycles, electrical supplies, hardware and cutlery, locomotives, [and] cotton goods."[5]

From 1895 to 1900, US total foreign trade grew about 30 percent, from about $1.7 billion to about $2.2 billion, with all but about $45 million of that growth in exports, and about one-half of that accounted for by manufactures exports, which more than doubled, from about $200 million to over $430 million, and rose from about 23 percent to about 31.5 percent of total US exports. By 1899–1900, in total exports, the US, Emory noted, "stands second only to the United Kingdom," and US exports "exceed those of Germany, with her splendidly organized industrial activity, by nearly $300,000,000."[6]

The US had become, as Vanderlip said, "a billion dollar country," that is, with annual exports regularly exceeding $1 billion. In the half-dozen years, 1895–1901, years in which US gross national product (GNP) grew from about $13 billion to about $20 billion, the US aggregate export surplus over imports, Vanderlip noted, amounted to about $2 billion, "while from the founding of our Government up to six years ago [1789–1895] the excess of our exports amounted to only $383,000,000, a balance, which we have recently equaled in eight months."[7] "All other commercial events of our time," Vanderlip observed, "are comparatively insignificant when measured against the figures of gigantic industrial development which the United States has in five or six years made in the world's trade, and particularly is that true when viewed in the light of the effect of that development upon the commercial conditions of other nations." On this last point, as Vanderlip further explained, "The natural accompaniment of our invasion of foreign fields heretofore held by European manufacturers has been that we, at the same time, have been able to supply more completely our own markets," so that even with rising US consumption "in the last half dozen prosperous years," there had been "no material increase in our imports." The overall result was that: "We have been successful competitors with foreign manufacturers both in their own field and in our home markets. Those foreign manufacturers have not only lost many profitable markets the world over, but they have been permitted to gain no new foothold in that greatest of all their markets – the United States." Or, as Emory put it: "As we advance along these lines, crowding our competitors more and more closely, not only in markets common to all, but in their own home markets, we shall be less and less able to evade those responsibilities which inevitably attend so active a participation in the world's affairs."[8]

In summary, by the last years of the 1890s, US industry, its efficiency honed by the rigors of the great depression of that decade, and by economies of scale and scope attained with corporate concentration and reorganization, was outproducing and underselling British and European industry in US markets, in British and European home markets, and in world markets elsewhere – a triple loss of markets, extant and prospective, for the British and Europeans. This portended not only a new and intense rivalry between the US and the other industrial powers, but also an intensification of rivalries and strains already current among Britain and the European powers, in the Middle East, in Africa, in Asia, in Latin America, and in Europe itself. The US was now implicated in the conflicts of the "Old World" along with the Old World powers themselves. This was at the heart of the "responsibilities" it could no longer "evade."

With such background information and perspective in mind, let us now return to the AEA panel of December 28, 1901 on "Meaning of the Recent Expansion of the Foreign Trade of the United States."[9]

BROOKS ADAMS

Drawing upon his previous published work, including, in particular, essays of the past three years, Brooks Adams began with history. He posited the premise of the economic basis of human history, and correlative premises that economics is a historical science, and that economics is the master historical science – a science of cause and effect in time, that is, in human affairs from past to present and future: "Every science is based on experience, and we can draw no inferences regarding the future save such as we deduce from the past." It was therefore necessary "that our inquiries into a subject such as this should begin at the beginning, no matter how remote that beginning may be." In this way, Adams was arguing that US history, its present circumstances, and its future prospects, were to be understood in the context, and as an outcome, of prevalent patterns of human history, not simply those of the US' own history, but those of world history since antiquity. The US was no exception to a universal human history, nor therefore to the lessons, principles, laws, or imperatives, of historical science.[10]

To Adams, accordingly, it was first necessary to "explain my conception of the scope of economics," lest "I might seem to wander" from the subject. Economics was "the study of competition among men . . . of that struggle for survival which is the primal cause of wars and revolutions, of the strife of classes, of financial panics, and finally of that steady change which goes on from age to age in the type of populations – a change occasioned by the elimination of such [human] organisms as are unable to adapt themselves to the demands of an ever varying environment." It followed that "economics embraces a large section of the whole field of human knowledge and experience," ranging from archaeology to "military, political, and religious history," and to "the history of jurisprudence and of institutions," and to "numismatics . . . mechanics, and . . . metallurgy." The economist also "should be profound in geography," should be "a linguist," and "Above all he should be a man of the world, familiar with the care of property, with the stock-market, and with methods of transportation and administration" (p. 80). Modestly, Adams said he could "lay claim to no such equipment," but he would "attempt only to suggest, my hope being to interest abler minds in certain phenomena which I deem vital to us all" (pp. 80–81). We might say, on Adams's behalf, and as Adams himself thought and could well have said, that history/economics as a science, or a study, of *social evolution*, was, like other sciences or disciplines, the work of many minds, effectively interacting, and that the US was to be understood in terms of evolutionary, or historical, processes (laws) of variability, or adaptation to changing circumstances, common to all societies and all peoples throughout history, without exception, and discoverable by the associated work of the many inquirers.[11]

In the larger perspective of world history, and given these universalist historical premises, "an inquiry into the 'meaning of the recent expansion'" of US foreign trade, "opens the gravest of economic problems," Adams warned, because given its character and dimensions (as prefatorily indicated above), "that expansion is, probably, only one amid innumerable effects of a displacement of the focus of human energy." Displacements of this kind and magnitude had "occurred periodically from the dawn of civilization, and of all phases of human development they are, perhaps, those which merit most to rivet our attention," and particularly because, as in this case of the late nineteenth century, "they have always been preceded by a wave of superb prosperity, and have left decay behind." Such displacements meant "a shifting of the [world's] social equilibrium," than which "no event is so far reaching . . . [and] none exacts a more practical treatment," because it centers in the basic "competition of life," for survival, in which the "weapons . . . range from the mighty army to the pettiest detail of the peasant's household." In this competition of life, "No economy is too small, no waste is too trifling to be neglected," for in human history, "communities rise and fall in proportion to their economy . . . [and] economy varies according to circumstances." What is economy? "Economy is adaptation to the conditions under which men compete, and these conditions are only learned through experience." Economics, as a historical (experiential) science in the study of competition for survival, was itself, then, vital to successful adaptation, "for at each passing moment nature is selecting those organisms which work cheapest, and rejecting those which are costly," and in this selection, nature is "omnipotent and merciless" (p. 81). Or, as Secretary of State John Hay phrased it, two months later, in his state eulogy of the assassinated President William McKinley, addressing the new US role in the world consequent upon its advanced stage of economic development, "The questions that are put to us we must answer without delay, without help – for the sphinx allows no one to pass," the sphinx, as Hay explained, being the "symbol of the hostile forces of omnipotent nature, who punishes with instant death our failure to understand her meaning." The US, no less than all other societies in history, was subject to the universal law of civilization and decay. Or, as Adams had plainly phrased it, "America enjoys no immunity from natural laws."[12]

To "begin at the beginning," Adams went back in time about 3,000 years to "the first recorded displacement of energy," recorded in that first work of history, the *Old Testament*. It could "serve as the prototype of all that have followed." It was the rise and fall of Nineveh, thirteenth to seventh centuries BC – today's Mosul, Iraq. Nineveh's imperial reach or interests stretched from Mesopotamia eastward to Persia and beyond, to Bactria (northeastern Afghanistan), the Punjab (Pakistan, India), Cashmir (Kashmir), central Asia, and China, and westward to the Mediterranean (p. 82) – the nexus of Asia and the West where at the opening of the twenty-first century AD, the US, Britain, and other "great powers" were deeply engaged.[13]

Ancient Nineveh (and Babylon at large) represented that "phase of development which we call civilization." Adams thought he could "assume that we shall agree" that this developmental phase called civilization "opened with the smelting of the metals," with which "man makes his sword, his plough, and his money . . . . [and] the tools with which he builds decked ships, and convenient wheeled vehicles." Peoples using metals – copper, bronze, iron – "evicted, enslaved or destroyed" those peoples "adhering to wood or stone," which proved "comparatively wasteful in war or peace." By ancient times, "the metals became a condition of existence in the more advanced regions of the world, and the position of the mines necessarily exercised a controlling influence over the current of international exchanges" (pp. 81–82).

In an "epoch when sea-going ships did not exist, and the Dardanelles were closed," Adams noted, Nineveh's "supremacy" resided not in itself having the "natural resources," the mines, but in "her geographical position, as the converging point," on the Tigris, of the two major land routes "leading from northeastern Asia to the Mediterranean," and thus in having the metals even without itself having the mines, and in controlling the West/Asia trade. The southern route passed over the road running through what later became Tehran, and thence to Nineveh (Mosul); the northern route, with short boat traffic on the Caspian and Black seas, proceeded south through Trebizond and alongside Lake Van (today's eastern Turkey), to Nineveh, "and from thence several routes led to the different Syrian ports" on the Mediterranean (today's Lebanon). "Therefore, in the main, the eastern trade went west by land, and accordingly the chief care of the Ninevite emperors was to police the roads along which this commerce flowed. Hence their endless campaigns both toward Syria and Armenia" (pp. 82–83).

Serving as the major Mediterranean ports of "the Mesopotamian empire," the Phoenician cities of Tyre and Sidon "rose with the rise of Babylon and Nineveh, and fell with their decay." The Phoenicians developed markets for "the commodities of the East" in the Mediterranean region, as well as "acceptable exchanges." "Slaves and metals were the only two European products" Asia would take in payment of its exports, "and of the two the metals were the more important." The Phoenicians immediately "grasped the situation," laying the basis of their "future opulence" by developing the mines of Cyprus (copper), and then "crowned their fortune by discovering the silver and gold of Spain, and the tin of Cornwall" (p. 83).

As revealed in their legends of the Minotaur and the Golden Fleece, which "tell plainly enough of their weakness, and of their aspirations," the Greeks understood that as long as they remained outside "the line of traffic," they were "condemned to poverty." So they "tried war," in order to enter upon "the race for supremacy." The Greeks "sacked Troy,[14] forced the Dardanelles, penetrated into the Black Sea," and from Miletus they spread settlements "along the coast of Asia Minor [Turkey], and, passing the Bosphorus, planted colonies at all the outlets" of the Asian trade. They thereby "opened direct water communication between the Oxus [River – in Afghanistan and Central Asia to the Aral Sea] and Gibraltar, by way of Corinth [Greece] and Syracuse [Sicily]." With the development of this system, "the lines of transportation straightened," and Nineveh "fell into eccentricity," and, as Adams said, "the chronology tells the rest." By 700 BC, the Greeks established their power "throughout the Euxine" (the Black Sea region), the prophet Nahum "foretold the destruction of Nineveh," which "fell in 606 BC and Babylon soon followed"; by 538 BC, the last Babylonian king "Belshazzar read the writing on the wall" (pp. 83–84).[15]

The Persians sought to succeed to the seat of empire, but "the disease which wasted Mesopotamia was inanition caused by the diversion of her trade." The Persians therefore needed to conquer the Greeks to take control of the lines of trade; hence their invasion of Greece, the battles of Marathon in 490 BC and Plataea in 479 BC, and from the defeats there, "Persia never rallied." Athens reached its zenith around 450 BC, Adams noted, and by 400 BC, Persia had "rotted to the core." In 331 BC, "the end came with the slaughter of Darius and the triumph of Alexander." From this history, Adams inferred that the Persian wars marked the movement of "the world's centre of energy . . . from Mesopotamia to the Ionian Sea," and that this "consolidation" became the basis of "the economic system which subsequently sustained the Roman empire" (p. 84). And as the saying went, we may add, all roads led to Rome (many of them built or improved by Rome).

The shift of empire from the Babylonians and Persians to the Greeks and Romans afforded an "example of a change of social equilibrium," that Adams found "valuable because of its simplicity" in following the paths of exchange. "The West had little beyond its metals. The East possessed the rest," with Arabia, India, and China supplying "spices, silk and gems." Europeans maintained "the balance of exchanges" with the export of gold, silver, and copper. But the Romans "were not inventive," they did not make improvements in mining, "the waste was prodigious," and they failed "in their attempt to open up Germany." The demand for metal rose, the supply did not keep up, and therefore, Adams argued, the Roman

Empire "had hardly been organized before it began to spend its capital."
It could neither "extend its source of supply, nor meet eastern competition" in agriculture and manufactures, and it went bankrupt "when the
mines of Spain failed" (p. 85).

This ancient history, Adams held, "may aid us in interpreting the
phenomena of the present time." He cited four lessons: (1) the evidence
tended to show that from antiquity "the need of metals stimulated men
to explore toward the west," and there "they found what they sought";
(2) as metals supply grew and new sources were found westward, "the
diameter of the economic system" enlarged, and so "the centre has been
displaced," and thus "the social equilibrium has been shaken"; (3) with
the disturbance of the social equilibrium, "the centre of the economic
system has moved," as the trade routes changed accordingly, throwing
"the ancient capitals" into "eccentricity," bringing "ruin for the city, and
annihilation for the population" (pp. 85–86).

Dispensing with Clausewitz's aphorism (that war is politics by other
means – perhaps as a rather empty truism with otherwise little distinctive
meaning), Adams cited as the *fourth* lesson that "war is as essentially
an instrument of commercial competition, as is trade itself; that, indeed,
war is only commercial competition in its intensest form."[16] Explaining
more incisively, and invoking an empiricist (experiential) authority,
Adams added, "All the facts point to the conclusion that war is regularly
kindled by the heat engendered by the impact upon an established economic system of a system which is consolidating." This meant that "the
outbreak of war at certain stages of development must be regarded as a
usual, if not an invariable phenomenon."[17]

As Adams proceeded, unlike in his book, *The Law of Civilization and
Decay*, he omitted reference to Byzantium, and to the rise, by war and
otherwise, in place of Rome (East and West), of the empire of Islam, Arab
and Ottoman, to a commercial and political hegemony in the Asia/West
intercourse, many centuries in duration. Here, under time constraints,
he skipped over this large and formatively consequential epoch, as he
also skipped over the Mongols and Ming China, to go directly from the
Roman empire to "the rise of England," with only scarce mention of
Italian and Spanish intrusions (and none of Portuguese and Dutch), and
then to the US.

Adams noted that "during the middle ages the financial metropolis lay
in northern Italy, as in a remote antiquity it had lain in Mesopotamia."
But this "equilibrium" lasted only until "the inflow of gold and silver
from Mexico and Peru" pushed "the centre of exchanges westward,

much as the inflow of the Spanish metals had projected it two thousand years before." Then in the sixteenth century, "England laid the basis of her future fortune by robbing Spanish treasure"; as Persia had attacked the Greeks, so Spain retaliated, and "the Armada met a defeat as decisive as Xerxes met at Salamis." The current of the exchanges then "flowed north," and by 1815, having vanquished France, its "chief rival," Britain "held an economic supremacy more absolute than that of Rome." The nineteenth-century British supremacy "surpassed the Roman because resting on broader foundations" (p. 86).

Britain became the center of the world economic system, fourfold, Adams explained, as "the world's distribution point like Nineveh, as "a carrier and explorer like Phoenicia," as "the world's banker like Rome" [or northern Italy], and, with "her supply of useful metals," as the world's leading manufacturer, enjoying "a substantial monopoly of manufacturing during two generations." In manufactures, Britain "undersold India," instead of being "drained by the East." Even in agriculture, British production "nearly sufficed" for its population "down to 1845" [1846, repeal of the Corn Laws, but with cheap imported supply thereafter], whereas "Roman agriculture failed after the Punic wars" (pp. 86–87).

Never before had an empire assembled "such [a] favorable combination of conditions," and "an equilibrium so stable defied attack." But it was soon "shaken," not by challenges in Europe or the East, but, Adams observed, "by the series of events which propelled the United States along the path which must presently end in her supremacy or her ruin." The California gold discovery of 1848 was the "first link in this chain of cause and effect . . . and upon that discovery has, perhaps, hinged the destiny of modern civilization." Before 1848, the US was a "poor country," with slow development and "overwhelming difficulties," without the capital to overcome its "immense distances" by efficient transportation, and thus unable to "compete with a narrow and indented peninsula like Europe." In short, "Her mass outweighed her energy and her capital." The gold influx wrought a "magical" change, particularly the dramatic rise in "the accumulation of capital," 1848–1860, corresponding with the output of the mines in the West – gold, then silver, copper, lead. The capital accumulation fed the installation of a "comprehensive railroad system," with all of its developmental implications (pp. 87–88).

The accelerated US economic development, and the new "stress of competition" it pressed upon England and Europe, corresponded once again with "the centre of metallic production . . . [being] projected westward," and with it "the seat of commercial exchanges." The result, as

Adams said, was that "the trade routes are straightening, London is falling into eccentricity, and Europe is being undersold." The chain of events was "nearly a reproduction of the decline of Nineveh," and in the context of historical cause and effect, "the process stands out with the logical precision of a natural law" (pp. 88–89).[18]

Adams proceeded with some further historical detail on US economic development and its impact on England and Europe in the period 1870s–1890s, showing that "the logical precision of a natural law" did not mean that a looming US economic supremacy was occurring *automatically* from the westward projection of metals production and corresponding changes in the patterns of trade, but from those happenings combined with a sine qua non of effective adaptations by the American people and their *economy* ("adaptation to the conditions under which men compete") to changing circumstances, that is, effective adaptations ("learned through experience") without which the economic supremacy, the seat of the world's exchanges, and the global primacy, would be lost, and passed to others more competitively (economically) adaptive. Thus, his caveat that the current trends "must presently end in her [US] supremacy or her ruin."

In 1873, as European currency conversion from silver to gold spread, "America's [European] creditors rejected her silver," which had represented, Adams noted, "a cash asset of upward of $35,000,000 annually." The US had to sell other commodities, "and the chief of these were farm products." But the fall in agricultural prices that had set in by the 1870s, "reduced the value of wheat and cotton alarmingly." "Ruin seemed impending," and the US "suffered keenly for years" (the severe depression, 1873–1877). In the event, however, the US "proved herself equal to the emergency," producing more cheaply than Europe, and at length it "has not been the [US] debtor, but the [English and European] creditor who has ultimately collapsed."[19] Railroads and ocean steam-shipping brought down "freights," so that American wheat sold readily across the Atlantic. "English farmers could not cope with the situation." Land went out of production, "rents broke, and soon the aristocratic classes stood on the brink of insolvency." To save their "encumbered real estate," the British landowners had to sell "personal property," and US securities were "the best property the British owned." They sold "in masses, until they exhausted the supply. Afterward they borrowed" (pp. 88–89). (And married.)

By 1900, the US could "now afford to lend," but that was because, at first, as Adams said, "American society shook to its base." With reduced proceeds from silver and other lower-priced commodities, the US "had to meet the deficiency with gold . . . [and] gold flowed eastward." In 1893 alone, Adams recounted, the US exported $87 million net of gold, "a sum probably larger than any community has been forced to part with under similar conditions." Americans had to adapt to the changing circumstances, including those of their own nation's economic development: "The crisis had to end in either insolvency [e.g., President Cleveland's bond flotations, the ending of silver coinage, and the continuing outflow of gold to 1896] or relief, and relief came through an exertion of energy, perhaps without a parallel" – that is, the corporate reorganization of the economy (pp. 89–90).

To speak of "the crisis of the 1890s" meant not a country simply in a disorderly uproar and confusion, but as Adams understood it, a crisis in the rigorous sense of a turning point, and in this case one bringing on a historic transformation. "In three years, America reorganized her whole social system by a process of consolidation, the result of which has been the so-called trust" – or in Vanderlip's words, "the great corporation" – and, as Adams went on to say, "the trust, in reality, is the highest type of administrative efficiency, and therefore of economy, which has, as yet, been attained."[20] The American people, through their corporate reconstruction of their economic system – their "social system" in Adams's equation – met the test of *economy* in the "competition of life," for survival and hence for supremacy. "By means of this consolidation the American people were enabled to utilize their mines to the full" – coal, and iron and nonferrous metals, alike – and "the centres of mineral production and of exchanges were forced westward," from Europe (Paris, Hamburg) and England (London) to New York. Touching more specifically upon leading characteristics of the new historical conditions, Adams hit the keynote of steel, the major metal of modern power and of modern society as such: "Only four years ago, in March, 1897, America completed her reorganization, for in that month the great consolidations of Pittsburgh first undersold Europe in steel." (And President McKinley was inaugurated.) With the rising system consolidating and the shifting of the world's social equilibrium in play, Adams observed, "the well known symptoms supervened." Referring, presumably (as in his published essays), to the Spanish–American War, the Sudan War, the Boer War, and the anti-Boxer intervention in China, Adams noted that "The first of these symptoms was war." This historical situation, however, was special: "The peculiarity of the present moment is its rapidity and intensity," and Adams observed, "this appears to be due to the amount of energy developed in the US, in proportion to the energy developed elsewhere." To characterize the US in these late nineteenth-century years in terms of "depression," "robber barons," "gilded age," "populism," etc., would rather parochially, and "American-centrically," miss the larger historical point: "The shock of the impact of the new [US] power seems overwhelming" (p. 90). A new world order (system) was emerging, or at the least, struggling to be born.[21]

Here let us listen to Secretary Hay, in his state eulogy of the fallen president, as if playing to Adams. Referring to "the vast economical developments" of the previous few years, Hay recalled that at the time of McKinley's election in 1896, "the country was suffering from a long period of depression," but his victory corresponded with "a great and momentous movement . . . along all the lines of industry and commerce," so that "In the very month of his inauguration [US] steel rails began to be sold at $18 a ton – one of the most significant facts of modern times," because it meant that "American industries had adjusted themselves to the long depression – that through the power of the race to organize and combine, stimulated by the conditions then prevailing, and perhaps by the prospect of legislation favorable to industry, Americans had begun to undersell the rest of the world. The movement went on without ceasing." The advance all along the line at home went with global projection. "All industries responded to the new stimulus and American trade set out on its new crusade, not to conquer the world, but to trade with it on terms advantageous to all concerned." Yet war came, and although with great expense, the US became all the more enriched. President McKinley's "four years of administration were costly; we carried on a war which, though brief [against Spain], was expensive." The US, Hay noted, "borrowed two hundred millions and [we] paid our own expenses" (Vanderlip's stewardship at Treasury), "without asking for indemnity" (in fact, on the contrary, the US made payment of $20 million to Spain in acceding to the Philippines and Guam); nevertheless, "the effective reduction of the debt now exceeds the total of the war bonds"; the US now paid $6 million less in interest than before the war, and "no bond of the United States yields the holder 2 per cent on its market value," as a result of which, combined with the nation's prodigious economic growth and efficiency at home and in markets abroad, "we have five hundred and forty-six millions [dollars] of gross gold in the Treasury."[22]

Adams put "the shock of the impact" of the rising US economic power starkly: with Pittsburgh underselling Europe in steel, "Immediately Spain and China disintegrated," while Britain had entered upon "a phase of decay corresponding pretty exactly to that which Spain passed through under Philip II," and Russia "collapsed."[23] Germany "sought relief by attacking China and attempting to absorb her mines" (in Shantung province, 1897–1898). Adams gave as "the reason for these catastrophes" the fact that "no nation so suddenly ever attained to such a commanding position as the United States now holds," and that "no nation ever succeeded in so short a time in developing such resources so cheaply." Its location and multiversity of resources and capacities, moreover, made for and magnified a historically unprecedented power. The US lay "between two continents with ports on either ocean connected by the most perfect of railroads." Its mountains did not, as in Asia, "make transportation costly"; its great lakes facilitated "penetrating the interior"; and it possesses "unlimited gold and silver, iron, coal and copper, with a fertile soil." More especially, combined with all these natural resources and advantages, the US had "an enterprising population," and its "whole social system, including industry, transportation and farming," was "administered with a precision elsewhere undreamed of." Hence, the US "enjoys not the advantages of Nineveh or Syracuse, of Rome, of Lombardy, or of England separately, but of all these combined, and her attack is proportionately cogent." It was consistent with all past historical experience, and all the more so in this instance, that "the centre of gravity of human society is shifting very rapidly, the seat of mineral production and of commercial exchanges is migrating westward, the lines of transportation are straightening to correspond, and London is ceasing to be the universal mart." Adams added: "As with Nineveh, so with London" (pp. 90–91).[24] Or as Hay reprised, giving notice to the joint session of Congress and, through the attending diplomatic corps, to the world: "The 'debtor nation' has become the chief creditor nation. The financial center of the world, which required thousands of years to journey from the Euphrates to the Thames and the Seine, seems passing to the Hudson between daybreak and dark." Provided, that is, the American people knew how to act, "for the sphinx allows no one to pass."[25]

Preparatory to treating the question of the American people acting, or adapting and competing, adequately, or with effective "economy," in the new historical conditions, Adams assessed the competitive capacities of the three powers at the time most commonly regarded as in serious contention against the US – Britain, Germany, and Russia. He made no reference here to France or Japan, most likely because at this point, in the common parlance, France seemed no longer, and Japan not yet, a sufficiently *great* power. He briefly specified the weaknesses of each of the recognized contenders, in turn.

Britain, Adams reiterated, had "literally eaten up" its US accumula-
tions, and now "lives by borrowing." Much of its nominal exports of
coal, ore, and provisions went to British bases and coaling stations, and
hence were "paid by Englishmen, and is dead loss." As its iron and copper
mines were failing, Britain had to import metals and at the same time
"pay Americans to feed her, and pay for the transport." Yet the British
"spend upon the basis of the lavish profits of old," now gone; hence,
"the drain of gold which once prostrated Rome, and afterward desolated
Spain." It always led to "pillage." Just as Philip and Alva had sought to
"make treasure flow" from Flanders and the Dutch, so now with "the
policy of Lord Salisbury's cabinet toward South Africa" and its mines,
in the Boer War. But England like Spain lacked the "military energy."
Adams left implicit what he had argued at length in his recent essays,
just published the year before as *America's Economic Supremacy*, that
Britain being in irrevocable decline and decay, its future lay either in ruin,
or in alliance with the US, the two as great maritime powers, against the
European continental powers, in Europe and in Asia, and in the transatlantic region (pp. 91, 92).

As for Germany, since the 1870s, having unified and enlarged itself
and defeated France, it "organized to meet English competition." Like
England, however, Adams noted, Germany "also has been perturbed"
by the shifting of the social equilibrium westward to the US. German
industry had vigorously developed and become profitable, but when
"American trusts entered the field this profit disappeared," and the
Germans "now comprehend that they must adjust their whole system
of agriculture, industry and transportation to a new [US] standard."[26]
Success was "problematical": Germany had neither "the bulk" nor the
mines the US possessed. "She must always buy her raw material." Even
the German beet sugar industry faced "destruction" from loss of the US
market to "Cuban competition." As with Britain, the prospect here also
was for a German resort to pillage, Adams specifying the mines of China
(p. 92). It may be added that Adams could be taken here to be antici-
pating the German pillaging eastward and westward in Europe and the
Mediterranean, in World Wars I and II.

From the shifting of the social equilibrium, Russia "suffered most,"
Adams held, with least competitive capacity among the powers: Russia's
"unwieldy shape and ill-situated ports make her transportation costly, and
. . . her population is hopelessly archaic and therefore wasteful." It was,
Adams observed, "the old struggle between the Stone Age, and the metals."
The Russian "vice" began at the "base," where "the communal land-tenure

still prevails." It indicated "an intellectual development more than three centuries behind the American," and just as, were "the Elizabethans resuscitated and made to compete with us they would assuredly starve," so "Russians starve." The Russian peasant, with "nothing but his grain . . . without money to buy machinery, or intelligence to use it, without railways, or tolerable roads, without even the stimulus which comes from sole ownership of the land they till, ground down by taxes and subject to military service, are made to compete with the capitalistic system of Dakota, the machinery and energy of Nebraska, and the Pennsylvania Railroad. The conclusion is foregone. They perish by thousands from inanition" (pp. 93, 94).

Russia's backwardness and consequent competitive incapacity were particularly manifested in its pre-modern system of officialdom and bureaucracy. Here Adams dwelt on a decisive characteristic distinguishing modern society from pre-modern society: "Administration is the last and highest product of civilization; a primitive community is primitive, precisely because it lacks the administrative faculty." The distinction Max Weber was later to make between the pre-modern "prebend" system and the salaried bureaucracy system of modern society, Adams here made: "The payment to officials of fixed salaries instead of fees, is an advanced economic conception . . . All primitive societies, however, prefer fees, hence the official does not work unless he is paid. Fees breed delay, waste and peculation." With such administrative backwardness, "all Russian undertakings are excessively wasteful." Russian railways, such as the Trans-Siberian, and industry alike, entangled in state enterprise and pre-modern bureaucracy, remained underdeveloped, inefficient, overpriced, and deeply in debt, to pay for which the Russian government taxed at home and borrowed abroad, with interest and principal flowing out when not in default. Rich in resources, yet Russia's backwardness kept it from benefiting from them in agriculture, mining, or industry, and it had to rely on foreign aid – "strangers to organize their plants," and loans "to keep the works employed," and to repay previous loans. Russia remained poor and effete, unable to take whatever advantage it had from its size, resources, and centralized government power. Under the impact of the sudden US rise, it "collapsed" (pp. 90, 93, 94).[27]

Having assayed current developments, in light of the history of displacements of the focus of human energy, and the corresponding shifts in the world's social equilibrium, "from the dawn of civilization" to recent times, Adams now concluded with such "inferences regarding the future," which toward the beginning of his paper he said, we can only "deduce from the past" (p. 81).

Inferring from the patterns established in the past and still at work, Adams saw conflict of unprecedented intensity and ferocity in the future, pitting Europe against the US, and war on a grand scale beyond any of the past – unless the knowledge from the experiential science of economics/history could yield ways and means, and the wisdom, to avoid it. "These symptoms of energy at home [US] and of collapse abroad," he maintained, "point to a readjustment of the social equilibrium on an unprecedented scale." Explaining further his inference from past history, he noted, "Unless all experience is to be reversed the ferocity of the struggle for survival must deepen until one of the two competing economic systems [that is, the US and the European] is destroyed." Whatever the other symptoms or signs, "the shadow of the approaching crisis" could be discerned in "the failure of the purchasing power of Europe which is reflected in our [US] declining exports" to Europe, coupled with the "threats of retaliation" by Europe against US trade, "which we daily hear." If the US were "to push her advantages home, and drive her rivals to extremity," it was likely that in the European retaliation, the US would "lie open to two methods of attack" – a Eurasian continental system excluding the US, and a European mining of China, thereby forcing the social equilibrium further westward beyond the US or its control (pp. 94–95).

As to the first method of attack, in Adams's words: "European nations singly or in combination may attempt commercial exclusion somewhat on the principle on which Napoleon acted against England; or they may adopt a policy which will lead to war, such for example as disregarding the Monroe Doctrine." Against European hostilities, the US was "vulnerable through her communications." As history showed, "Like all centres of international exchanges the United States must preserve her outlets open else she will suffocate, and these outlets now embrace both [the Atlantic and the Pacific] oceans." It was on this "same principle" that the kings of Nineveh "for centuries, waged ceaseless war against the Syrians and Egyptians on the west, and the Armenians on the north, to control the roads to the Black Sea and the Mediterranean" (p. 95), and now, as this implied and as Mahan (and others) drove home, the need of the US to control its global sea lanes.[28] In line with this strategic point, it may be noted that the United States at this time was beginning to develop a two-ocean naval power, served by the Spanish–American War's establishing US naval presence in the Caribbean/Atlantic and the Pacific, the negotiation and renegotiation of the Hay–Pauncefote treaty with Britain, giving the US complete control over an interocean isthmian canal, and continued building of US naval power, especially in capital ships.[29]

Europe's second "method of attack" was by "opening regions which shall be to America what America has already been to Europe," and thereby "to force mineral production once more westward." Adams specified "northern China." Germany was already active in Shantung province, but "the provinces of Shansi and Honan," a region "not unduly large, or distant from the sea, or costly to develop, or unhealthy," held stores of coal and iron "unparalleled in value." Adams postulated that if "such a people as the Germans could subdue those provinces, police them, organize them on the American basis, with labor trained and directed by Europeans versed in the American system, there seems to be no reason why America should not be undersold." Hence, China was the key to the future, or, as Adams unabashedly put it: "The problem of future civilization, therefore, promises rather to turn upon the capacity of Europeans to partition and reorganize China, and upon the attitude which the US may assume toward the experiment, than upon natural physical difficulties" (p. 95). Hence, we may observe, by the time of Adams's presentation at this panel: the US "Open Door" initiatives in China, which included insistence upon sustaining Chinese national integrity and its control over its own resources, with US rights to participate in their development, all of which strengthened by the US presence in the Philippines, and its strong engagement in the anti-Boxer intervention and the diplomatic (including indemnity) aftermath.

Adams ended his discourse, returning to its beginning, assigning economics to its ethical and scientific work, without sentimentality, of guiding human events in modern times through a remorseless history from past to future. As he said, "Here then, I apprehend, lies the field of usefulness for modern economics." Its subject was not simply technical questions of supply and demand, interest rates and money supply, and the like, but "these complex questions involving peace and war, prosperity and ruin," which were indeed "the profoundest which can absorb the mind." It was, in short, on a par with the depth otherwise associated with religion and philosophy. On these questions "hinges the existence both of individuals and nations." In terms at the core of the western philosophical and scientific tradition, as we may plausibly assume Adams was acutely aware, he said, "If economics, dealing with such questions in the light of the past, can in some degree illuminate the future, economics will not have toiled in vain" (pp. 95–96).

Adams punctuated his view with the statement that "We are debating no scholastic issue, but the burning topic of all time." With specific reference to the historical position at which the US had arrived, Adams returned now to his warning that its impending supremacy carried with it great risk of ruin. "Every rising power has been beset by opponents whom fear and greed have incited to destroy her, and the landmarks of history are the battles which have decided this struggle for survival." He invited his audience to "Think of the siege of Troy [Greeks vs. Nineveh], of Marathon [Greeks vs. Persians], of Arbela [Greeks (Alexander) vs. Persians (Darius III)], of Zama [202 BC, Rome (Scipio Africanus) vs. Carthage (Hannibal)]. Think of the sacks of Constantinople [1204, West vs. Byzantium and Islam; 1453, Islam vs. Byzantium and West], and of Antwerp [1576, Spain vs. the Low Countries]; think of the Armada [1588, Spain vs. England], of Blenheim [1704, Britain (Marlborough) vs. France (Louis XIV) and Bavarian allies], of Trafalgar [1805, Britain (Nelson) vs. France (Napoleon)] and of Manila [1898, US (McKinley, TR, Adm. Dewey; and implicitly Britain) vs. Spain (and implicitly Germany)]." On each of these battles, Adams held, "hung the fates of empires and of millions of men and women." The US was no less implicated in, and its prospects no less ultimately determined by, the course of human history, and the great landmark battles, than was Nineveh and every other people, nation, and empire of the past. Unblinkingly, Adams noted, "From the dawn of time to yesterday, experience has but one lesson to teach us, the lesson that the conflagration kindled by the shock of two rival economic systems has uniformly been quenched in blood" (p. 96). We may ask, given the ensuing history of the twentieth century, can it be said that Adams was wrong? Could it be that, as he averred, there was science (method) in this human history (madness) after all?

Science, however, can possibly avert ruinous conflict. "Economics can have no aim so high," said Adams, "as to strive to shield our country from this ancient destiny by marking the path to danger." Science might dispel the Fates and Fortuna alike. "Peril exists not for the sagacious and strong, but only for the feeble and the rash. If we would prosper we must be cautious and be armed." An axiom President Theodore Roosevelt reiterated and implemented in policy (speak softly, and carry a big stick). Strategically, Adams advised, "We must be willing alike to yield and to strike. If we cannot make ourselves beloved, at least by concessions [e.g., reciprocity and tariff reductions as advocated by President McKinley and others] we can make it profitable to live with us in peace." Nevertheless, armed strength was integral to effective economy: "On the other hand by preparation we can cause all to fear us, and guard against attack." In conclusion, Adams stated, "The prudent man will never fight unless in the last extremity, but if he must he will take care that victory shall be sure" (p. 96).[30] Thus, economics. Thus, "Meaning of the Recent Expansion of the Foreign Trade of the United States." According to Brooks Adams. (The Good News and the Bad.)

DISCUSSANTS

Conant

Charles A. Conant began his discussion by saying that the "address of Mr. Brooks Adams is so interesting, both in matter and manner," and it gave "such a dazzling panoramic vision of the movement of world history," that it "requires some courage to contest any of his broad conclusions." Indeed, Conant stated, "With many of these conclusions I am in agreement." He agreed with Adams's major formulation of past and current history: "The struggle among the nations for commercial supremacy is a reality which has grown more stern as the struggle has become more intense with the improvement of machinery, the increase in the mass of capital seeking investment, and the contest for remote islands and pestilential marshes under the equator in the national hunger for land and competitive opportunities."[31] As Conant had earlier written, in 1899, "The civilized nations of the world are entering a contest for financial and commercial supremacy upon a grander scale than any in the past, and upon a field which is being rapidly extended over the decadent and undeveloped nations." Like Adams's natural-law, evolutionary view of history, Conant had also written, regarding this contest, "Society, in the long run, instinctively acts along the lines of natural development."[32]

By the time of the panel, in other words, Conant/Adams agreements, as well as subsidiary disagreements and differences in perspectives on present and future trends, were a matter of public record and common if diffuse knowledge, as were the two New England Yankees' prestige and standing in US foreign-policy-making councils. The panel afforded a sharper focus. Their publications had often run synchronously and often on the same or parallel tracks. Their major treatises both appeared in the US in 1896: Adams's *The Law of Civilization and Decay*, and Conant's *A History of Modern Banks of Issue: With An Account of the Economic Crises of the Present Century* (New York and London: G. P. Putnam's Sons, 1896; 1st edition, including four chapters, 100 pages, on crises and their causes and on specific nineteenth-century crises through that of the 1890s). Again in the same year, this time 1900, were published both Adams's *America's Economic Supremacy* (Macmillan, New York) and Conant's *The United States in the Orient: The Nature of the Economic Problem* (Houghton, Mifflin, Boston, and New York). Each volume collected essays published in leading public-issue magazines in the years 1898–1900, addressing common subjects of world politics and the US role therein, and with many common viewpoints. Among these essays, Adams's "The Spanish War and the Equilibrium of the World" appeared in *Forum*, August 1898, and Conant's "The Economic Basis of Imperialism," the next month, September 1898, in *North American Review*. Adams's "The New Struggle for Life among Nations" appeared in *McClure's* in April 1899 (after appearing in *Fortnightly Review* in England in February 1899); and both Adams's "England's Decadence in the West Indies" and Conant's "The Struggle for Commercial Empire" appeared together in the June 1899 issue of *Forum*. Conant's "Russia as a World Power" had appeared in *North American Review* in February 1899, and Adams's "Russia's Interest in China," in *Atlantic Monthly* in September 1900; Conant's "Can New Openings Be Found for Capital?" had earlier appeared also in *Atlantic Monthly*, in November 1899; and his two-part essay, "The United States as a World Power" appeared consecutively in the July and August 1900 issues of *Forum*, the first subtitled, "The Nature of the Economic and Political Problem," and the second, "Their [the US'] Advantages in the Competition for Commercial Empire."[33] The year 1900 also saw the publication, along with the Adams and Conant collections, of Paul S. Reinsch's *World Politics at the End of the Nineteenth Century: As Influenced by the Oriental Situation* (Macmillan), with similar subjects and views, including such topics as "The Transition from Nationalism to National Imperialism in the Nineteenth Century," "The Opening of China," "The Consequences of the Opening of China in World Politics," "German Imperial Politics," "The Nationalism of Bismarck and the Imperialism of William II," and "The Position of the United States as a Factor in Oriental Politics." Reinsch's influential article in Page's *World's Work*, "The New Conquest of the World," appeared in February 1901, emphasizing (like Conant in his earlier essays) the distinctive characteristics of modern capitalist imperialism centered in surplus capital and global development, the same month as Conant's "Crises and Their Management" appeared in *Yale Review* (editors included economist Irving Fisher, and economist and Yale President Arthur Twining Hadley).

A listing of publications, such as this, taken in a context of similar expressed thinking and policy making by leaders like McKinley, Hay, Root, Taft, T. Roosevelt, Gage, and Vanderlip, and the interplay in these years of analyses and views, not only by Adams, Conant, and Reinsch, but also by numerous other authors, in books and public opinion and scholarly journals is indicative of the broad and ongoing public discourse on international affairs and US foreign-policy formation by the time of the AEA panel, and also of a shared set of thinking evolving along with an emergent social-institutional milieu shaping US foreign-policy making around the turn of the twentieth century. As the eminent economist John Bates Clark wrote, in his combined review of the Conant and Adams collections and Josiah Strong's *Expansion under New World Conditions* (the review appearing in the scholarly *Political Science Quarterly* of March 1901), "These three books have a general likeness to one another," and in treating "the newly acquired power of the United States to produce manufactured goods and to sell them in the markets of the world," and in showing "the necessity for keeping the Asiatic markets open," the authors "reach conclusions that the people of America have generally ratified as sound, and they present many striking facts in support of them."[34]

At the AEA panel, Conant now continued his dialogue with Adams by registering a disagreement, or the need for some revision, within the larger common outlook. Adams, he said, "gives too great an importance to the part played by money and the precious metals among the forces contributing to national greatness." Not to see that "the ebb and flow of the precious metals is a consequence and not a cause of national prosperity" was "putting the cart before the horse." It was not "possession of mines," but "producing power," that brought and retained precious metals. "The vital element in national greatness," Conant argued, "is the capacity to produce goods with economy." A nation that "solves this problem of economical production . . . may snap its fingers in the faces of its competitors," and indeed draw "their gold into its exchequer, in spite of every artificial device which they may employ to hold it," as England with its "manufacturing and agricultural energy" and its "commercial policy," without producing "scarcely an ounce of gold or silver," drew away the gold and silver extracted by Spain from the mines it possessed in Mexico and Peru "three centuries ago, and . . . continued to attract to London the gold of the world" ever since. Hence, "the mere possession of mines of gold and silver is a minor element in the struggle for national power" (pp. 102–103).

In these views, Conant and Adams were not really at odds. Adams, as we have seen, not only recognized, but strongly emphasized, economy in production and a controlling power in trade relations ("commercial policy"), as the condition of the effective use and sustained retention of metals, precious and otherwise, and thus of national or imperial wealth and power. Conant, for his part (as we have seen in Chapter 1), recognized and emphasized the role of precious metals, as an asset and as the basis of an efficient currency, in the attainment of effective economy, and in the development of national or imperial wealth and power. Conant, in effect, acknowledged the essential agreement between himself and Adams by immediately noting that "a great commercial nation needs the precious metals for carrying on her exchanges and would be more or less paralyzed without them," and also in noting that "Silver and gold may be a valuable asset in themselves, as they were for our country when the mines of California were opened" (here specifically reiterating Adams's point), and indeed, Conant added, "as they were for Australia in contributing to her [recent] great development" (p. 103). In his 1899 essay, "The Struggle for Commercial Empire," Conant had made a similar point with respect to German development: "In 1870 Germany was a comparatively poor country. It was not merely the direct transfer of $1,000,000,000 [$1 billion] in credits from France, by way of a war indemnity, which enriched her, but the stimulus this event gave to her industrial development . . . [and] the result has been an enormous manufacturing development at home, and the accumulation of capital which has permitted large investments abroad."[35] Here at the panel Conant, in effect, further acknowledged that Adams understood all this in citing "one of Mr. Adams's own illustrations," that of Spain as "the possessor of the riches of Mexico and Peru, but . . . [which] could not hold them long against the seductive power of English manufacturing and agricultural energy." Note also Conant's use of Adams's key term, "energy" (p. 103).

Two gambits may be conjectured to have been at work here in Conant's ostensible disagreement, and Adams indulged his fellow Bostonian and renowned, if junior, authority without demurrer (as he would not Seligman and Gardner later in the panel discussion).[36] First, Conant was taking this occasion, among scholars and experts, to register a rejection of "monetarist" explanations of prices and market relations, central to arguments of gold-bug sound currency doctrinaires on the one side, and on the other, of populist and silverite inflationists in their appeals to debtor-producers as against creditor-bankers or "monopolists." He was thereby at the same time repeating a rebuking of Adams, as Roosevelt had earlier (note 19), for lending support to such ideas and politics, and more immediately, against which Conant was then contending in the upcoming congressional deliberations on his Philippine currency and banking reform plans (Chapter 1); although by the time of the AEA panel, the populist-inflationist issues were receding from the center of US politics, and in his published writings in the previous few years Adams no longer had been engaging much, if any, interest in them.[37] Second, and equally important to his present purposes, Conant was deploying the ostensible disagreement as a way to focus on major characteristics of the modern industrial-capitalist economy that embodied trends different from the past and augured a future variation, even if not a total break, from rigid repetition of cyclical patterns of human history. In this latter sense, there was in Conant's thinking (and in that of other discussants) some genuine disagreement with Adams, giving the panel a range of views foretelling larger twentieth-century trends.

Conant proceeded with the role of capital, delineating more precisely what "economy" meant under modern world conditions. There was the saying, he began, that "'gold was a coward'," in that it followed "the shining path of commercial success," but in the industrializing age, this meant that the "true magnet which draws gold into any country" was not simply commerce, but "the possession of capital." In present circumstances, capital was "much more effective in the form of manufacturing machinery, railways and steamship lines, than in the form of precious metals." Such as these were its "efficient forms," by which "capital commands the precious metals and draws them from the hands of the most persistent misers" (pp. 103–104).

Conant was here agreeing with Adams on the essential importance of "economy," and in specifying that the "capacity for economical production is a vastly better heritage for any people than a mountain of silver or a river whose bed shines with gold." He agreed with Adams, as well, that economy of production was a matter of not only the hardware of plant and technology, but also the software of "administration," in business alike as in government. Capital was of this dual (tangible and intangible) nature. In addition to its material embodiment in plant and equipment, it also had its immaterial embodiment, not alone in "individual efficiency, although that is most important," but also, under modern conditions, in the "capacity for organization, invention and the combining of the factors of production" – both the individual entrepreneur and the social corporation. In this twice-dual characteristic (hardware/software, individual/social), capital yielded "a high scale of efficiency," and this meant in turn, the "capacity for producing goods at the lowest cost." Lowest cost, however, was "not the result merely of a low scale of wages."

Conant was here implying a revision of Adams (and, in effect, disagreement with William Graham Sumner and like-minded economists), by emphasizing that the rising efficiency characteristic of modern capital meant that lowest cost went not with cheap labor, but with rising-value labor and rising standards of living, for the working class as well as for capitalists and the middle classes, and that this was particularly so in the US, and more so in the US than elsewhere in the world (p. 104).

This was a point made at length by the first discussant, George E. Roberts, who had just preceded Conant. In reinforcing it, Conant combined it with the evolutionary, or historical, perspective he held in common with Adams, and, for that matter, with Hay and the others. The new productive powers, he said, "seem to have reached their culmination to-day in the Anglo-Saxon race and pre-eminently among the people of the United States." This was not a matter of genetics, but of historical circumstance (hence, the word "to-day"), just as productive supremacy in the past had resided with other "races," and would so in the future.[38] In the present case of the US, according to Conant, it was through "farming on a large scale, through railway combinations which stagger the world by their immensity, through the consolidation of banks, through the elimination of weak manufacturing concerns, and the concentration of the highest efficiency in modern machinery," that "the average producing power of the American people had become greater than that of any other." On this basis, Americans were "beginning to undersell all other peoples in the markets of the world" (p. 104).

To some large extent, these trends in productive efficiency, were "the result of the organizing capacity of a few minds," namely, "our captains of industry," with their "audacious spirit and inventive genius," and the gains would be substantial "even if the productive capacity of the ordinary worker were the same in America as in Germany, and the same in Germany as in Japan or the Philippines." But in the US case, the rising productive power was prodigiously compounded, because "to this great capacity for organization" there was now "added a higher individual intelligence among the workers" (who, as Conant knew, were largely non-"Anglo-Saxon"), "with a resulting increase of capacity to accomplish results, and a higher standard of well-being, increasing both physical and intellectual power" (today, commonly referred to as "human capital"), which would propel the US to "a continuing series of triumphs in time to come" (pp. 104, 105).

Let us recall here Secretary of State Hay's phrasing, "through the power of the race to organize and combine . . . Americans had begun to undersell the rest of the world," and then also note here the formulation in 1899 of Hay's assistant secretary of state, David Jayne Hill: "We may have reason as a people to be proud of our Anglo-Saxon origin," but the US consisted of "the most cosmopolitan population in the world." It was a population that "has largely assimilated our laws and institutions, and has shed its blood in the common cause of maintaining our heritage of liberty and union." Americans, Hill said, could not "listen with patience to any word that limits our great achievements as a people to a single race." To do so would be to wrongly "stigmatize the intelligence and patriotism of our good and faithful fellow-citizens whose lineage goes back to unselfish Ireland, or thrifty Germany, or patriotic France, or industrious Holland, or patient Sweden, or long-suffering Africa," all of whose "tributaries have flowed into the great stream of our national greatness." The US and its people were part of a universal history. "If there is a larger word than 'American,'" Hill continued, "it is that great unfathomed word 'human,' which implies that, irrespective of stages of culture, which are the expressions of historical development, there is an underlying unity of nature that opens the door of hope for all mankind."[39]

At the panel, Conant expressed this universalist theme, as he had in his writings. At present and for some time to come, in his view, "Anglo-Saxons" and "Caucasians" were the paramount conveyors of progressive development, or modern civilization, and thus the agency of a higher stage of human evolution. That paramount agency would in all likelihood eventually pass to others as progressive development inexorably spread across the globe. In agreement with Adams, Conant thought this cyclical rise and decline "natural," a process of necessity, not of choice, but in disagreement with Adams, he saw this as a necessity positively to be chosen, not as a fatal outcome to be feared, and if portending a decline of the power of one's own "race" or "civilization," not to be resisted, but, as part of the process of progressive evolution in humanity's development, to be welcomed, or at least receptively anticipated. This is how he phrased it: "It is truly the function of modern economics, as Mr. Adams contends, to seek out the causes of national greatness and endeavor to teach them to coming generations." Yet, Conant observed, "in a broad sense . . . it is doubtful if the recipe for perpetual life will ever be found for nations any more than for individuals." Human history, *in general*, cumulatively progressed via life cycles of individuals and peoples, or societies, *in particular*. "Birth, youth, vigorous manhood, and then decay have marked the history of all the great states of antiquity, and in spite of occasional eccentricities seem in our own day to be pursuing the same round" (p. 105).

Thus spake also Adams. But now with some revision by Conant. Modern means of production, transportation, and communications could partially reverse or delay decline, and indeed restore progressive development where it had long ceased, and introduce it where unknown. If in present times, "the movement of national life from the beginnings up to the zenith of achievement and then downward into the abyss of despair are less clearly marked than in antiquity," it was, explained Conant, "partly because the close communion of all parts of the earth [given modern means of production, transportation, and communication] enables a dying nation to absorb a little of the energy of modern life from her vigorous competitors." Thus it was that in recent years, "we have witnessed the regeneration of Japan from a civilization long petrified and dying," and have seen "Algeria and Egypt lifted from the coffin of mediaeval barbarism and breathing the breath of modern life," and likewise have seen "proposals to give a new birth to the moribund empire of China" (p. 105).

Given the always-changing circumstances of history, agreed Conant with Adams, Americans could not rest in "the confident belief that our future is secure," because "National prosperity has often been sapped at the roots by events having but a remote connection with national character." Like Adams, Conant noted that the "change in routes of trade has isolated communities which were once the focus of the world's exchanges," and an "environment . . . favorable to economic progress under one set of conditions has failed under a new set of conditions." For some time, until recently, it was the maritime countries, "with an extended and sinuous coast line," and with "many inlets and landing places," that were "most fortunately placed for the control of trade." But with modern railways, "great interior areas were suddenly thrown open to development, changing coastlines and rivers into subordinate factors," and making continental systems once more potent in competing for control of world trade. In addition, just as "steam power on the ocean worked its revolution," so now "electricity promises to work new revolutions in its turn." Future inventions "yet beyond our power of comprehension" might well "destroy the value of every dock at Liverpool or New York, or make waste iron of the world's four hundred thousand miles of rail" (of which, by 1901, US railways, with about 180,000 miles, accounted for just under one-half). "Against such conditions," Conant noted, "even national energy may struggle in vain, if out of the logic of events the new inventions do not spring from the brain and hand of the [currently] energetic and governing race." Historical circumstances, and adaptive responses, not genetic pedigree, selected and governed the governing (pp. 105–106).

Historical circumstances, such as they were at the turn of the twentieth century, meant that "for the present, and probably for several generations to come," by virtue of their own long and laborious historical experience, that is, by "the civilization which has been built up through the seven centuries of English free speaking and unfettered thinking since Magna Charta," indeed, "through even the twenty-five centuries which link modern civilization with the arts of Greece and Rome," Conant explained, like Adams going back to beginnings, and thus invoking a still longer period of preparation and a more diverse lineage than Britain alone, "the Anglo-Saxon peoples are the masters of energy, the inventive genius, the power of organization and combination of the world" (p. 106). As Conant had already indicated, that should not be taken to mean a permanent American – or "Anglo-Saxon" – supremacy in world affairs, nor to mean regret at its loss, nor an intent or a hope to prolong or perpetuate it beyond its appropriate time in a universal-human pattern of progressive development, a pattern in which supremacy or leadership passed from people to people, society to society, in accordance with varying historical circumstances and adaptive responses.

In his review of the Adams and Conant books earlier that year, John Bates Clark had drawn particular attention to a worried concern for future implications of "facts which must be reckoned with in deciding what is wise American policy, political and commercial, under the conditions which prevail at the beginning of the new century." Regarding Conant's "major premise," the congestive dysfunction of surplus capital in the US and other industrial countries, and the need "for a long interval . . . [in which to] relieve the situation in America by sending capital to the undeveloped areas of the world," Clark noted that "the time must ultimately come when they too will begin to feel the glut of capital," and there would be "no further areas to which the productive fund can be exported," bringing on " a condition much to be dreaded and for which no remedy is suggested." Here was Clark's conundrum: He affirmed the "general soundness" of Conant's "plea for outlets for exportation," and especially of Conant's "recognition of the fact that the opening of foreign countries" meant not only "a chance to sell goods with profit, but [also] . . . to invest our own capital with an even larger and more permanent profit." Precisely this soundness, however, implied dire consequences begging thought. But, Clark noted, "the ulterior effects of this investment and of the development of the resources of the countries to which the capital is to go," although "much to be dreaded," Conant "does not discuss," except insofar as he "finds solace in the reflection that the date of the world-wide glut of wealth is perhaps so remote as to make it unnecessary now to take the coming condition into account." In the same dreadful vein, Clark noted that Adams had briefly expressed an awareness of "the remote consequences of the forcible opening of Asia," and had stated that it might well be in "the interest of America, if China were to 'remain quiescent.'" Clark observed that there was "much involved in the development of the dormant energies of China besides an outlet for surplus goods and surplus capital," that "some of the remoter effects are to be of a kind that America will not welcome," and that Adams would have rendered his readers "a large service" if he had "more fully discussed" such implications.[40]

Actually, both Adams and Conant had addressed these matters in a way consistent with their respective outlooks, albeit perhaps not with that of Clark.

Notes

1. In reference to the programming and scheduling information in the previous two paragraphs: Publications of the American Economic Association, Third Series, Vol. III, No. 1: *Papers and Proceedings of the Fourteenth Annual Meeting*, Washington, DC, December 27–30, 1901 (published February 1902, for the American Economic Association by the Macmillan Co., New York), hereafter cited as AEA, 1901. All the six sessions were plenary. The program listed Conant as "Washington Correspondent of the New York *Journal of Commerce*," although he was still serving as Special Commissioner of the War Department for Philippine affairs, and was in transition from journalist to his new position as banker at the Morton Trust Co. of New York. The *Wall Street Journal* had debuted in 1889, and was up and coming, but the *Journal of Commerce* was still the preeminent US business daily that the *Wall Street Journal* later became and is today. Conant subsequently wrote columns for the *WSJ*, including a series of unsigned editorials on the need for central banking in the US. Conant's own family line, matching the Adams's and then some, went back nine generations to Roger Conant, acting Governor of Salem, Mass. (Spring 1625–June 1628) before the arrival of Governor John Endicott, indeed before John Winthrop's Massachusetts Bay Colony (1630).

2. In his Chicago Commercial Club address, two months later, Vanderlip could likewise assume a similar common knowledge among the business, civic, intellectual, and political leaders in attendance (while still citing and discussing some of the salient details): "The statistics . . . which mark with definiteness our advances in industrial competition, and our control of market after market . . . are familiar to all of you, I presume." Vanderlip, "The Americanization of the World" (Prelude, note 1), p. 3.

3. Walter Hines Page, the prominent North Carolina journalist (correspondent for Pulitzer's *New York World*), editor previously of the *Atlantic Monthly*, *litterateur*, and "progressive" Southern Democrat, would later play a major role in securing Woodrow Wilson's Democratic party presidential nomination in 1912, and in Wilson's successful election campaign, and he then became Wilson's Ambassador to Britain. Regarding the name of Page's magazine: in 1899, Theodore Roosevelt, affirming US global geopolitical policies related to the Spanish–American War and its aftermath and implications, had called upon Americans to "do our share of the world's work." Speech at the Hamilton Club, Chicago, April 10, 1899: "The Strenuous Life," at Roosevelt, *The Strenuous Life: Essays and Addresses* (New York: Century Co., 1903), pp. 4–10.

4. Frederic Emory, "Our Growth as a World Power," *World's Work*, I: 1 (November 1900), pp. 65–72, at pp. 67–68. Or, as Vanderlip put it in his Chicago address ("Americanization," p. 4): "The total of these exports is certainly startling, but the real significance is not so much in the total as in the character . . . It is the increase in manufactured products that offer the striking feature . . . Those increases show that we have suddenly taken our place in the very first rank of the industrial nations of the earth, and while we have lost nothing of our supremacy as an exporter of food products, we have gained astoundingly in the sales of the products of our workshops." For a later scholarly study corroborative of these earlier perceptions, see Matthew Simon and David E. Novack, "Some Dimensions of the American Commercial Invasion of Europe, 1871–1914: An Introductory Essay," *Journal of Economic History*, XXIV: 4 (December 1964), pp. 590–605, reporting, for example, that from 1895 to 1914, "the paramount feature is, of course, the spectacular rise of the exports of semifinished and finished manufactures," with total US exports rising 240% and manufactures exports rising nearly 500%; and manufactures rising from under 20% to over 34% of total US exports, while foodstuffs declined from about 45% to 20% (pp. 601–602). Also in this period, 1895–1914, "it was the entire world rather than Europe alone which became the basic outlet for American manufactured goods," the increase to Europe quite substantial at 354%, that to the rest of the world even higher at 433% (pp. 604, 605). Also, the US percentage increase in manufactures exports, comparative to that of other leading industrial countries, was substantially larger; in the years 1892–1912, the US increase was 457.3%, the German, even itself coming on strongly, less than half that, at 208.3%, the UK, 126.5%, and the French, 108,5% (p. 602, and Tables 1 and 2, pp. 594–597).

5. "Review of the World's Commerce," in Department of State, Bureau of Foreign Commerce, *Commercial Relations*, 1896–1897, House. Doc. No. 483 (Washington, DC: GPO, 1898), 2 vols., I, pp. 19–23.

6. Emory, "Our Growth as a World Power," pp. 67, 69, 70, 71.

7. Vanderlip, "Americanization," p. 3. Secretary of State John Hay, five days after Vanderlip's address, cited similar statistics in his state eulogy of President McKinley (February 27, 1902): "But, coming to the development of our trade in the four McKinley years, we seem to be entering the realm of fable.

In the last fiscal year our excess of exports over imports was $664,592,826. In the last four years it was $2,354,442,213. These figures are so stupendous that they mean little to a careless reader – but consider! The excess of exports over imports for the whole preceding period from 1790 to 1897 – from Washington to McKinley – was only $356,808,822. The most extravagant promises made by the sanguine McKinley advocates five years ago are left out of sight by these sober facts." *Cong. Rec.*, 35: 57th, 1st, p. 2201 (see note 12 for full citation and more context). Brooks Adams himself had also displayed and discussed such statistics, e.g., in his article, "Reciprocity or the Alternative," *Atlantic Monthly* (August 1901): "Between 1897 and 1901 the average excess of American exports over imports has risen to $510,000,000 yearly. The amount tends to increase . . ." Export surpluses of these magnitudes continued, even allowing for price inflation that set in after 1897, at about $3.4 billion, 1902–1908, and $2.7 billion, 1909–1914, and at yet higher magnitudes during the years of World War I. Cf. Department of Commerce, *Annual Report*, Report of the Chief of the Bureau of Foreign Commerce, 1915 (Wash., DC: GPO, 1915), Table, p. 244.

8. Vanderlip, "Americanization," p. 3; Emory, "Our Growth as a World Power," p. 67. Also, making the same point, Adams, in his essay, "Reciprocity or the Alternative," had written: "On the present basis, there seems no reason to doubt that, as time goes on, America will drive Europe more and more from neutral markets, and will, if she makes the effort, flood Europe herself with goods at prices with which Europeans cannot compete." Hence, "the European regards America as a dangerous and relentless foe." Cf. Worthington Chauncey Ford, "The Commercial Policy of Europe," AEA, 1901, pp. 118–166. This was the paper, with a focus on European responses to the "American invasion," delivered and discussed directly after the Brooks Adams panel at the AEA session on December 28, 1901; Adams was a discussant on the Ford paper (commenting it corroborated his views); Ford was chief of the Department of Statistics of the Boston Public Library, one of the leading US economic statisticians, and well known to Adams and Conant, as well as to others; indeed, Adams and Ford were close friends. Cf. also David E. Novack and Matthew Simon, "Commercial Responses to the American Export Invasion, 1871–1914: An Essay in Attitudinal History," *Explorations in Entrepreneurial History*, 2nd ser., III: 2 (Fall–Summer 1966), pp. 121–147.

9. The alert reader will have noticed the omission of the definite article, "The," before "Meaning," at the head of the title, and will presumably have pondered "The Meaning" of the omission.

10. AEA, 1901, pp. 80–96, at p. 81. Hereafter, in this section, all the quotes and paraphrases from this paper by Brooks Adams will be referenced in the text by parenthetical page number(s), instead of by note.

11. As by others often noted, we may again note here, that by 1900 economics, even with the onset of neoclassical marginal-utility, monetarist, fiscal, and business-cycle trends, was not yet generally thought of as primarily a "technology" (or specialty-expertise) of micro- and macroeconomic measurement and management, on the one hand, and of market analysis, on the other. Accordingly, university and college departments in the field of economics

were still routinely named Departments of Political Economy (often tied to other related fields), and individual faculty titled as professors of economics and politics or of political economy (plus); although specialty genres began to emerge as graduate programs in, for example, finance and public administration. By the latter part of the twentieth century, if not sooner, economics as in Adams's meaning and as in his time commonly apprehended, came more to be thought of, not as economics as such, but as economic history, or a species of social history, or just part of history, and as overlapping with sociology, anthropology, archaeology, technology, and other related fields. Except that, cliometrics, as developed and deployed, for example, by Simon Kuznets, Milton Friedman, Anna Jacobson Schwartz, Stanley Engerman, Robert Fogel, *et al.*, business-cycle, growth, and fiscal studies running, for example, through Wesley C. Mitchell, Joseph A. Schumpeter, W. W. Rostow, Herbert Stein, *et al.*, and organization studies by, for example, Adolf A. Berle, Gardiner C. Means, Peter F. Drucker, Alfred D. Chandler, Jr., *et al.*, have achieved, to some large degree, if not a synthesis, at least an interweaving, of the historical and specialty trends, perhaps even the preliminary outlines of a "unified field."

12. "Reciprocity or the Alternative," Hay's eulogy, delivered on February 27, 1902, before a joint session of Congress, with members of the cabinet, the Supreme Court, and the Washington, DC, diplomatic corps (plus the royal Prince Henry of Prussia, and other invited guests) in attendance, is at *Congressional Record*, Vol. 35, Parts 3–5, 57th Congress, 1st Session, pp. 2197–2202, quotation at p. 2202. Brooks Adams's book, *The Law of Civilization and Decay* (first published in 1895 in London by Sonnenschein), had been published in the US in 1896, by Macmillan (which also published the AEA's proceedings); it was reviewed at length and in depth by Theodore Roosevelt in the Jan. 1897 issue of *Forum* magazine, and the ideas and issues in both the book and the review, along with those in Adams's widely read essays, some published in 1900 (Macmillan) as *America's Economic Supremacy*, and others about to be published as *The New Empire* (1902), were much in the minds of his AEA discussants and audience.

13. Here, I am using BC and AD, instead of BCE and CE, for uniformity with the common usage at Brooks Adams's time, and with his and others' actual usage. The ancient history, including dates, as recounted here, is as Adams rendered it, not as rendered by other historians then and since; this applies as well to subsequent history treated by Adams and the other panel participants (except where I explicitly intervene). Also, it may be noted that for Adams's purposes here, the "beginning" was with Nineveh, as "the first *recorded* displacement of energy," although that beginning skipped over earlier beginnings, in Egypt, among others.

14. Some historians date the Trojan War at the early twelfth century BC, *c.* the 1170s–1180s (fall of Troy, *c.* 1183), about the time of the Hebrews' exodus from Egypt and their conquest and settlement in Canaan. Cf. William McNeil, *The Rise of the West* (University of Chicago Press, 1963), p. 192.

15. Actually, Daniel, summoned by Belshazzar, deciphered the writing and read it to the king. Belshazzar was the son of Nebuchadnezzar (reign, 605–562 BC),

who had forced Jews into the Babylonian captivity. The writing was: Mene, Mene, Tekel, Upharsin. Daniel at first said to the king: ". . . thou hast praised the gods of silver, and gold, of brass, iron [n.b.: gods of metals], wood, and stone, which see not, nor hear, nor know: and the God in whose hand thy breath is . . . hast thou not glorified." Then he read the writing to the king. Mene: "God hath numbered thy kingdom, and finished it." Tekel: "Thou art weighed in the balances, and art found wanting." Upharsin (Peres): "Thy kingdom is divided, and given to the Medes and Persians." Then it is recorded: "In that night was Belshazzar the king of the Chaldeans slain." Daniel, 5: 23–31 (Bible, King James Version).

16. Cf. Emory's statement in his November 1900 *World's Work* article, "Our Growth as a World Power," (note 4, above) p. 67: "Commerce is in itself a peaceful occupation and draws its very sustenance from the continued amity of nations. But it were childish to pretend that there are not occasions when a trading nation must assert its dignity or protect its rights with the mailed hand. As in the case of individuals, a nation trading largely must have power of one kind or another at its back, and consequently it is easy to see that, without leaning toward jingoism, imperialism, or any other of the catch words meant to indicate a preponderance of the military spirit, this country is being forced by its material development to provide itself with the proper weapons of defence." And note Adam Smith's observation: "Commerce, which ought naturally to be among nations, as among individuals, a bond of union and friendship, has become the most fertile source of discord and animosity." *Wealth of Nations*, as quoted at W. W. Rostow, *Theorists of Economic Growth from David Hume to the Present* (New York: Oxford University Press, 1990), p. 504.

17. Or, as Adams had phrased it in his article, "Reciprocity or the Alternative," published four months before the panel, in the *Atlantic Monthly* of August 1901, "Each year society inclines to accept more unreservedly the theory that war is only an extreme phase of economic competition; and if this postulate be correct, it follows that international competition, if carried far enough, must end in war." Note and compare President Woodrow Wilson's subsequent statements regarding the causes of modern war, and of World War I in particular, in his assessment of the US peacekeeping task after the war (correlating strongly with Points 2 and 3 of his Fourteen Points): (1) "Special alliances and economic rivalries and hostilities have been the prolific source in the modern world of the plans and passions that produce war. It would be an insecure peace that did not exclude them in definite and binding terms," September 27, 1918; (2) "Is there any man here or woman – let me say is there any child – who does not know that the seed of war in the modern world is industrial and commercial rivalry? . . . This was a commercial and industrial war," September 5, 1919. Arthur S. Link, ed., *The Papers of Woodrow Wilson* (Princeton University Press, 1985, 1990, Vols. 51, 63). We may interject here the following provisional inference or implication, one that Wilson and other US leaders had grasped: if war is commercial competition in its most intense form, and if war results from the impact of a rising (consolidating) economic system upon an established economic system, and

hence if war is usual at certain stages of development that in essence embrace unevenness in the stages as between the rising and established systems, then if the "system" can become global, rather than geopolitically segmented in rival subglobal systems, war may be avoided (that is, big or epochal wars of the historical scale here in question), indeed, enduringly superseded, and so may the rise-and-fall-cycle of empires, or civilizations. This point does actually emerge, if not phrased precisely this way, in the ensuing panel discussion of Adams's paper, as the reader will soon see, and we will come back to it again further on in Part Two, and also at the end of the book.

18. Note that Adams skips again, under panel time constraints, this time skipping over the US–Mexico war and the US Civil War. It could be said, in terms of Adams's framework, that it was precisely the accelerated economic development in the years 1848–1857 that brought on the Civil War by 1860, as the "consolidating" system of the "North" clashed with the "established" system of the "South," among other things contending for control of the gold and other metals of California and the western territories, wrested from Mexico, with the "usual" or "invariable" war, and the victory of the "North," the result. At the same time, and more globally, the two wars can be viewed as part of the process of the US system as a whole "consolidating" vis-à-vis England and Europe.

19. Germany went on gold (with the indemnity it took from France after their war of 1870–1871), and so did the European countries of the Latin Union (Austria, Italy, and others), and also in 1873, the US demonetized silver ("the Crime of '73'" in populist political argot), preparatory to putting the dollar on gold. In his review of Adams's *Law of Civilization and Decay*, Theodore Roosevelt (*Forum*, January 1897, pp. 574–589) had criticized Adams's view that the US lender-creditors were eviscerating the producer-debtors with a gold-standard currency and consequent falling prices, much as in a declining Roman Empire, the creditors had destroyed the producer-debtors, and that the US accordingly risked a similar decline. Roosevelt argued that in the US, by contrast, the producers were vigorous and powerful, credit and land were easily attainable and cheap, and if anything, US producer-debtors exploited and often impoverished the lender-creditors. Members of Adams's audience might here have noticed an intriguing alignment of views with the now new US president, in this assessment by Adams of US–Europe relations.

20. Cf. Vanderlip: "The foundation of this great prosperity which we are now enjoying [since 1896] was laid in the rigid economies which followed 1893 ..."; also, referring to "the great corporation" and the economies associated with "specialization in manufacturing, concentration, combinations, and trusts." "Americanization," (note 1, p. vxiii).

21. Cf. Emory, "Our Growth as A World Power" (November 1900), pp. 66–67: under the subhead, "Economy the Cause of Leadership": "The influence which we are now most forcibly exerting ... springs from the increasing economy of production. For many years this economy took the form of new processes of manufacture or improved machinery; but now looms up the mighty problem of organized economy of capital in the form of the so-called trusts. There are trusts in Europe, especially in Great Britain [actually, more

typically, cartels, rather than the consolidated corporations in the US], but the world is watching a simplification of capitalistic processes in the United States which is marvelously akin to that simplification of industrial processes which has, with astonishing quickness, placed us far in the front of what might be termed the great staples of manufacture. Without entering into the question of the merits or the evils of combinations of capital, we may assume that a country which adds to the greatest efficiency of the human unit of production with the aid of labor-saving machinery, the least waste of invested capital, and draws from within its own borders the most abundant supplies of raw material and fuel, must, of necessity, outstrip any competitor. This has happened in the case of the United States in so marked a degree within the past few years that the great manufacturing nations of the world are addressing themselves most seriously to the effort to imitate or to improve upon our processes and apparatus."

22. Hay, Eulogy, February 27, 1902, *Cong. Rec.* 35: 57th, 1st, pp. 2200–2201. Respecting "the prospect of legislation favorable to industry," Hay singled out "The Dingley bill [which] was speedily framed and set in operation," that is, the tariff act of 1897, which raised rates above the somewhat reduced rates of the Gorman tariff of 1893, passed during the Democratic Cleveland administration. Regarding the war financing, see Frank A. Vanderlip, "Lessons of Our War Loan," *Forum*, XXVI (September 1898), pp. 27–36; and cf. Vanderlip's remarks at "Americanization" (pp. 8–9), five days before Hay's Eulogy: "One of the mile posts that most significantly marks our progress toward the first ranks of financial strength is the position which has been reached by our Government securities. They are, as you all know, now on a basis which marks the highest Government credit the world has ever known, and a credit incomparably higher than can be shown by any other nation. The various issues of United States bonds now sell on a basis which nets the investor between 1½ per cent to about 1.9 per cent . . . An English consol pays 2¾ per cent and sells at 94 . . . France . . . sells her own 3 per cent rents at par. The Imperial German Empire, with a debt of but one-half our own, has just made an issue of 3 per cent bonds at 89½. Russian 4's sell below par, and Italian issues return the same rate . . . in spite of the fact that we have successfully fought an expensive war with an old world nation, purchased for $20,000,000 territory which has cost many more millions to retain . . . and in spite of five years of the most generous appropriations Congress has ever made . . . do you know that, under Lyman J. Gage's administration of the Treasury, the annual interest charge on Government bonds [a total outstanding of nearly $1 billion – cited previously by Vanderlip] was reduced from over $40,000,000 to less than $29,000,000. Is not that a sort of financiering that will make the world look up to us even more than does the creation of billion dollar corporations." (Vanderlip was here referring to the recently formed US Steel Corporation, capitalized at over $1.3 billion.)

23. In September 1899, Russian bank and industrial stocks "crashed," declining 20 percent–50 percent, with strong reverberations in Germany and Belgium whose capitalists had made heavy investments in these Russian sectors. Conant, *History of Modern Banks of Issue*, p. 705. Russia's military collapse

in the war with Japan, 1904–1905, and the quasi-revolution of 1905, were not far off.

24. Cf. Rudyard Kipling (Briton married to an American) in his "Recessional" of 1897 (on Queen Victoria's fiftieth year of reign):

> Far-called, our navies melt away;
> On dune and headland sinks and fire:
> Lo, all our pomp of yesterday
> Is one with Nineveh and Tyre!
> Judge of the nations, spare us yet,
> Lest we forget, lest we forget!

25. Hay, Eulogy, February 27, 1902, *Cong. Rec.*, 35: 57th, 1st, p. 2201, 2202.

26. Cf. Conant, *History of Modern Banks of Issue*, pp. 705–706: "In Germany efforts [in 1899] to maintain high prices for iron and coal were made by the large syndicates [cartels] by curtailing production, but they were only partially effective." Also, weakened by the Russian stock losses, German banks with fixed investments in industry and real estate suspended payments. By Autumn 1900, two large German mortgage banks failed and a panic in the mortgage bond market ensued. In late 1900–1901, the Dresdner Creditinstalt and the Bank of Leipzig (est. 1839) both closed, and there was a run on the banks of Saxony. From January 1, 1899 to mid-October 1901, the stocks of German electrical enterprises and tramways sank by 61 percent. More normal conditions returned in Germany in early 1902 (that is, after this AEA panel).

27. The question of modern administration vs. primitive officialdom, or salaried vs. fee-taking officials and bureaucrats, corresponds with present-day issues of corruption vs. honest, efficient, and transparent civil-service and business practices, an issue still of large consequence in the modernization efforts of China, Russia, Mexico, India, and other countries, and prominent, for example, as played out at the UN in its Oil-for-Food Iraq program (Volcker Report, 2005), and many of its other programs, and in the anticorruption efforts of Paul Wolfowitz at the World Bank (mid-2005–mid-2007), fiercely resisted within the bank and among its clients, resulting in Wolfowitz's forced departure, along with the ongoing harassment of WB's anticorruption officer (INT chief) Suzanne Rich Folsom and her deputies, resulting in their departure as well (January 2008, in spite of another Volcker Report). Cf. Bob Davis, "World Bank's Watchdog Criticizes the Lender's Efforts to Fight Corruption," *Wall Street Journal*, May 22, 2008, p. A10: "The World Bank's in-house watchdog [Independent Evaluation Group – IEG] said the bank's effort to set up anti-corruption commissions and ethics codes to combat graft in developing nations has been largely a flop . . . [Par.] Mr. [James] Wolfensohn's successor, Paul Wolfowitz, made corruption-fighting a major part of his agenda . . . The current World Bank president, Robert Zoellick, has tried to win over the staff, after Mr. Wolfowitz resigned under pressure, and has made several high-profile efforts to fight corruption in bank lending programs." In Adams's sense, by the very nature of their membership, composed of "developed" and "less developed" countries, the UN and the WB each inherited the combined characteristics of an officialdom/bureaucracy both salaried *and* fee-taking, yielding modern-day institutions that in many

of their functions operate under "primitive administration" with fabulously expensive and chronically debilitating inefficiency (or in Adams's words, "delay, waste and peculation"). In the pre-World War I years, the administrative reform of the Chinese government and bureaucracy, suited to modern market and political development, was a major objective of US policy, in the US initiatives regarding railroads, indemnity administration and remission, currency reform, Manchurian economic development, government and fiscal reorganization, and it incurred fierce, sustained resistance from Chinese Imperial, national, and provincial officials, which effectively stymied all the US programs. The US efforts met, as well, with obstruction by governments and business interests of the other powers in their not wanting to risk special relations they had developed with Chinese officials and business interests, and, especially in the case of Russia and Japan, not wanting China to become a strong unified nation with a modern state. The US is working with China today toward realizing these early twentieth-century US objectives, and now, in terms of overall current trend, with some large degree of success, although far from complete. It may be recalled that one of the first priorities of US policy in the Philippines was to install a modern civil service system, and that Governor Taft had been a leading civil service activist in the US in the 1880s and 1890s. It may also be recalled that Theodore Roosevelt, in the 1890s, served as a member of the US Civil Service Commission, part of the US movement to modernize its own governing institutions and to make them more suited to the modern market society, as against what were popularly, and often risibly, referred to as "spoils," "graft," and "machine politics" (e.g., as subsequently chronicled in lurid, if fond, detail by Lincoln Steffens in his 1903 series, "The Shame of the Cities," for *McClure's*), but which had serious implications for maximizing US competitive "economy." Adams gave a nod to this issue in US politics by remarking: "The fee system even yet lurks in America" (p. 93). And, we may remark, even yet.

28. Cf. words Secretary of the Treasury Leslie M. Shaw, four months after this AEA panel, on April 26, 1902, speaking on the nation's history down to the war with Spain, at the banquet commemorating the 80th anniversary of President/General Ulysses S. Grant's birth, held by the Americans Club of Pittsburgh, the leading Republican organization of western Pennsylvania, with US Attorney-General Philander C. Knox (later, President Taft's secretary of state) acting as toastmaster (as reported in Pulitzer's Sunday *New York World*, April 27, 1902, dateline, Pittsburgh, April 26): "Just across our border Spain for a hundred years had heaped cruelties upon a weak and defenseless people [Cuba]. Without pleading a personal grievance, the United States, by the unanimous vote of both houses of Congress, voluntarily intervened in behalf of the oppressed. [Par.] Why did we not do this [during the] one hundred years before? The corpuscles of American blood were always red, the Anglo-Saxons and their Teutonic kinfolk were always humane. Our altruism had been appealed to again and again, but in vain. [Par.] Disguise it as we will, deny it as we may, the element of self-interest was a factor in the equation in 1898. We were masters of our own markets and were reaching out for new ones, Yes, commercialism, if you please, had touched us; and so

it was that our self-interest as well as our unselfishness were appealed to. Then we gave notice to the world that we proposed to police the street on which we lived, and we challenged him who doubted our right to step into the open. [Par.] The trend of thought and of events had been toward a stronger central government. If the door set ajar in the spring of 1898 by the unanimous vote of both houses of Congress ever swings wide on its hinges the United States will police not only the street on which it lives but the entire western hemisphere, and with it all countries and all islands washed by the Pacific. I give not audience to the thought without misgivings, and I mention it only as the logical sequence of the trend of our national development. [Par.] American wealth, American energy, plus Hawaii, which is ours, plus the Philippine Islands, which are ours, plus the isthmian canal, which we will surely construct, plus a merchant marine, which we will surely build, transfers the sovereignty of the Pacific Ocean from the Union Jack to the Stars and Stripes." Roosevelt appointed Shaw to succeed Gage at Treasury. An eminent midwestern Republican leader, Shaw had been governor of Iowa, and also Permanent Chairman of the Indianapolis Monetary Convention of 1898 (hence, like Gage, associated with Conant in monetary and banking reform efforts). Shaw would become, to that time, one of the four longest serving US treasury secretaries, and since 1846 the longest (January 16, 1902–March 4, 1907), and one of the more policy-significant, directing countercyclical treasury monetary operations in lieu of a central bank that the US still lacked. Regarding Shaw's relatively long tenure and policy significance, see A. Piatt Andrew, "The Treasury and the Banks under Secretary Shaw," *Quarterly Journal of Economics*, XXI (Aug. 1907), pp. 519–566.

29. The US navy had four first-class battleships in 1898, 20 by late 1907. The sixteen battleships of "TR's Great White Fleet" embarked from Hampton Roads, VA, on December 16, 1907, for its 43,000-mile global voyage of over a year (returning to the US in February 1909), giving notice to the world of US intended sea-lane policing power. En route, the fleet passed southward through the Caribbean, visited Rio de Janeiro, Brazil, Buenos Aires, Argentina, continued around Cape Horn and northward along the west coast of South America, visiting ports in Chile, Peru, and Mexico; the fleet crossed the Pacific and visited at Hawaii, New Zealand, Australia (Sydney), China, the Philippines, and Yokohama (where it received an escort of 16 companion Japanese battleships); it then sailed south and westward from the Pacific Ocean to the Indian Ocean, the Red Sea, through the Suez Canal into the Mediterranean Sea, brought earthquake disaster-relief to Messina, Sicily, and visited Marseilles, before returning home. Zimmerman, *First Great Triumph*, pp. 3–6, 276. Note, a century later, the formulation of US Navy Commander James Kraska: "maintaining a stable regime that ensures global maritime maneuverability and mobility is considered a cornerstone of the nation's [US] economic and national security." In *International Journal of Marine and Constitutional Law*, quoted at *Wall Street Journal*, August 13, 2007, p. A14, Mary Anastasia O'Grady, "Americas" Column: "Northern Rights." Note also the statement by former Secretaries of State James A. Baker III and George P. Shultz, urging that the US, as "the world's pre-eminent maritime

power," accede to the Convention of the Law of the Sea, adding their support of Senate treaty ratification to that of former President William J. Clinton, incumbent President George W. Bush, and the current Joint Chiefs of Staff. Baker and Shultz explained that the treaty "will be a boon for our national security and our economic interests"; it "will codify our maritime rights and give us new tools to advance national interests"; it will "increase our ability to wage the war on terror," assure "maximum maritime naval and air mobility, which is essential for our military forces to operate effectively," and provide "the stability and framework for our forces, weapons and materials to be deployed without hindrance – ensuring our ability to navigate past critical choke points throughout the world" [e.g., Strait of Hormuz, Strait of Malacca]. Baker and Shultz, "Why the 'Law of the Sea' Is a Good Deal," *WSJ*, Op-Ed, September 26, 2007, p. A 21. And note the opposition to treaty ratification, on grounds the Convention would seriously thwart such US national security and economic interests, by William P. Clark and Edwin Meese (National Security Adviser and Attorney-General, respectively, under President Reagan), in their coauthored "Reagan and the Law of the Sea," *WSJ*, Op-Ed, October 8, 2007, p. A19. Also see, rebutting Clark and Meese, and agreeing with Baker, Shultz, and other treaty supporters, letter to the editor, *WSJ*, October 22, 2007, p. A17, by Prof. of Law (Univ. of Miami, FL) Bernard H. Oxman, vice-chair of the US delegation to the Law of the Sea Conference under presidents Nixon, Ford, Carter, and Reagan; and *WSJ* lead editorial opposing treaty ratification, November 3–4, 2007, p. A8. Also, regarding events a century later, it may be noted that in September 2007, for the first time in history, naval ships of China, now rising as a great maritime/commercial nation, made port calls at German, French, Italian, and British ports; and that Chinese admirals were becoming frequent guests on US naval ships. In December 2007, the Chinese government turned away US naval ships from calling at Hong Kong, although subsequently rescinding the denial, but too late for the departed ships to return. (Cf. Bret Stephens, "Global View: Why TR Claimed the Seas," *WSJ*, December 18, 2007, p. A20.)

30. In his "Reciprocity or the Alternative" essay published in the *Atlantic Monthly* four months before the AEA panel, Brooks Adams had written, "To be *opulent, unarmed, and aggressive* is to put a premium upon them [i.e., upon "combinations" and "reprisals" of attacking adversaries]," also that "Destruction has awaited . . . the braggart who would be at once *rich, aggressive, and unarmed*," and that the US, with its growing and aggressive engagement in world economic and political affairs, would need a strong and ready army, "well-fortified coasts and colonies, and an effective transport service. More especially, she needs *a navy*." [Emphasis added.] Earlier, in 1900, Adams had written: ". . . All signs now point to the approaching supremacy of the United States, but supremacy has always entailed its sacrifices as well as its triumphs, and fortune has seldom smiled on those who, besides being energetic and industrious, have not been armed, organized, and bold." ("The Decay of England," ch. 5, pp. 142–192, in Adams, *America's Economic Supremacy*, NY: Macmillan, 1900, at p. 192.) On September 27, 1901, scarcely two weeks in the office of president, and preparing his first

Annual Message to Congress, Theodore Roosevelt wrote to his friend ("Dear Brooks"), requesting some consultation: "Before I finish my message I would like to see you, for I intend (although in rather guarded phrases) to put in one or two ideas of your *Atlantic Monthly* article." Roosevelt sent in the message on December 3, 1901, so that by the time of the AEA panel in Washington, DC, on the morning of December 28, it was of public record and widespread notice, doubtlessly known and a matter of discussion among many, if not all, of those attending the panel. The new president joined Hay, Root, Adams, Conant, Vanderlip, Reinsch, Mahan, Emory, and such others, in relating the nation's new foreign policy objectives to its own recent (in TR's words) "tremendous and highly complex industrial development," which was proceeding "with ever accelerated rapidity," and which "make foreign markets essential," and relating all this, in turn, to the need for US engagement in the development of Asia, China in particular, and "the 'open door' with all that it implies," and thus to the need for building US military power, and especially naval power; and he joined the others in holding that upon doing so or not doing so rested whether the US was to rise or decline as a nation and in world affairs. Drawing upon Adams's words, with some repositioning, but not so "guardedly," Roosevelt stated: "The American people must either build and maintain *an adequate navy* or else make up their minds definitely to accept a secondary position in international affairs, not merely in political, but in commercial, matters. It has been well said that there is no surer way of courting national disaster than to be '*opulent, aggressive, and unarmed*'" [emphasis added]. Adams and Roosevelt, at William A. Williams, ed., *The Shaping of American Diplomacy* (Chicago: Rand McNally and Co., 1970, 2nd edn.) Vol. I, pp. 422–426.

31. AEA, 1901, p. 102. As with Adams's paper, quotations and paraphrases from the discussants' statements will hereafter be referenced in the text by parenthetical page number(s), instead of by note. It may be noted here that Adams's paper ran 17 pages (80–96) in the AEA's printed record, and the "Discussion" section ran longer, at 21 pages (97–117). For thematic coherence, the discussants will be treated here in an order different from their appearance in the printed record. As printed, Roberts's discussion came first (5½ pages), then in order, that of Conant (about 6 pages), Willis (1½ pages), Seligman (4 pages), Gardner (2+ pages), and Crowell (2 pages). Conant and Seligman spoke directly to major points of Adams's paper, and so it makes thematic sense to convey their discussions first (Conant, then Seligman). Roberts spoke obliquely or supplementally to Adams's presentation, yet with directly relevant views; his discussion will be conveyed next. These three discussions were also the most extended of the six recorded. The three others' will be conveyed, in part, in the course of the treatment of Conant, Seligman, and Roberts, and in part, on their own.

32. Conant, "The Struggle for Commercial Empire," *Forum*, June 1899, at Conant, *United States in the Orient*, pp. 61, 63. This is the book by Conant that Taft cited in his testimony at the 1902 Senate hearings.

33. An example of Conant and Adams effectively engaged in explicit dialogue prior to the panel is to be seen in Conant's "New Openings" essay

(November 1899), where he comments: "Prior to the extension of European influence in Africa and recent development in China, society was reaching the state of economic congestion portrayed by Mr. Brooks Adams in his interesting work, 'The Law of Civilization and Decay,' and his more recent article [Feb., April 1899] . . . 'The New Struggle for Life among the Nations.' [*sic*] . . . " *United States in the Orient*, p. 98. Also, see Conant, "The Struggle for Commercial Empire," at ibid., pp. 61–64. Kipling's "The White Man's Burden," appeared in *McClure's*, February 1899.

34. "Reviews," *Political Science Quarterly*, XVI: March 1, 1901, pp. 142–144, at p. 144. It might also be noted here, as indicative of the authors' status, or impact, as "influentials," that Adams's *Law of Civilization and Decay* went through five printings by 1903; Conant's *History of Modern Banks of Issue*, four editions by 1909, five by 1915; and Reinsch's *World Politics*, four editions by 1904.

35. Conant, "The Struggle for Commercial Empire," *Forum* (June 1899), at *United States in the Orient*, pp. 65–66.

36. At the time of the panel, Conant was 40 years old, Adams 53; and Conant had opened his remarks with words of deference and respect, as well as of significant agreement, as we have seen.

37. In June 1895, just before its first publication in England (October 1895), Brooks had written his brother Henry Adams, regarding readership prospects in the US for *The Law of Civilization and Decay*, that "my best hope is with the socialists, the silver-men, and the debtors." Brooks to Henry, June 30, 1895, quoted and discussed at Charles A. Beard, "Introduction," in the Vintage Books (New York) edition, 1955, p. xiv, note 3. In Conant's earlier 1899 "New Openings" essay, after noting Adams's understanding that "economic congestion" was a major problem for the industrial nations, Conant had also criticized Adams's monetarism, stating, "The congestion has not, as he [Adams] seems to believe, very much to do with the supply of gold and silver, the mere tools of exchange; it has to do with the subject of exchange – the great mass of capital seeking employment, and unable to find it at home" (*United States in the Orient*, p. 98). Regarding Conant's views on money and prices, and their relation to his opposing political populism, cf. M. J. Sklar, *Corporate Reconstruction*, pp. 71, 77. Conant had been the unsuccessful "gold" Democratic candidate for Congress in 1894, in the "Harvard" district; he had been a delegate to the Gold Democratic Party convention in 1896, in Indianapolis; and as advisory secretary to the Executive Committee of the Indianapolis Monetary Commission, he had helped formulate provisions of the Currency (Gold Standard) Act of 1900, and worked with the McKinley administration for its passage (Chapter 1).

38. Conant and Adams, like others, and as was common at the time, used the term "race" not only to mean the then relatively new (and today genomically discredited) categories of late nineteenth-century biology and anthropology (e.g., "Caucasian"), or categorization by putative skin-color (as in the US), but also what today is more usually thought of as nationality or broad culture (ethnicity). They referred, for example, to the English race, the French race, the German race, the Spanish race, the Italian race, etc. In their

usage, "Anglo-Saxon" meant essentially the dominant sociopolitical strata in the UK and the US, and in such offshoots as Australia, New Zealand, and British Canada. Cf. Emory, "Our Growth as a World Power" (note 4), pp, 65, 66; and David J. Hill (US assistant secretary of state), "The War and the Extension of Civilization," *Forum*, XXVI (February 1899), pp. 650–655.

39. Hill, "The War and the Extension of Civilization," pp. 654–655. Hill served as Hay's assistant secretary of state in 1898–1903, and sometimes as acting secretary in Hay's absence; he had particular responsibility for Asian and Chinese affairs. Officially, he was second assistant secretary, second to the venerable, perennial First Assistant Secretary Alvey A. Adee. Hill had been president of Bucknell University, 1879–1888, presiding over the introduction of coeducation there in 1883; he was also president of the University of Rochester, 1888–1896. He later served as Roosevelt's minister to Switzerland, 1903–1905, and to the Netherlands, 1905–1908, and as Taft's ambassador to Germany, 1909–1911. He also served as US delegate to the Second Hague Peace Conference of 1907 (the first, 1899), and in 1907 he became a member for the US of the administrative council of the Permanent Court of Arbitration (Hague Tribunal). In all, Hill served under Presidents McKinley, Roosevelt, and Taft, and under their Secretaries of State Hay, Elihu Root, and Philander C. Knox.

40. J. B. Clark, Review, *PSQ*, XVI (March 1901), pp. 142, 143, 144.

PART TWO

THE FOUNDERS' AMERICAN CENTURY:
THE TALE ONCE-TOLD

CHAPTER 3

World History: Evolving Cycles of Empires

Having indicated thinking among twentieth-century foreign-policy founders through a sampling of direct quotation, in Chapters 1 and 2, as well as in the Prelude, let me now further convey the set of thinking by composite summary of its content, presented in the form of numbered propositional statements, divided into this and the following two chapters, addressing world history, US history, and twentieth-century world politics and the US role. Please keep in mind that the propositional statements represent my composite characterization of the thinking summarized, and (except for bracketed insertions) *not* my own assertion of fact, and *not* my own views, which whether in agreement or disagreement are here irrelevant.

(1) A plausible framework of interpretation warrants the view, and its serving as a working focus of applied thought, that since some point in antiquity, human world history, in that part of its record as a process of cumulative evolution, has involved a succession of greater empires, moving geographically, not always but in the long run, and in line with comparative economic advantage, from east to west. The seat of each greater empire, in turn, was located at, or controlled, the current center of major world commerce, which at a certain point in history became that between Asia and the West. The cumulative-evolutionary process quickened and intensified as the seat of empire and the seat of world commerce, or its control, have in essence coincided.

(2) Landmark wars and revolutionary changes in human history came with contests for the seat of empire, or challenges posed by rising to established seats of empire. Imperial systems controlling trade routes across land and inland waterways between the West and Asia predominated until ocean navigation began to become viable in the West for commercial traffic

and projection of power, sometime in the fifteenth century, and with the Columbian revolution, became more and more highly developed. The shifting in the seat of empire away from a land-based Arab-Ottoman-Islamic system became contested by rival oceangoing Christian powers – Portugal, Spain, the Netherlands, France, and Britain – for control of Western commerce with Asia via oceanic routes, a contest which also brought the *Western* Hemisphere into a massive transatlantic system, and into the world-empire evolutionary process.[1]

(3) By Elizabethan times, in the sixteenth century, it was becoming, and thereafter remained, a vital national interest of Britain to control the Mediterranean and transatlantic sea-lanes, and maintain a balance of power in Europe, in order to attain and then keep British maritime supremacy, and to prevent the recreation of a land-based Eurasian system. Napoleon's continental program represented a challenge by a prospective land-based Eurasian system to the British maritime West–Asia system. If successful, it would have established the primacy of a continental Eurasian system, underwritten growing French/European naval power, and thereby both strategically and economically marginalized Britain and absorbed the transatlantic system. The French Napoleonic challenge (the last pre-industrial challenge), including the effort to control Egypt and Iberia, and hence Europe's Mediterranean–Asia link, precipitated the climactic warfare that resulted in British world supremacy after 1815. British supremacy included industrialization at a pace ahead of all others, with use of metals and energy of modern power, of iron, coal, steel, steam power, plus science and engineering. British supremacy brought a global ascendancy of the maritime system, sustained by British naval dominance, including an enhanced US security and role in a rising transatlantic system, as well as British naval dominance in the Mediterranean, Indian Ocean, and Arabian Sea, along with projection of British naval power into the Pacific Far East. Thereafter, Britain continued to have an abiding interest in a balance of power in world politics, especially on the Eurasian continent, that would prevent the reconstruction of a land-based Eurasian system, whether controlled by one great power or an alliance of powers. As a country with strong transatlantic, Caribbean, Pacific, and, in short, global maritime interests, and with a vital geopolitical interest in preventing European recolonizing in the Western Hemisphere (Monroe Doctrine), the US shared with Britain basic foreign policy objectives.

(4) British world ascendancy after 1815, or the Pax Britannica, came also to be known as the "British Century," although it peaked and began to enter upon a *relative* decline in something less than a century,

by the 1870s–1890s. It was in these decades that the international spread of industrialization, along with the development of railways and tele-communications, made it once again possible for a continental or land-route system, this time German-centered, but with prospective French and Russian components, to pose a serious challenge to the maritime system for the world's seat of empire. This brought on the disruption of the post-1815 world equilibrium, and inaugurated another landmark struggle over the shift in the seat of empire, a struggle in the outcome of which the US had a vital national interest. Note the accelerated pace of rising and declining imperial power – decades instead of centuries given modern means of production. By the closing years of the nineteenth century, the new struggle, shaped by a growing Anglo-German rivalry, with France and Russia oscillating, of rising, contesting spheres of influence in Africa and Asia, augured instability, strife, wars, and revolutions, on a world scale, unless the anticipated cost or destructiveness of modern military conflict deterred or muted the struggle, or alternatively, unless governments could find peaceful methods of empire-shifting, or ways of moving world history beyond empire-shifting altogether.

(5) The advent of modern industrializing capitalism and its spread beyond Britain to other countries marked the beginning of a basic depar-ture from past human history, or past evolutionary development. The point of departure first crystallized in Britain, western Europe, parts of central Europe, the US, and Canada – that is, largely in the northern transatlantic world – by the 1870s–1890s. It consisted in the very nature of modern industrializing capitalism: with private property and markets, extension and intensification of machine production, railways, steam-ships, telecommunications, and managerial and organizational innova-tions, including those in credit and capital markets, modern capitalism represented the nullification of Malthusian scarcity, in principle and in actuality, because it created an abundance economy of international proportions and accelerated the pace of economic development without past precedent, in which production (agricultural as well as industrial) exceeded population growth on a sustained basis, and in which not only goods, but also capital, in the form of productive capacities and savings and investment funds, came to be in chronic surplus in relation to effec-tive demand, and in some cases even in relation to reasonable use.

The epochal departure spurred new principles of economic and his-torical theory, such as, in economics, neoclassical marginal utility theory and business cycle theory, and in history, evolutionary–anthropological theory, paralleling and in some large degree informed by evolutionary theory in biology and geology. In the northern transatlantic system, until the 1870s–1890s, except for short-term episodes, the demand for goods and productive capacities generally matched or exceeded supply. During the 1870s–1890s, except for short-term episodes, supply began chronically to exceed demand, and there was strong reason to believe it would continue to do so. The long-term condition of surplus productive capacities implied the potential deepening, expansion, and perhaps acceleration of the cumulative-evolutionary dimension in human history. Might it also mean an actual receding, and the ultimate ending, of the cyclical dimension, that is, a receding and ending of the recurrent shifting of the world seat of empire, and with it the recurrent rise and fall of empires or civilizations?

(6) With the transportation and communications revolution, modern industrial capitalism brought into being, by the late nineteenth century, the beginnings of the first truly worldwide economy in history, as distinguished from the age-old, shifting, intercontinental trade routes and trade relations, centered on metals, slaves, staple commodities, weaponry, and select consumer goods. Investment capital, free labor (i.e., unencumbered wage labor), and modern productive enterprise, as well as trade, became international in flow and location, on a scale, and at an accelerating pace, that made a basic difference in kind from past worldwide commercial relations, however extended and vast they may have been.

Modern capitalism became the driving force in combining strong nationalisms in Britain, Europe, the US, and Japan with globe-spanning, rival national imperialisms of a new type by the late nineteenth century. This rivalry would form the substance of world politics moving into the twentieth century, but with a significant difference from the past. By its very nature, modern capitalism, with its surplus not merely of goods but, more importantly and distinctively, of productive and investment capacities, shifted the focus of rivalry for the seat of empire from trade routes as such to the extension of production, investment, and financial activity on a global scale. The capacity to control and protect land and sea routes would continue to be essential, as in the past, for military-strategic power, and for securing trade in goods and movement of people, but now also as the vital geo-strategic condition of protecting and extending communications, and of claiming, extending, and securing a due share of global developmental opportunities. Colonial possessions, spheres of interest, protectorates, and the like, into which the larger part of the world was carved by the great powers by the end of the nineteenth century, were now connected, along with trade and strategic interests, with methods of claiming, extending, securing, and pre-empting developmental and investment opportunities. In the modern context, to speak of "trade" and "markets," "trade expansion" and "market expansion," was to speak of a market system not simply of trade in goods, but of developmental *investment*, without which the trade itself, especially in higher technology categories, could not be long sustained, let alone grow.

(7) The transhistorical West–Asia relation remained decisive in the location of the modern world's seat of empire, as indeed the scope of the British Empire attested, not only because of the growing trade, but now also because of the looming centrality of developmental investment and therefore the centrality of Asia, especially China, India, and the Pacific and Indian Ocean arenas, in future global development, given their wealth of resources, their large populations, and hence their incomparable potential for development activity. The rivalries and conflicts among the European powers, now joined by the US and Japan, would, as in the past, ultimately turn upon the West–Asia relation. As in the past, therefore, but now more intensively, given the developmental imperatives of the surplus-capital condition, relations with China and the rest of Asia were of primary strategic significance in world politics, and would remain so in the twentieth century and beyond. Would a continental Eurasian system arise and triumph over a maritime system? Could a balance of power in Europe be maintained sufficient to deter the attempt to assemble such a continental system? Would Asia be closed off to the US by European and Japanese colonial or sphere-of-interest empires? Would Asia be closed off to the West altogether by a resistant traditionalism or by a rising Japan? Would the seat of world empire continue its course westward across the Atlantic Ocean to the US and the Pacific arena? In any of these cases, could war be avoided? What would be the conditions of peace *consistent with* continuing world development and progressive human evolution?

(8) Modern world development, if sustained, made capital the driving force of current history. The substance and role of capital were best to be understood not primarily in terms of money, credit, and exchange, which were perennial in the history of civilization, although these were essential components of the modern market system. Rather, the substance and role of capital were to be understood in terms of applied know-how, taking the shape of scientific, technical, organizational, managerial, and productive capacities, and actualized in private property, contractual association, and market relations, which in their function and progressive evolution were nurtured, protected, and facilitated by appropriate education, custom, morals, law, and government.

(9) Those societies endowed with, or acquiring, these characteristics represented modern civilization, and were the most advanced along the cumulative-evolutionary path of human development. By the 1880s–1890s, they were currently located in Britain, large parts of western and central Europe, and the US; Japan was moving impressively nearer to taking its place among the modern societies, Russia (Witte's reform programs) was trying to, so was Mexico (the Diaz regime), and in China, India, and the Middle East, indigenous modernizing trends (with Christian missionary help) were stirring. Of these societies, the Anglo-American, or "Anglo-Saxon," was the most advanced. The advanced "races" or societies of the West, impelled by the necessities of their own continuing development, by rivalry among themselves, and by moral obligation, were beginning, and would continue, to instruct Asia and the rest of the world, in their advancing to the stage of modern civilization. The West would do this by introducing, guiding, and for some time controlling, the development of the non-Western and other less advanced societies along modern economic and political lines. This was the substance of modern imperialism: developmental capitalist imperialism, which, while sharing some characteristics with past imperialisms, nevertheless represented entirely different characteristics and a basic departure from past history. Its central dynamic drove it beyond the tribute, extractive, export-import, annexation activity of the older nomadic, territorial, settler, and commercial imperialisms, to the venting of the developed societies' surplus capacities upon the less developed, in a process transforming – revolutionizing – the latter from traditional to modernizing societies. Older imperialist practices persisted within the framework of the new, and as legacies of the past. Unless attended to and constrained, the mixture could result in grave injury, if not unprecedented devastation and cruelty, to the people of less developed societies. Nevertheless, no society or people had a right of exemption from modern development: the preservation of modern civilization in the West through its incessant development, and hence the continuing advance of human evolution, required a universal modernizing development process in the East, in Africa, in Latin America, that is, on a global scale.

Note

1. During discussion of an earlier, shorter version of this work (published in 1999; see end of p.123, note 1 for citation) at the Dartmouth College (Hanover, NH, March 28–31, 1996) International Conference on Postimperialism: New

Research for a New Millennium, Gerard Chaliand (director of the European Center for the Study of Conflicts, Paris, and author [inter alia] of *Strategic Atlas: A Comparative Geopolitics of the World Powers*, 1992) noted similarities between the Americans' thinking summarized here and that of the eminent British geopolitical thinker of the time, Halford J. Mackinder. Chaliand also remarked on the thinking's Eurocentric perspective. Subsequently, and entirely independently, in private correspondence, Walter LaFeber (professor of History, Cornell University, and among the leading historians of US foreign relations) also noted this similarity and the relevance of Mackinder's thought to understanding twentieth-century US foreign relations. The similarity makes it that much more significant that all the substantial components of the Americans' thinking had been laid out in published and unpublished work by the years 1898–1902 (in some cases, earlier) – that is, well before the publication of Mackinder's classic essay: "The Geographical Pivot of History," *Geographical Journal*, 23: 4 (1904), pp. 421–437. Mackinder presented his essay to a meeting of the Royal Geographical Society on January 25, 1904. The discussion following it included comments by Spencer Wilkinson and other notables, which were published along with the essay (ibid., pp. 437–444). The similarity between the American and British trends of thought is better understood not in terms of priority (who influenced whom?) but, rather, as part of a long-evolving transatlantic outlook that Americans shared in, from their colonial and early national times, and that, by the opening of the twentieth century, they were themselves coming noticeably to reshape from the standpoint of the US' new position in world affairs. (Mackinder, e.g., cites Mahan in "Geographical Pivot," at pp. 432–433.) Upon closer scrutiny, it becomes evident that the Americans' views were less cyclically geostatic and more historical-dynamic in substance; they were future-oriented, with a central emphasis on the role of modernizing capitalism in pointing to new kinds and paths of world development; they looked toward the prospect of an inclusive global system; and they anticipated, as Mackinder's views at that time conspicuously did not, a leading role for the US in the reshaping of world affairs. Indeed, it may be more accurate to say that the Americans' views were less Eurocentric than quite plainly "Americocentric," yet not American Exceptionalist. In passing it might be noted that Mackinder was not some "conservative imperialist" but a man of the Left – a London School of Economics "Fabian" socialist; and it may be remembered that Lenin once described G. B. Shaw as "a good man fallen among Fabians."

CHAPTER 4

US History: In the Evolving Cycle

(1) An industrializing capitalist society, the US during the 1870s–1890s had attained to an advanced modern stage of development, with an abundance economy and a sustained capital surplus in the form not only of goods and funds, but also of productive capacities with rising efficiencies. Indeed, in its productive development, the US was, by the end of the nineteenth century, the most advanced among the modern capitalist nations, not in every particular, for example, its monetary and banking system needed revision, and agro-peonage and racist annulment of the rule of law still prevailed in the South, with extensions in the North and West, but in overall trend of its ongoing development: its industry, agricultural output, railways, telecommunications, economies of scale, quality of labor force, public education, traditions of individualism, enterprise, and self-reliance, and political institutions of liberty, rule of law, and self-government.

(2) The realities of modern industrial capitalism in the US rendered obsolete that aspect of classical economic theory centered upon Say's Law that production creates its own demand, so that competitive markets yield supply–demand equilibrium at full employment. By the 1870s–1890s, the pace of growth and rising efficiencies, in a fiercely competitive market system, combined with huge concentrations of fixed capital and labor forces not easily mobile, which further intensified competitive pressures, made surplus capital and consequent disequilibrium and recurrent crises of excess capacity, disemployment, and unemployment (of capital *and* labor), a normal feature, indeed the mark, of progressive development. (In effect, Carnegie's Law – of market-share maximization via down-pricing and incessant reinvestment in rising efficiencies; Marx's organic comprehension of capital with its transformation of values; and Schumpeter's

"creative destruction" superseded Say's Law.) This very progress of rising efficiency and economic growth in a competitive-market system, however, endangered further development, because it brought with it wrenching price and profit deflation (Marx's "declining rate of profit," Ricardo-Mill's feared "stationary state," later Hansen's "stagnation"), severe "boom-bust" market cycles (1850s, 1870s, 1880s, 1890s), crises of socioeconomic distress and dislocation, political turmoil, strong tendencies of popular political and cultural reaction against rising efficiencies and markets as such, and hence, the risk of retrogressive popular *and* investor resistance to further progressive development of the nation as a modern civilization – in effect, pitting individual liberty and political democracy against modern progress, modern civilization. The US would either continue progressing, in a manner consistent with liberty and democracy, or it would succumb to the age-old cycle of rise and decline as a civilization, as well as to the Polybian cycle of political forms. With such retrogression would likely come the forfeiture of the seat of world empire, either in enervating civil strife and wars small and large, or to another modern world power with US subordination to its dominance in world affairs, in either case, combining external and internal sources of decline.

(3) If the US were to continue on the path of progressive evolution, the crises of modernization would have to be made to serve further development, rather than sinking the nation in economic breakdowns and sociopolitical turmoil. Ways and means were to be devised for managing and moderating crises so that they could become periodic episodes of a softened business cycle stimulative of further innovation and rising efficiencies. In effect serving this purpose, business leaders (taking cues from the railroads) were reorganizing major sectors of the economy along the lines of large corporations that combined concentration, diversification, and integration of production, marketing, and investment activity. In so doing, they were replacing older competitive market practices with the more modern practices of combining competition with association and cooperation, as the new basis of sustaining and developing the property-market system and individual liberty, within a framework of political democracy. (In effect, Rockefeller's and Morgan's Law – of risk management and innovation via combination and cooperation – now superseded Carnegie's Law, in perfecting the superseding of Say's Law.)

The new system of large corporations and managed (or administered) markets sought to realign supply more closely with demand, stabilize prices, moderate the business cycle, and consequently soften the impact and shorten the duration of crises. If the new system itself, however, were not to become the nemesis of ongoing progressive development, its functioning had to be made consistent with vigorous entrepreneurial initiative, growing productive capacities, economies of scale, rising efficiencies, and ample employment at rising per capita real income. It therefore had to be regulated by government against unfair market and labor practices, against monopolistic complacency and rigidities, and, in particular, regulated to keep markets open to new entries or "potential competition," and accordingly it had to be complemented with sources of competitive supply and rising demand, both from abroad and at home. Globalization and social reform, including measures for rising living standards and growing public expenditures, were the conditions of continuing progressive national development.

(4) The large corporation as it was emerging in the US was suited to this kind of continuing domestic progress, and in addition, with its divisional variabilities, vertical integration, and centralized authority, it was especially suited to global enterprise. It was a vital part of the solution of the "social problem" at home. It was, at the same time, the distinctively American solution to the global market problem, where market meant not simply trade but also investment and the transfer of modern organizational and productive capacities. To forbid corporate consolidations or "bigness," to forbid business-regulated markets, would therefore be retrogressive (as Presidents McKinley, Roosevelt, Taft, Wilson, and their effective policy-making colleagues, in common, understood). The law should regulate, not forbid, the new corporation property-production-market system, keeping it open to competitive new investment, entrepreneurial initiative, and incessant innovation, and in so doing, making it socially serviceable and politically accountable.

(5) Along with the corporate reorganization of the property-production-market system, continuing progressive evolution required other institutional adaptations in the US, among them, in addition to sound "antitrust" law, changes in law or practices related to reforming the money and banking system (including installing a central banking system), tariffs and taxation, conditions of labor, social welfare, military organization and capacities, President–Congress relations, government administration, electoral rules, and party politics – that is, the continuing reform, or modernization, of the nation's institutions (which in the event, occurred to significant degrees along all these lines, hence, historians' rubrics, "Progressivism," "Progressive Movement," and "Progressive Era").

(6) The corporate reorganization of the property-production-market system, involving globalization and social reform, represented the alternative

to a monopolistic plutocracy, on the one hand, and a retrogressive populism, on the other, either of which would run counter to ongoing progressive development. It also offered the alternative to an equally unprogressive state-command political economy – one characterized by far-reaching government-directed supply and demand management, income allocation, and investment activity, whether it took the form of a state-command capitalism or a state-command socialism, or some combination of the two. Instead, the alternative combined corporate reorganization with *positive* government, or government regulation – as against state-command – with a view to securing ongoing progressive development. The latter included Western liberal democracy, understood in terms of the political tradition of the supremacy of society over the state, constitutionally empowered, yet limited, government serving society (the sovereign people) under the rule of law, individual and associational liberty, widespread suffrage, representative legislatures, elected executives, an "independent judiciary," separation of powers with checks and balances, civic pluralism, and equalitarian principles and aspirations. Within this liberal-democratic tradition and framework, including positive government, US major party politics, as the twentieth century moved on, would encompass, whether along or across formal party lines, (1) a "party" of capitalism, internationalism, and imperialism, and (2) a "party" of social justice, emphasizing the equitable distribution of the gains from the policies of the first "party"; or, respectively, a "party" of production and a "party" of distribution, in general bringing into political interplay, dialogue, competition, and complementarity, the various principles, social relations, outcomes, and values associated with capitalism *and* socialism, as the great shaping forces of the modernizing world.

(7) In adaptation to the nation's evolving modern development, US foreign policies needed to be recast beyond mere continental and hemispheric horizons (isolationism), and refocused on a global perspective suited to the US moving from the status of a great continental and regional power to that of a great world power. US control of the Caribbean Sea, and the US construction and control of an isthmian canal, would provide direct maritime access to Asia from East Coast and Gulf ports, and would be for the US what the Mediterranean Sea, the Middle East land bridge, and the Suez Canal were for Britain in establishing and projecting global power. In this context, US foreign policies would need to be framed in terms of the US assuming a major world leadership role in the spreading of modern economic and political development, and hence in terms of the US acknowledging and shouldering the responsibilities that went with such world leadership.

CHAPTER 5

Twentieth-Century World Politics and the US Role: Moving Beyond the Cycle to Universal Evolution

(1) The point of departure of human evolution represented by modern industrializing capitalism emerged at a time in world history, as it was bound to, when the age-old rivalry and succession of empires still prevailed. It was a time, moreover, when the rivalry had become unprecedented in its global scale and destructive military capacities. The evolutionary departure might now not begin, caught in the cyclical conflict and succession of empires, or it might now come into the world and open an epoch of global cumulative evolution released from the older cyclical constraints. In either case, wars and revolutions could be expected, and the great challenge of statecraft would be to facilitate and manage the shifting of the seat of empire and its phasing out, and the corresponding revolutionary changes toward modern civilization, with as little war or violent conflict, and with as much international concord and peaceful process, as possible.

(2) Modern capitalist imperialism differed from the older nomadic, agrarian, tribute, settler, extractive, and commercial forms, or phases, of imperialism, in that it involved the breakthrough productive efficiencies of applied science and steam-electricity-steel technology, combined with a worldwide extension of the modern business system – or, the modern investment system – all of which went far beyond (although by no means exclusively, everywhere, or all at once) annexation, emigrant settlement, labor levies, resource and wealth extraction, or trade pure and simple. It meant the transfer, installation, and development of plant, skills, technique, management, wage-labor, commoditization of land and resources, monetary and banking systems, contractual relations and private property, contract and property law, administrative capacities, and governmental

institutions and fiscal practices, from and by the industrial-developed countries, to and in the less developed countries. It meant, that is, the global spread of modern production, market, and political institutions to the less developed societies, with or without their consent, under Western controls and tutelage, with or without formal annexation.[1] As all this implies, it also meant transforming or revolutionizing traditional (pre-modern) societies throughout the world and, to that extent, a growing global uniformity of an evolving general society-type, although in each case adapted to differences in culture and historical circumstances. The basic intent and effect, accordingly, was not to keep these societies backward, but to move them progressively along a universal evolutionary scale – with social dislocations and travails, as well as rising benefits and wealth, similar to those experienced by Western societies in their own evolution along modernizing lines. It implied the eventual assumption of self-governing nation-statehood by the less developed countries as they became more developed and modernized and, consequently, a passage from imperialism to post-imperialism in world history, provided that interimperialist rivalries could be diminished or ended, and prevented from short-circuiting the process.[2]

(3) By the opening of the twentieth century, several national imperialisms divided up the world's developmental opportunities in a multipolar array that a still pre-eminent, but relatively declining, British power could no longer guide, lead, or manage by itself. Several though these national imperialisms were, nevertheless, as in times past, two basic types were locked in rivalry: the sea-power system versus the land-power system. As it happened, by historical circumstances, Britain and the US ("Anglo-Saxons") represented the most powerful of the maritime type in the West, and a rising Japan in the East; Russia and Germany represented the most powerful of the land-power type. (France, no longer by itself capable of forming a world empire system, would join with the Germans or the Russians, or with a German-Russian-French system. In World War I, France went with the maritime US/UK system with great devastation to itself. In World War II, France in effect went with the German Continental system, which made a bid to organize a German/Russian Continental system with French and Italian junior partnership.) Historically, Western maritime empires were associated with relatively more openness and democracy (e.g., Athens, Netherlands, Britain), land-power empires with exclusiveness and authoritarianism (e.g., China, Persia, Rome, Arab, Ottoman, Spain [Spain's empire was noncontiguous, overseas, but not effectively maritime, hence always vulnerable to attack and progressively

debilitated after the sixteenth century], Russia, Austro-Hungarian, Bourbon and Napoleonic France). The British and US maritime, open-empire systems stood for open markets, liberty, individualism, self-government, and democracy; the Russian or a German land-power, closed-empire system stood for restricted markets, conformity, and centralized authority. The British–US system represented the "Western" principles of individualism, liberty, and constitutional democracy; the Russian or a German system represented the "Eastern" principles of collectivism, state command, and autocracy.

(4) The maritime open system was best suited to a global modernization process sufficient to employ the surplus capacities of the advanced capitalist societies. The land-power closed system would retard or prevent global modernization, because of its antidemocratic and illiberal character, and because it would divide the world into closed empires, each of which would prove insufficient by itself to absorb capital surpluses, leaving the industrial societies in a general state of congestion and stunted evolution or outright decay. Most likely, therefore, the closed system would also result in continuing rivalries and wars of competitive empire expansion, as well as social retrogression and counterrevolution.[3] The conflict between the maritime and land-power systems and its amelioration or resolution would be the substance and task of world politics in the ensuing decades of the new century, and upon its outcome hung the fate of human freedom and progressive evolution.

(5) The US should align itself in world politics with Britain in extending and strengthening the maritime system, containing or dissolving the land-power system, and in particular, preventing the creation of a German or German–Russian, or German–Russian–French, Eurasian Continental empire that would shut the Anglo-Americans out of Europe, the Near East, more and more of Asia, and other areas of the world. After the Russo–Japanese War of 1904–1905, it was evident that the danger to the maritime system came from a German-dominated Eurasian system, not from Russia by itself or as dominant (the Franco–Prussian War, 1870–1871, determined German primacy in western and central Europe and in either joining or subordinating Russian in the formation of a Continental-Eurasian system), and that a further danger came from a Japanese-dominated closed Asian system that might contend against, or join with, a Russian or a German system, and that in any case would eventually be capable of contending against the Anglo-Americans with sea power as well as land power. The Britain–Japan alliance treaty of 1902 sought to keep Japan tied into a maritime-open system, while also

releasing British naval power for concentration against Germany in the Mediterranean, the North Sea, and the Atlantic.

(6) The US should seek acceptance of the "Open Door" principle among the great powers, offering them variable shares in global development, in proportion to their differing productive and investment capacities, instead of closed empires or spheres of interest – variable *shares* instead of fixed *spheres*. Although the US, as the single largest economy, might have the largest share, still the proportions were subject to change, and the shares arrangement would make room for all the national imperialisms to thrive, eventually leading to their peaceful cooperation in an open system of global development, rather than predatory or militaristic rivalry, and to the gradual assumption of self-government on the part of less developed societies as they attained to modernization. Given its wealth of resources and great population, and strong great-power engagement in its affairs, a unified and developing China was key to the establishment of the "Open Door" principle in Asia and thus globally: a modernizing "Open Door" China was key to great-power peace and worldwide progress, and thus of central importance in US foreign-policy objectives. The "Open Door," in sum, would mean modern development – and corresponding revolutionary change – on a world scale, with non-state-command systems, that is, increasingly, nation-state social democracies combining open-market economies, transnational enterprise, and positive government, in national and international affairs.

(7) With a general acceptance of the "Open Door" among the great powers, the world could pass from interimperial rivalries and war to a global system of progress and peace, from a past human history of imperialism to a post-imperialism future (and from "balance of power" to "collective security"). It would depart from the age-old empire-cycle of world history and enter a more unencumbered cumulative-evolutionary human history, in which a pluralism of cultures, societies, and nations would contribute to, and enrich, an increasingly common global society-type and a global universal humanity: *e pluribus unum: novus ordo seclorum.* Thus may history and prophecy meet. Until then, keep the powder dry.

Notes

1. To Joseph A. Schumpeter's view that imperialism was an "atavistic" survival in the modern epoch "from earlier ages ... or ... from past rather than present relations of production," and that it was not consistent in principle or proper ultimate practice with capitalism, the Americans would have responded

that yes, Schumpeter was on to something important, but he was jump-
ing the gun; that there were different kinds of *imperialisms* in history, not
Imperialism; that modern capitalism brought into being a new kind of imperialism that was developmental and modernizing; that this new capitalist
imperialism established the conditions of its own demise and a passage to a
post-imperialist age, or stage of human development. This was a way of thinking about modern imperialism that Schumpeter himself could be expected to
have understood, given his own belief that capitalism, as it developed, established the conditions of its own demise at the hands of its internally generated
socialism. On this latter point, Schumpeter was both wrong and (for reasons other than his own) right: Capitalism *has* generated socialism, but as its
cooperating partner, not as its replacement, in the shaping and development
of modern society – something anticipated in components of the Americans'
thought. In a similar vein, a cogent argument may be made that global affairs
at this point in history, by the opening of the twenty-first century, are a mix
of imperialism and post-imperialism, with the latter increasingly superseding
the former, but not yet entirely, and whether irrevocably it remains to be
seen. For Schumpeter's view of imperialism as an atavistic survival, and for
the words quoted above, see Joseph A. Schumpeter, *Imperialism and Social
Classes* (New York: Augustus M. Kelley, 1951), pp. 84–85, 90–91. The best
conceptual (and strongly research-based) treatment of modern theories of
imperialism and their relation to modern capitalism and post-imperialism
is to be found in Parrini, "Theories of Imperialism," in *Redefining the Past*,
pp. 65–83, and Parrini, "Charles A. Conant, Economic Crises, and Foreign
Policy, 1896–1903," in *Behind the Throne*, pp. 21–52. See also Parrini and
M. J. Sklar, "New Thinking about the Market, 1896–1904," *Journal of Economic
History*, 43: 3 (1983), pp. 559–578; M. J. Sklar, *Corporate Reconstruction*,
ch. 2, esp. pp. 57–85. For some of my own previous writing on the mixings
of capitalism, socialism, imperialism, and post-imperialism, see M. J. Sklar,
United States as a Developing Country, esp. chs. 1, 3, 4, 7; "The Open Door,
Imperialism, and Postimperialism: Origins of US Twentieth-Century Foreign
Relations, Circa 1900," ch. 11 (pp. 317–336) in *Postimperialism and World
Politics*; "Capitalism and Socialism in the Emergence of Modern America:
The Formative Era, 1890–1916," ch. 22 (pp. 304–321), in *Reconstructing
History*, eds., Elizabeth Fox-Genovese and Elisabeth Lasch-Quinn (New York:
Routledge, 1999); and "Thoughts on Capitalism and Socialism: Utopian and
Realistic," *Journal of the Gilded Age and Progressive Era*, 2:4 (October 2003),
pp. 361–376.

2. It may be noticed that this American outlook is essentially at odds with such
outlooks as those associated with "core-periphery" and "dependency" models
for interpreting world politics. It is also essentially at odds with such "clash
of civilizations" outlooks as that associated with Samuel P. Huntington: first,
because the American outlook saw empire as in principle both intra- and
cross-civilizational; second, because it saw international conflict largely in
universal evolutionary-development terms, not in cultural-religious or "civilizational" terms; third, because accordingly, it did not read world history as a
record of recurrent conflicts of perennial civilizations; and fourth, because it

anticipated that humanity's historical evolution could pass beyond a cyclical rise and fall of empires or civilizations. For Huntington's views, as originally presented, see Samuel P. Huntington, "The Clash of Civilizations?" *Foreign Affairs* 72: 3 (1993), pp. 22–49; and see also the discussion by Fouad Ajami and others, "Responses to Samuel P. Huntington's 'The Clash of Civilizations?'," *Foreign Affairs*, 72: 4 (1993), pp. 2–26, and Huntington's reply, "If Not Civilizations, What? Paradigms of the Post-Cold War World," *Foreign Affairs* 72: 5 (1993), pp. 186–194; and Huntington's subsequent book, *The Clash of Civilizations and the Remaking of World Order* (New York: Simon and Schuster, 1996). Indicative of its intellectual appeal, from article to book, Huntington's "Clash of Civilizations" went from the interrogatory to the declaratory.

3. Closed-system control of too large a part of the world economy would so severely limit, as in effect close, the open system. In principle, the open system had to become universal, or nearly so. Lenin rejected the possibility of a capitalist universal open system (in his view, universality was possible only under socialism), and he equally rejected the possibility of peaceful cooperation among closed capitalist empires (in this latter respect, Lenin's views were similar to those of the Americans), and he virulently attacked Karl Kautsky for pointing to any such possibility. Lenin expected, instead, chronic closed-empire rivalries and wars, and welcomed them for their revolutionary potential. This interimperial conflict was what the Americans warned against and wanted to prevent or get beyond. Lenin believed that Imperialism was the "highest" (and "last") stage of capitalism; see V. I. Lenin, *Imperialism, the Highest Stage of Capitalism: A Popular Outline* (1917; reprint, New York: International Publishers, 1933). The Americans would say that modern capitalism brought on a highest and latest kind of *imperialism* (hopefully the last) in human history, preparing the world for a future of post-imperialism and universal progressive development, more revolutionary than the future that Lenin stood for. Note, also, that like Lenin, Schumpeter thought in terms of *Imperialism* instead of the Americans' *imperialisms*.

PART THREE

HISTORY'S AMERICAN CENTURY:
THE TALE TWICE-TOLD

CHAPTER 6

1898 to 1941: American Century –
Birth and Awkward Youth

At the outset of this discussion, I proposed that the twentieth-century foreign-policy founders' thinking, as displayed and summarized in the Prelude and Parts One and Two, and its manifestation in policy and events, might serve to suggest some interesting lines of historical inquiry, namely: to what extent did early twentieth-century US foreign-policy thinking *anticipate* major trends in twentieth-century world politics and the US role in them? To what extent did these trends, as they arrived at the century's end and were tending beyond it, *realize*, and may indeed have been *generated* and *shaped* by, US foreign-policy objectives since the early twentieth century? To what extent, accordingly, was the US not merely *reactive*, but positively *proactive*, in twentieth-century world affairs? To what extent was the US role revolutionary, and in fact the decisively revolutionary force, in world affairs? To what extent, in light of these inquiries, and in what way(s), is the term "American Century" historically meaningful? The discussion here in Part Three addresses these matters by scouting ways in which major trends and events in world politics and world affairs during the twentieth century, and at the outset of the twenty-first, may be cogently understood within the framework of the early twentieth-century Americans' set of thinking – that is, as if from inside the composite mind as it might look into its own future through a crystal ball, or "look down from above" upon its "career" in the course of twentieth- and early twenty-first-century world affairs: a kind of Phenomenology of Mind (American).

For this purpose, I continue with the propositional format I used in Part Two for displaying the mind at work at the beginning of the century, but now the propositions will be *my own* thinking inferring from, and applying, the earlier thinking, and *not* summaries of thinking by others.

I have divided the set of propositions into four subsets, addressed in this and the following three chapters: 1898 to 1941: American Century – Birth and Awkward Youth; World War and Cold War: American Century – Young Adulthood; Post-Cold War and 9/11: American Century Arrived; American Century Fulfilled and Revoked, or Nullified: From Empires to a Universal Humanity? Or Cycles Forever? The propositions are provisional and, necessarily for present abbreviated purposes, selective in events and trends treated (many others could be included), and so are neither definitive nor exhaustive, but meant to be exploratory and suggestive. The idea is to arrive at testable hypotheses about the meaning of the "American Century" and its implications.

Before proceeding to the subsets, let me state a general overview to begin with, by way of "full disclosure," so that the reader may consider the following critically, and with appropriate grains of salt. Taking into account objectives, alignments, allies, and adversaries, we can readily discern some sturdy patterns of continuity in the US role in twentieth-century world affairs. The patterns, moreover, tend to confirm that US leaders' thinking at around the twentieth century's beginning anticipated, generated, and shaped, to some impressively large extent, the course of world affairs during the century, and as they are tending into the twenty-first. Whether a matter of historical selection or intelligent design, the record suggests that instead of viewing US political leadership in the twentieth century as by and large having been vaingloriously moralistic, naively idealistic, venally interest-centered, or parochially illusionary, it may be more interesting, if not more accurate, to view it as having been, to a significant degree, consistent, effective, broad-minded, and sophisticated, in outlook, principles, objectives, and achievement, comparing favorably in these respects with other ruling or governing leaderships in world history – and in scope of perspective, effectiveness of fulfillment, and global scale, perhaps unprecedented. The common picture of the "sophisticated European" and the "hayseed Uncle Sam," the Old World "culturally cultivated" and the New World "cockeyed cowboy," may not exactly capture the reality. This is not a question of good or bad, praise or blame; rather, it is that of posing plausible hypotheses toward arriving at a historically valid assessment. If the course of world affairs correlated closely with the Americans' thinking, can it have been entirely by chance, inadvertence, or absence of mind? Even if so, that would itself be remarkable and of no small interest to historians, and not only to those who see Providential Design in the world and America as God's Country – or, the Great Satan.

(1) Viewing the period as a whole, we may summarize as follows: with the "British Century" in decline by 1900, the world balance of power dissolving, and the contest over the shift in the seat of world empire once again in play, the conflict among national imperialisms resumed, along the lines of the open maritime system versus the closed land-power system, or more generally, open versus closed systems. The struggle for the ascendancy of the one type of system over the other – by war, or by other means – did indeed make up the great task and substance of world politics in much of the twentieth century. In the late 1890s and the very early years of the twentieth century, the US did become an Atlantic-Caribbean-Pacific power, and a major player in Asian affairs, especially in relation to China, and in an intensifying engagement of both cooperation and rivalry with Japan. The US and Britain did move into closer alignment in the years from the mid-1890s to 1914, and thereafter ally with one another in the conflict of national imperialisms, on behalf of the maritime open-empire system, in two world wars, the first principally against Germany, the second principally against Germany and Japan, to prevent the establishment of closed Eurasian and Asian systems (whether in rivalry or alliance).[1] So long as the contest for the seat of empire continued and remained unsettled, war, civil war, and insurrectionary violence punctuated world affairs, but now on an unprecedented global scale.

(2) In the pre-World War I period, the US builds the Panama Canal; expands the battleship navy; consolidates power in the Caribbean and naval base system in the Pacific. The US supports Japan versus Russia in Manchuria, Korea, then parries Russia/Japan in China/Manchuria and takes a lead in Chinese development affairs. The Spanish Empire collapses; Qing dynasty crumbling; Ottoman Empire disintegrating; Balkans in upheaval with Austro-Hungarian Empire tottering; Boer War. Revolutionary movements or revolutions in Cuba, the Philippines, Hawaii, China, Mexico, Ireland, Turkey, Russia, Hapsburg Empire. The rise of Social Democrats in France, Germany, and Italy, Labor Party in England, and Irish nationalists.

(3) World War I may not have made the world safe for democracy, nor did it prove to be the war to end all wars, but in even the inconclusive victory of the maritime over the land-based system, it dealt mortal blows to traditional monarchy and aristocracy in Europe, and brought the dissolution of two German-aligned land-based lesser empires, the Austro-Hungarian and the Ottoman. Germany lost its monarchy, the vitality of its aristocracy, its overseas colonies, and much else, but maintained its national entity. Imperial Russia, in a virtual disintegration, lost

its monarchy and aristocracy, and some of its domain – Poland and the Baltic states, but otherwise, under the Communist regime, it recovered and retained most of the geophysical empire acquired under the czars, restyled as the Soviet Union. Turkey emerged as a new secular nation-state from the dissolved Ottoman Empire, and Britain and France, through League-mandates and spheres of influence, divided the rest of it. Britain also consolidated its sphere of dominance in Iran. Middle Eastern Islam entered a historic nadir of influence and power, losing not only to European intrusion, as before, but now also to nationalist-modernizing movements and trends. New independent self-governing nation-states emerged in central and eastern Europe (including the Baltic states and Yugoslavia).

Modernizing developmental forces grew stronger in society, culture, politics, and government in the new states and mandates, as well as in Iran, at the same time intensifying old and new class conflicts, and stirring simmering traditionalist, and boiling national and ethnic, resentments and aspirations. In Asia, Japan, having previously annexed Formosa (1895) and Korea (1910), extended its power and investment activity on the northern Asian mainland (especially Manchuria) and Formosa (Taiwan), and after the 1911 Revolution ending the Manchu Imperial Dynasty, China continued in chronic social strife and civil war, in which, by the 1920s, two rival promodernizing forces (those led, respectively, by the Kuomintang and the Communist Party), after failing to coalesce, fought against each other, against traditionalist forces, and by the 1930s against the Japanese invaders.

(4) President Woodrow Wilson's Fourteen Points, including the League of Nations proposal (the latter not originating with him), was a response, incisive and immediate, to Lenin's challenge of revealing the secret treaties and calling for worldwide anti-imperialist movements for self-determination. But it also correlated strongly with the long-term US objective of moving world politics beyond interimperial rivalries, and toward cooperative sharing of world development activity. Wilson's program was not "idealistic" but "ideology-realistic." It was a realistic alignment of the US in the already strong and widespread national movements of the time, a realistic positioning of the US as a leader in the world revolutionary-nationalist trend, the better, at the same time, of serving the US long-term objective of dissolving closed empires. And it was a realistic understanding that in the modern world of mass politics and mass armies (and informed by the lessons of the American Revolution, French Revolution, Napoleonic Wars, and the US Civil War), there could be no successful (or ethical) program – domestic and international – that was

not also aligned with democratizing public opinion, and, where necessary and appropriate, with national self-determination and social revolution.

The question for statecraft was how best to engage and guide it all so that national self-determination, anti-imperialism, and revolution would be progressive and consistent with an open global system (or "Open Door" world). Wilson's was one comprehensive approach – in effect, the social-democratic or open global system approach – if still in its early stages. Lenin's, in effect, became the other – the state-command/totalitarian, closed-system approach (although aspiring to world reach) subsequently to be joined in that approach by German Nazism, Italian Fascism, Japanese Pan-Asianism, and Arab/Iranian pan-Islamism. Wilson's peace-settlement policies are better understood in this way than as either a cynical play on ideas of others (e.g., Lodge, Grey), an opportunistic parrying of the Leninist challenge, or some idiosyncratic idealism of a peculiarly moralist president.[2]

World War I and its outcome, however, failed to establish a new sustained balance of power, and it failed to produce a predominant world power as a new seat of empire with global pacifying and stabilizing capacities. Even with many of the Fourteen Points implemented and a League of Nations formed, they were therefore to no avail in moving the world toward a sustained realization of US objectives, and this would still have been the case had the US become a formal member of the League. Although the US came out of the war as the single wealthiest nation (as it had been before the war, but now more so), as a world-creditor on a scale unprecedented in history, and, at least potentially, with the single largest military capacity, it was not sufficiently powerful, in unified will and effective force (especially after post-war military demobilization), to dictate the peace and establish a stable seat of world empire, no less to impose a peaceful shifting of the seat of world empire, or to move the world beyond the shifting altogether.

(5) Hence vigorous US diplomatic efforts in the 1920s in Europe, Asia, and Latin America on behalf of revitalizing and establishing an open global system (German reparations revisions, investment in German reconstruction and reintegration with the transatlantic economy, Washington conference dealing with naval armaments in the Pacific especially vis-à-vis Japan, active engagement in the Caribbean, Central American, Mexican, and South American economic and political affairs) failed to produce a stable world balance of power or a dominant seat of empire. The inter-war years by the 1930s saw the effective suspension of even a partial global open system and a not unrelated worldwide economic breakdown,

with the resurgence of German power under Hitler; lesser but indelible Italian power plays in Africa and the Balkans under Mussolini; the continued expansion of Japanese power in Asia (including annexation of Manchuria and occupation of parts of China proper); and the consolidation and development of the Soviet system in the former czarist empire. A state-command, closed-empire system (or systems), by 1939, stood on the verge of worldwide victory.

After the failure of British efforts (under Neville Chamberlain) to arrange a balance-of-power understanding with Germany that would leave at least part of the world for the open-empire system ("appeasement"), Britain, rallied by Churchill, took its stand against the German Eurasian threat, and once again the US (once again belatedly), under FDR (and as Luce advocated)[3] aligned itself with Britain, this time as the acknowledged senior partner, and with massive military operations, in Asia against Japan, as well as against Germany and Italy in North Africa, the Mediterranean region, and Europe. This time the US committed itself as an allied, not simply associated, power, joining more solidly in an alliance of "United Nations." World War II and its aftermath were much more truly worldwide than World War I and its aftermath, and hence more definitive in its results. The Anglo-American alliance joined with the Soviet closed empire and with KMT-CP China against the immediately more dangerous German and Japanese challenges. The World War II victory of the quadruple US-British-Soviet-Chinese coalition put an end, at least for the duration, to German and Japanese efforts to establish closed-empire systems. The US ended the war in the Pacific with the atomic bombing of Hiroshima and Nagasaki, and thus became with the war's end not only the greatest military (land, sea, and air forces) power in the world (and in world history) but also the only nuclear power. Unlike the aftermath of World War I, the US was now willing and able to assume a world leadership role.

(6) After the war, the US took the lead in reorganizing West Germany and Japan along the lines of more modern political and economic institutions, and reoriented them to membership in a greater transatlantic and transpacific open-empire system. The US secured western Europe's and West Germany's inclusion in the transatlantic system by diplomacy, massive governmental economic aid and private investment, and a sustained military presence, in western Europe, West Germany, and the Mediterranean. It also acted similarly, in Asia, with Japan, keeping troops and naval power there and elsewhere in East Asia. With US encouragement or pressure, and with capacities of coercion and legitimacy low or nil, the older western European and British colonial empires entered

the process of dissolving and yielding up new independent self-governing nation-states, by and large with "westernized" political leaderships oriented at least ostensibly in verbiage and stated intent to modernizing national development. The US now joined a United Nations that the US had prominently helped to establish, and in which it remained an active and leading participant. It succeeded to Britain ("Truman Doctrine," US-Spain-Portugal accord, the Iran démarche, US-Saudi alignment, and the Suez intervention) in securing the Mediterranean and the Middle East-Suez-Persian Gulf connection with Asia, and moved toward a similar succession to Japanese, British, French, and Dutch power in East Asia. A US "empire" in service of inaugurating a global "Open Door" system.

(7) After effective suspension and very nearly a long-term demise in the interwar years, the open system reestablished itself, during World War II and in the decade after the end of the war, on a greater worldwide basis than before, and with greater strength and stability. The half-century of wars and revolutions finally accomplished a definitive shift of the open system's seat of empire to the US. If the "American Century" is taken in the sense of the US becoming not merely a world power but the dominant world power and seat of empire, then the first forty years or so of the century may be considered the time of gestation, birth, and awkward youth, and World War II and its aftermath the time of young adulthood.

(8) World War II and its aftermath, however, did not produce a one-seat-of-empire world regime. The Soviet Union emerged from World War II as the new seat of a land-based closed-empire system astride eastern and parts of central Europe and by late 1949 in alliance with Communist Party-ruled China. The Cold War following the world wars resumed once again the conflict between a maritime open-empire system, led by the US in alliance with Britain and others, and a closed-empire, continental Eurasian system led by the Soviet Union and China, which then splintered in conflict within the first decade after 1949 (Yugoslavia, Hungary, Romania, Albania, China) instead of maintaining unity or close cooperation. The Sino-Soviet rivalry was consistent with the US Open Door view that closed empires tend to become engaged in conflict with one another, not only with open systems.

(9) With western Europe tied strongly into the transatlantic open system, and with the Sino-Soviet split, the imminence of a systemically disruptive challenge by a closed Eurasian system, this time controlled from Moscow instead of Berlin, subsided, but the threat of a closed Asian system, controlled by China instead of Japan, remained. The Mediterranean/Suez/Middle Eastern land bridge connection to Asia required constant

and difficult tending and the region also became strategic because of its oil. The West–Asia connection, and the growth and health of the open system, were at risk. The capital surplus problem was eased by the massive investments needed for post-war reconstruction in western Europe and Japan, but the very success of reconstruction meant that it could not be the long-term solution. The further opening of Asia remained essential to the health of the open system. After World War II, to the twentieth century's end and the opening years of the twenty-first, the US engaged in five military conflicts involving massive commitments of armed force, all in Asia (Korea, Vietnam, Kuwait-Iraq, Afghanistan, Iraq 2), in response to the threat of an Asian, or sub-Asian, closure that might then extend beyond Asia to Europe and Latin America.[4]

Notes

1. In this regard, it is significant that before the outbreak of World War I, the US military command, that is, the Navy General Board, had two specific major war plans – one against Japan and one against Germany. See Richard D. Challener, *Admirals, Generals, and American Foreign Policy, 1898–1914* (Princeton University Press, 1973), pp. 29, 30, and ch. 1 passim.

2. Wilson was not an "idealist" proponent of either an imminent general dismantling of empires or a national self-determination, and he "realistically" assumed as appropriate and necessary a Big Power dominance in world affairs. In his "Bases of Peace" work sheet of February 1917 (cited in Chapter 1, note 21), he stipulated, "Mutual guarantee of territorial integrity." In his consultative feedback, Secretary of State Lansing queried: "Does this provide for the adequate expansion of territory as a result of increased population or an accumulation of capital desiring investment in territory under national control? That is, should not some provision be made for future colonization?" In response, Wilson added the words: "Such a guarantee would not affect natural expansion peaceably accomplished." Also, regarding military power, Wilson stipulated, "Mutual agreement to limit armaments, whether on land or sea, to the necessities of internal order (including, of course, the internal order of an empire) [Wilson's parenthesis] and the probable demands of cooperation in making good the foregoing guarantees and agreements. Note. PROVIDED the nations which take part in these covenants may reasonably be regarded as representing the major force of mankind." (Reasonably translated: US–UK military predominance, i.e., US in "making good" and the UK in having the largest worldwide empire.) Also, Wilson was a "realist" about how much could be expected initially from such international agreements as he was proposing; he wrote to Lansing, as they worked on the "Bases": "All that we can hope for is to agree upon definite things and rely on experience and subsequent exchanges of treaty agreement to develop [the agreements] and remove the practical difficulties." The Versailles Treaty and League of

Nations charter that Wilson and House attained embodied and affirmed the Fourteen Points program by and large, and maintenance of empires (i.e., those of the US and the allies), Big Power dominance in world affairs, and the realist anticipations of subsequent negotiated adjustments. Hence, he did not regard the military dominance or US constitutional authority in military deployments as unduly violated or compromised, although his handling of Senate reservations on these and other points was less than adroit, indeed deeply flawed, in part from his illness, and in part from his concern that the US not appear improperly imperious. The colossal losses, upheavals, and trauma of World War I added now to the opportunity of laying the foundations of an "Open Door" world order and brought Wilson to embrace a greater degree of mutuality (or multilateralism) in US international relations than before, but this was not, at the time, uniquely "Wilsonian" either within the US or in other countries of the world. This was more a matter of the US, as it moved in status from great regional power to great world power, *joining in* a growing European multilateralist trend, tracing back to Augsburg (1555), Westphalia (1648), and Utrecht (1713), which had come to a first larger culmination in the "Concert of Europe" born of the Congress of Vienna (1815) and smaller demi-culminations in multisided alliances and ententes thereafter. See Bobbitt, *The Shield of Achilles* (Chapter 1, note 61), esp. Book II, Part II (chs. 17–23). What *was* distinctive in *US policy* was the pursuit of an "Open Door" internationalism, open rather than closed empires, and ultimately an open global system moving beyond empires toward a "commonwealth" of nation-states (or League of Nations), alias the "American Century," but this US pursuit did not *originate* with Wilson, although he played a major role (however flawed, as with others) in its ongoing development.

3. See Prelude, note 6.

4. It is of some relevance to note that of the US' eight major wars from 1898 to 2006, seven involved direct large-scale engagement in Asia: Spanish–American, World War II, Korea, Vietnam, Kuwait-Iraq, Afghanistan, Iraq. World War I, also, had its Asian dimension. It involved US and British efforts at containing an expanding control over China by the ally Japan (parrying the 21 Demands; bringing China into the war against Germany for some leverage with the ally Japan; and in other ways). That failing, after World War I, at the Washington Naval Conference in 1921–1922, Britain ended the 1902 treaty alliance with Japan, and there and subsequently Britain and the US tried unsuccessfully to contain Japan's naval power and Asian expansion. Of the seven wars in Asia, the Vietnam War was the least consistent, if at all, with an *effective* pursuit of US long-term objectives, and positively damaging to its world power, prestige, and influence, as well as to its own unity of purpose and political stability. The war also represented the greatest departure from the US' usual practice in foreign relations of acting prudently and from sound judgment and reliable knowledge, and taking care not to permit ends to justify disproportionate means. Other such departures (although not on as great a scale, but no less serious in terms of principle) include the conquest of the Philippines, 1899–1902, and "McCarthyism" in both its domestic and international dimensions; other examples may also be cited.

Robert S. McNamara's book, *In Retrospect: The Tragedy and Lessons of Vietnam* (New York: Random House, 1995), would seem strongly to corroborate this assessment of the Vietnam War, as does Henry Kissinger's statement in 1997 that, for reasons of prudence he specified, and although disagreeing in some important respects with McNamara, he thought the war was a "mistake." See *Third Annual Conference*, 1997 (full citation, Prelude, note 8) pp. 36–37, and former Secretary of State Warren Christopher's related remarks, ibid., p. 37.

CHAPTER 7

World War and Cold War: American Century – Young Adulthood

(1) In contrast to World War I and its outcome, World War II and its outcome established a new sustained balance of power, in a bipolarity in the seat of empire, which served as the framework of a stable world order, known as the Cold War, for almost the rest of the twentieth century. The transatlantic and transpacific open system included the world's most productive and wealthiest countries and their aligned less developed countries; hence it was sufficiently global to provide both strategic security and a sufficiently large field of development for the deployment of the system's surplus capital, especially with the added post-war reconstruction, catch-up, and social-reform demands. But by the late 1960s–1970s, congestive strains became increasingly apparent in the trilateral relations among the US, western Europe, and Japan. Having neither the advantages nor the problems of surplus capital, the Soviet–China closed systems were less economically dynamic, and their lethargy in effect contributed to maintaining stability in the bipolar balance of power in world affairs. It was a measure of the strength and durability of this stability that the two systems avoided direct military conflict even in the face of numerous inflammatory conflicts, such as those associated with Berlin (1948, 1962), Korea, Taiwan, Iran, Guatemala, Hungary, Poland, Suez, Cuba, Vietnam, Czechoslovakia, the Congo, Angola, Afghanistan, Chile, and Nicaragua. There was no lack of severe conflicts, no extended time of placidity from 1945 to 1991; yet the basic stability in great power relations held. Among less developed countries not effectively controlled by either side, some aligned with the state-command closed system as the best route out of the older imperialism and onto modern development; others aligned with the open system for similar purposes, or for protection against Soviet or

Chinese power; and some treated with both sides or, by choice or coercion, switched back and forth. Stable as the Cold War balance-of-power system was, in the absence of nuclear weapons on both sides, it may well be that from miscalculation or political pressures, some one of the many crises might have brought on direct great-power military conflict, if not World War III. This came closest with US–China force engagements in the Korean War in the early nuclear age, and close enough, with the US blockade, in the Cuba missile crisis a decade later.

Some refer to the Cold War as World War III, and to the current conflict with Islamist Imperialism as World War IV. Worldwide conflict, however, may lead to world war but is not the same as world war, so in my view the Cold War should not be conceived of as World War III, but rather as the framework of worldwide conflict without a world war – though with many wars, little and big. The conflict with Islamic Imperialism may qualify as World War III, depending on its course of development. A renewed conflict with Russia and its allies (including possibly an opportunist alliance with Islamic Imperialism or elements of it) may also lead to a World War III. Nevertheless, the nonnuclear circumstances previously indicated, and further indicated in (2) and (3) below, were quite compelling reasons for the stability of the Cold War balance: not truly "a long peace," nor "a long war" (nor a "World War III"), but, precisely with all the conflicts, a protracted struggle within a durable balance.

(2) Other dimensions of the Cold War system may be noted. First, it is of some significance that the leaders of neither side believed, *in principle*, in direct military means of expansion, as had the World War II leaders of Germany, Italy, and Japan. Each side, for the most part, resorted to use of a large military force of its own to deter direct hostilities, and to prevent losses, rather than to make gains. Second, although bipolar in overall form, the Cold War system was more than two-dimensional and the protagonists understood it to be. The Cold War was not only about the US-led open system and the Soviet (China)-led closed system containing one another, but it was also about containing the two former enemies and now new members of the open system, Germany and Japan, a containing in which both sides had a vital interest. The post-war division of Germany served that purpose, with all the bumps and frictions, to the practical satisfaction of both sides and evidently to all of Europe, and to many Germans themselves. East Germany being a less developed country, its inclusion in the Soviet bloc would not contribute significantly to strengthening designs for a Soviet–German Eurasian continental system, and so it was acceptable to the West. The inclusion of West Germany

in the US-led system (NATO and EU) effectively integrated the powerful industrial part of Germany into the transatlantic and more broadly global system, at the same time limiting and controlling West German military capacities, thereby eviscerating, if not extinguishing, German continental proclivities, and so it was acceptable to the Soviets as well as to the other European countries east and west. The sustained US military presence in Europe after World War II served less as a direct counterforce to Soviet military aggression on the ground than to secure Europe against German revanchism and to strengthen western European transatlantic and global ties and interests, as against pro-Soviet proclivities, and continental nationalist rivalries and ambitions.[1] In this context, the Soviets (whatever the rhetoric and nuisance politics) were not seriously interested in expelling US military force from Europe.

A somewhat similar situation, more completely after the testing of the Korean War, characterized the balance of forces in Asia. Under US protection and suzerainty, demilitarized, and reorganized politically along modified-liberal lines, Japan's reconstruction and long-term economic development were reoriented away from the Asian continent by strong political and economic ties with the US, the transatlantic system, and a rejuvenating transpacific system, and thus to its inclusion, with an increasingly growing role as a major component, in the global open system. This was acceptable to the Soviet Union, for whom a Japan-controlled Asian empire was dangerous, whether standing alone or in alliance with a German empire. This was also acceptable to China, for whom Japan had been the power in the twentieth century most dangerous to its national integrity and survival, and this was the case no less with a Communist than with a Kuomintang regime. China also had a strong interest in a US deterrent to Soviet power on its borders and in East Asia more broadly. Like the Soviets, moreover, China had neither the advantages nor the problems of surplus capital; its own security and internal development, not external economic or geopolitical expansion, were on its agenda.

On the US side, its long-held "Open Door" objective in China was to preserve and strengthen China's national entity, against disintegration or outright foreign control or partition, and this purpose the Communist regime served. (In the unsuccessful Marshall mission to China after World War II, the US had tried to effect a KMT-CP coalition government as the basis of a strong national regime.) In addition, the Communist regime was committed to modernizing development, another long-held US objective, and even if under autarchic, deeply flawed, indeed murderous, state-command auspices, nevertheless yielding a national unity and modernizing conditions favorable eventually to engagement in the open global system, especially as the Communist regime resisted domination by the Soviet Union and then split with it openly. A Communist China, accordingly, represented no threat of the building of a greater Eurasian system. Hence, the Communist control of China, but not of other parts of Asia, was acceptable to the US.

(3) Another dimension of the Cold War system is worth considering as a reason for its stability. The Cold War was not only a "Capitalist-West" vs. "Communist-East" conflict, but also a "Social-Democratic"/"Socialist-West" vs. "Communist-East" conflict, or in more simplistic conventional terms, it was not only a "Left–Right" conflict, but also a "Left–Left" conflict. With twentieth-century roots in the Russian Menshevik-Bolshevik split (paralleled by similar splits in western countries, including the US), and crystallizing with the establishment of the Soviet regime during and after World War I, world pro-socialist politics divided along several lines (among them some predating 1900), but generally between liberal-democratic socialists and vanguard-party state-command socialists. State-command socialists, in turn, divided between Communist socialists professing class-based universal-human principles, on the one hand, and *Volk-* or race-based national socialists, on the other (i.e., German Nazism, Italian Fascism, Japanese Yamato-Shinto Nationalism). The Communist and nationalist socialists came close to combining in a state-command closed Eurasian system against the open system, upon the Hitler–Stalin pact, the German conquest of France and the Low Countries, and the German–Italian–Japanese alliance. German National Socialist imperialism was of a retrograde, plundering, extractive, enslaving, and exterminating type, which, combined with modern technologies of production and destruction, was monstrous in methods, scale, objectives, and results. It was not of the modern developmental type. (Similar qualities characterize fascist Ba'athist/Islamist Arab-Persian imperialism of the late twentieth–early twenty-first century.) Japanese national imperialism combined retrograde and developmental characteristics.

Both the European and Asian versions of national imperialism posed a dire threat, and a particularly heinous one by Western progressive-humanistic standards, to both open-system capitalism and democratic socialism, and hence to prospects for universal-human cumulative evolution. Democratic socialists, liberals, and open-system capitalists and their constituencies joined together, and then also with the Communist socialists, in World War II, to defeat the European and Japanese national-racist closed-system imperialisms. In the ensuing Cold War, democratic socialists renewed and maintained the World War II coalition with liberals and open-system capitalists, now against Communist state-command, closed-empire socialism. The "West," or the open system, was immeasurably strengthened by its mixed capitalist/socialist institutions, relations, and constituencies, both in its internal affairs and in its appeal to people in the closed system. The "East," or the state-command, closed and monolithic (totalitarian) system, was severely and ultimately fatally weakened by its retardation and obstruction of its own societies' internal development, and consequently its declining appeal to progressives within these societies, and its increasingly limited appeal, including to the Left, in the West.

(4) It is a common mistake to think of the "Western" open-market societies as "capitalist." Rather, they are, and have been shaped since the early twentieth century as, mixed capitalist/socialist societies, in *both* their market *and* government sectors, as well as in their civic, public, and intellectual spheres. "Western" socialism, like "Western" capitalism, has been predominantly *associational* (and in the political-theory sense, corporatist only in an attenuated form in associational processes of collective bargaining and civil law). The associational character of Western capitalism and socialism accords with the strong civil society (including market relations) and political democracy characteristic of advanced, more developed societies. Communist socialism (like Nazi and fascist socialism) is corporatist, with party-state command and quasi-communal obligations, restrictions, and rights, in accordance with "pre-modern" conditions of less developed societies. Western Communist and sectarian Left identification with state-command corporatism represented a retrograde "anticapitalism" and "anti-imperialism" (hardly consistent with Marx's own thinking) that easily degenerated into "Third Worldist" reactionary obscurantism and an inverted nationalism, i.e., *anti*-America (instead of *pro*).

In this connection, prevalent US political leadership in the twentieth century, by and large, has taken care to ensure that political democracy not be pitted against modern development, and accordingly has embraced policies for managing and moderating the business cycle, subjecting the market system to social accountability, and supplementing it with public policies of welfare and social justice, thereby strengthening and institutionalizing working-class and middle-class interests in relation to managerial and capitalist interests. In effect, US political leadership since the early twentieth century has been combining, in an evolving incremental manner, interests and programs of the "party of production" (capitalism) and those of the "party of distribution" (socialism) (see also Chapters 4

and 6), within a framework of constitutional, or liberal, democracy, generally involving strong positive government, but not state command.
The positive-government/state-command distinction is crucial, not one
of degree but of kind, and is not grasped by those who confuse positive
government, or "big government," with "statism" or state command and
who confuse modern corporations with "corporatism." It may be said
that in the US, this course of positive government and capitalist/social-
ist mix was stayed during the twentieth century by an evolving political
leadership coalition of "social capitalists" and "liberal socialists" both
within and across formal party lines, similar to governing leaderships
in other developed and developing countries. (Hence, purist prosocialist
and purist "free market" libertarian "3rd" parties can get little traction in
elections.) In this respect, as in many others touching basic characteristics
in the evolution of modern societies, the US is no "Exception."[2]

(5) By the late 1960s–early 1980s, with western Europe reconstructed,
and Germany and Japan having become once again major economic
powers, capital surplus and productive congestion resumed its "normal"
role in the vigorously developing open system, along with their corresponding strains, a situation analogous to that of the 1870s–1890s. The
system on the whole needed to expand its sphere, so that shares could
grow, be added, and, where appropriate, be redistributed. This was the
time of European concerns, a second time around since 1898–1914,
about the "American Invasion," US concerns about international trade
and payments deficits (for the first time since the early 1890s), monetary
instability and the final steps in the demise of the gold standard, rising
unemployment rates, European and US concerns about the "Japanese
Invasion," inflation with sluggish growth ("stagflation"), worries about
"social malaise," social-cultural rebelliousness and political turbulence in
western societies, and trilateral questioning about "The Governability of
Democracies."[3]

As in the 1870s–1890s, the market societies underwent more or less
wrenching economic restructuring in the 1970s–1990s, along with efforts
at reforming, revitalizing, and deepening the open system and extending
its global reach. Already by 1969–1990 US leaders were thinking that an
easing of Cold War conflict in less developed countries might lend stability and access conducive to developmental investment; and some opening
of the closed systems' domains (the Soviet Union, eastern Europe, China)
to Western trade and investment would be of even greater significance
for globalization. Serving this purpose were the Nixon–Kissinger initiatives of "détente" and "linkage" with the Soviets (tacitly affirming and

subsuming West German *Ostpolitik*), and steps toward reestablishing normal relations with China. The China initiative marked a resumption of *active* pursuit by the US of its "Open Door" objectives with respect to China and their global implications.

The Communist systems, for their part, although ostensibly confident and stable in the 1970s, and seemingly "on the march" in world affairs, especially in less developed countries, against a defensive open system, had reached a developmental impasse. State-command systems could work with dramatic results, or "success," in the age of steel-coal-oil-electricity productive forces, but could not transact the passage to the higher technology productive forces of a post-industrial state of development, and still less to the electronic-digital-information age. While the open-system market societies were able to respond to the surplus-capital, post-industrial, and technology-transition crises as creative occasions for restructuring and innovation, which to a large extent dissident social movements in democratic environments fostered and facilitated (wittingly and unwittingly), the Communist systems handled their own developmental barriers in their customary state-command ways, either by the traditional practices of suppressing overt crises, along with social and technological stagnation (for example, the Brezhnev era), or with "mobilizing the masses" in chaotic and developmentally ineffective or destructive crises, like the "Great Leap Forward" and the "Cultural Revolution." The state-command Communist systems were "good" at the old heavy industry, and laggard or a failure not only at the digital-information technology but also at consumer goods and services, health care, and environmental protection, essential interests of an industrializing working class and professional middle class, which did indeed grow and develop under Communist-style modernization. In the larger historical perspective, in other (Marxian) words, the communist systems proved a failure at the restructuring and innovation suited to advancing to a higher level of productive forces, as the "West" was doing.

The Communist governments needed the "West," that is, the aid of the open system, for restructuring, innovation, and continued development. With its surplus capital and the need to make the open system more global, the "West" was ready, *on terms*, to oblige. Here, with the Nixon-Kissinger initiatives, resided the beginning of the end of the Cold War, for which neither Nixon nor Kissinger have been accorded due acknowledgment, although "conservative" critics strongly denounced Nixon-Kissinger's "détente" policy as going "soft" on the Soviets and Communism. Conservative writers later contrasted the Nixon-Kissinger "soft" policy with Reagan's "hard" policy, but miss the essential similarity and continuity in the overall project of drawing the Soviets and China into the global modernizing system. It was to the mutual interest of both sides – or, should we say, *all* sides: US–Europe–Soviet Union–China–Japan. "East" and "West" needed each other – as they had through much of past human history.

(6) Indicative of its strength, the mutual interest in modernizing development endured zigs and zags, setbacks, hostile rhetoric, and political-military conflicts, in central and eastern Europe, in Africa, in Central Asia, in the Middle East, and in Latin America. Under effective management by the Reagan–Shultz–Baker–Bush–Powell, and the Bush–Baker–Eagleburger–Powell leaderships (note Baker's, Bush's, and Powell's transadministration engagement, and hence their importance, in the work of closing down the Cold War, and note also Eagleburger's influential diplomatic and deputy State Department positions, along with his association with Kissinger, as indicative, among many other indicators, of continuity with the Nixon–Kissinger policies), on the US side, and the Gorbachev–Shevardnadze and the Deng Xiaoping leaderships on the Soviet and Chinese sides, by 1989–1990 (roughly) the Cold War was ended, and with it the Cold War system of world order. The ensuing years brought the open system substantially *closer* to a complete globalization, in a world of over 190 independent nation-states moving into a post-imperialism age, and toward a transnational global political economy, all told corresponding rather strongly with the US century-long "Open Door" quest. A new world order – *novus ordo seclorum* – was arriving, or, it remained to be put in place, lest an old order of multilateral conflict and empire-shifting return. In this sense, the "American Century" was only just begun.

(7) Compared with the world wars and massive destruction of lives and productive capacities of that phase of the protracted conflict between open and closed systems occupying the first half of the century, the Cold War phase during most of the second half of the century, for all its violence in "small wars," mass terror and murder, famine, revolutions, and civil or communal conflicts, brought wars around the world, and huge loss of life, but no world war, that is, no war directly among the great powers, while presiding over a continuous and massive growth and development (instead of the destruction of World Wars I and II) of global productive capacities and actual output, and the Cold War ended entirely peacefully in the relations among the great powers. Although we live in an age, in the "West," of deep and widespread cynicism among the intelligentsia, artists, celebrities, and journalists, about their own societies' leaders and institutions, a luxury among those accustomed to

enjoying both fulsome liberty and assured security, the pacific ending of the Cold War was a signal achievement of modern political leaderships and institutions, unprecedented in human history – indeed revolutionary, in that sense at least. It was an achievement which has gone, by and large, unnoticed and unappreciated, especially by the intelligentsia, if not foremost by many historians, who seem least historically aware, perhaps because having become so accustomed to their peace, they blame its interruption on their own leaders, who are trying to sustain it, instead of on the actual enemies and destroyers of that peace. Hence their demonizing of Bush, Rumsfeld, Cheney, Ashcroft, Gonzales, Romney, Lieberman, Palin (not to mention Israel), and their indulgence of Arab/Persian Fascism and Islamic Imperialism, a repeat of appeasement in the 1930s of Nazi Germany and "anti-imperialism" attacks against "warmongering" Churchill and FDR.

The Pacific Cold War outcome and the cascading cynicism together may be taken as a piece of evidence in favor of the view that world history may be moving beyond the old cycle of decline-and-fall of empires, or civilizations, to an ongoing progressive-cumulative evolution, as the "American Century" outlook anticipated, unless an undeterrable complacency rearm and reempower a cyclical retrogression. Indeed, a major reason for the relatively peaceful outcome of the Cold War was that (unlike Jihadi-Islamism) Communism, as an ideology, was itself cumulative-evolutionary, prodevelopment, internationalist, and universal-human, in its *central principles*, in contrast nevertheless as they were with Communists' practices, the practical realities they incurred, and their makeshift "anti-West" and "anti-imperialism" propaganda. In effect, and in professed intent, Communism acted in the "East" (and elsewhere) as a "Westernizing," that is, a modernizing, force. (For example, it was Communist Vietnam that put an end to the mass-murdering, anti-modernizing Khmer Rouge regime in Cambodia.) Enough of the Communist leaders in the Soviet Union, eastern Europe, and China were sufficiently committed to evolutionary, universal-human principles to choose development over the preservation of a closed-empire, state-command system, which – in their own (Marxian) words and theory – came to be "a fetter on the forces of production," that is, a fetter on modern development, and which, therefore, again in their own theory, comprised backward, reactionary, and counterrevolutionary social relations needing to be discarded or overthrown. In this respect, whatever the terminology, the Communists and the Americans – and the "West" in general – shared in common some key basic principles of an evolutionary-development outlook.

It is plausible to think that the shared outlook was of some major significance, given nuclear weapons, in the US and the Soviet Union's never going to war directly against one another. Their mutual commitment to modern development, and shared horror at risking its destruction ("Mutual Assured Destruction"), played a decisive role, for example, in the peaceful resolution of the Cuba missile crisis of 1962 – among other examples that may readily come to mind. It was also a key factor in the US–UK–Russia–China alignment – however provisional and porous – against anti-modernization Jihadi-Islamist imperialism (aka "terrorism") – a quadruple alignment that ran through much of the earlier twentieth century, through World Wars I and II, as we have seen, that in effect was resumed in the 1980s–1990s, and that may well be decisive to continuing nonempire modern development in world history.

Notes

1. US military ground forces in Europe, however, did serve indirectly as an effective deterrent to a Soviet military thrust into western Europe, because it would engage NATO forces, including US forces, and risk a nuclear response by the US. The US forces (again, with NATO Treaty validation) also strengthened western European political-economic resolve against internal pro-Soviet Communist movements and against alignment with the Soviet Union in international affairs. But it was generally understood that NATO ground forces as such could not withstand a major Soviet ground invasion.

2. Elsewhere, I have explored further the matters of the capitalism-socialism mix, associationalism vs. corporatism, and positive government vs. state command: *Corporate Reconstruction*, chs. 1, 7, et passim; *United States as a Developing Country*, chs. 1, 2, 7; "Capitalism and Socialism in the Emergence of Modern America: The Formative Era, 1890s–1916," in *Reconstructing History*, ch. 22, pp. 304–321; and "Thoughts on Capitalism and Socialism: Utopian and Realistic," *JGAPE*, October 2003, pp. 361–376.

3. Michel J. Crozier, Samuel P. Huntington, and Joji Watanuki, "The Governability of Democracies," Report of the Trilateral Task Force on the Governability of Democracies, May 1975 (for discussion at the Trilateral Commission meeting in Kyoto, Japan, May 30–31, 1975), bound typescript. Huntington was as persuasively appealing and impressively erudite about this as subsequently with "Clash of Civilizations," and in both cases somewhat less than reliably prophetic.

CHAPTER 8

Post-Cold War and 9/11: American Century Arrived

(1) Global-spanning modernizing development was indeed the great "task" of the twentieth century, central to world politics and world affairs, with the open and closed systems essentially in competition for dominance in controlling the work and the distribution of its fruits. As also anticipated in the early twentieth-century American thought, the great conflicts of the century, their outcome, and the prospects of future world politics largely turned, even more intensively given modern capacities, on two intersecting axes: (i) the balance or imbalance of power in Europe as it related to the prevention or the establishment of a closed continental Eurasian system; and (ii) the West–Asia relation, and whether it was to be controlled by a closed Eurasian system, or by an open global system that secured the Asia-transatlantic connection; or whether it was to be severely restricted, if not cut altogether, by a closed Asian system. On both axes, the special US–Britain relationship was of decisive importance, and it endured throughout the century, with staying power going into the first years of the twenty-first century, as expressed in the US–UK alignment in the Afghanistan and Iraq wars, and related affairs.

(2) With respect to the European balance of power and the Eurasian question, the post-World War II division of Germany, combined with NATO and the European Union, by anchoring West Germany firmly in western Europe and the transatlantic system and establishing strong US–British–German ties, accomplished a durable balance of power secure against either a Russian-, or a German-, or a Russian/German-, or a Russian/German/French-controlled Eurasian system. The durable security allowed France to assume, without prohibitive risk, a Gaullist posture of "independence" – i.e., safely *within* NATO, the EC, and EU. The

very stability of the Cold War system's balance of power raised fear about
its end. Would the end of the Cold War system make West Germany or a
reunited Germany the predominant power in Europe and revive its continental ambitions? Would it facilitate a German–Russian, or German–
French–Russian, entente controlling a new continental system?[1] What
new balance-of-power or collective security system would effectively
replace the Cold War system's dual containment function?

The framework of a prospective new system emerged, in the 1990s,
in substantial informal and institutional changes, commitments, and
arrangements, including the following: (i) the abandonment by Russia
of the party-state-command system, and the commitment by the Russian
government to moving Russia in the direction of becoming a "normal"
modernizing country, with a rule-of-law market system and a presiden-
tial-parliamentary government, belonging to Europe, rather than a closed
Eurasia, and to the transatlantic and the greater global open system;
(ii) an institutionalizing of this European and global orientation by such
means as the greater activation of the Helsinki Accords, Russia's associate relationship with NATO, its participation with the G-7 powers in
the G-8, its opening to international capital investment and its access
to such international monetary, financial, and development facilities as
the IMF and the European Development Bank; (iii) the sustained commitment of the German government, and a now reunified Germany, to
the transatlantic community, as against continentalism, a commitment
institutionalized in its membership in NATO, in the European Union, and
in the European Monetary Union with a common currency and central
bank; (iv) the continued strong commitment of the US to engagement in
European affairs, including maintaining US military forces in Europe,
another source of reassurance to western Europe, eastern Europe, and
Russia against fears of German power and ambitions, and to eastern
and western Europe against fears of Russian power and ambitions;
(v) the expansion of NATO and EU eastward, less as a thrust or a
protection against Russia than as a means of strengthening the framework of keeping Germany, and hence Europe, committed to the open
global system via the transatlantic network of relations, and as an
added antidote to, or vaccination against, a German reversion to Eurasian
continental strategies, either against France and Russia or with them.
This, in turn, facilitated an ongoing integration of Russia into greater
Europe, and strengthened the capacities for keeping all the countries
of the world, including Russia and China, committed to the global
open system.[2]

(3) With respect to Asia and the West–Asia relation: having been forced by defeat in World War II to abandon the quest for a closed Asian empire, Japan resumed its modern development, but now as a member of the global open system, notwithstanding its less than complete reciprocity in opening its own economy. Japan became not only one of the open system's major advanced components, but also one the world's wealthiest nations – by the 1980s–1990s second only to the US. In general, Asian political leadership in effect affirmed the "Western" idea of there being no exemption from modern development, that is, the basic cumulative-evolutionary outlook of stages of political-economic development, with universal-human norms relating to institutional structures and human rights, although with significant variations in interpretation, expression, and implementation. (See Chapter 9, note 4 and related text, below.) As with such movements elsewhere, Chinese Kuomintang nationalism and Marxian Communism both had acted to plant this set of modernization thinking strongly in China's intellectual and cultural life, and this together with China's massive entry into the global open system, its policies so far in repatriated Hong Kong, and its growing economic relations with Taiwan and southeast Asia, reinforced this outlook throughout Asia. The global impact of the Asian financial-economic crisis of 1997–1998 indicated the extent to which Asia, or the West–Asia relation, stood indeed at the center of world affairs and world politics. But also, it was a distinctive mark of progress in Asia's modernizing development, just as such crises, appropriately managed as occasions of "creative destruction" and reconstruction, have been in Western development. Accordingly, this crisis became a stimulus for restructuring in some of the major Asian political-economies, including India, away from an "Asian model" of strong state direction in the economy (analogous to the West's mercantilist phases), toward greater market fluidity and openness, governmental and other institutional reforms, and stronger integration into the global open system.[3] This, I think, explains why the IMF and the US Treasury Department (the US government) treated the 1997–1998 situation not simply as a monetary question of immediately stabilizing currency exchange values, but as an opportunity for deeper and broader "modernizing" institutional change.[4]

(4) Opposition to the open global system in favor of restoring closed-system regimes remained alive and influential in the 1990s in the politics of Russia and China,[5] as in other countries, including in the "West." No outcome in history is preordained, but if Russia or China had chosen a closed-system course, in the absence of a greater Eurasian system,

it would seriously have risked, or in effect abandoned, its own ongoing development. And for what? The resumption of a closed, underdeveloped, sclerotic empire? A reversion to a cyclical, closed-empire strategy was most conceivable as a policy of anti-development. By the 1990s, antidevelopment outlooks and politics still abounded, in the "West" as well as in the "East," sometimes in such secular garb as antiglobalism, sometimes in such sacred garb as Jihadi-Islamism, but they became weak-running currents in Russia and China. In Iran and the Arab Middle East they ran more strongly, but ambivalently and on the defensive, although a chillingly tyrannical, venomous, belligerent, and technologically morbid defensive, and by 2001 had moved to an aggressive imperialist offensive. The closed-system proponents are seriously weakened by their unwillingness, or their inability convincingly, to square their "nationalism," "antiglobalism," or "pan-Islamism" with modern development, and hence with either their society's enjoying positive strength and power in world affairs (as against negative powers of energy curtailments or of frightfully destructive weaponry) or with the demands and interests of large and vital sectors of their populations. By the opening years of the twenty-first century, the prevalent Russian and Chinese political leaderships, as well as that of India, with broad consensual constituencies among their people, had committed themselves to policies of modernizing development in an open global system; so have most political leaderships elsewhere throughout the world, with varying degrees of popular consent.

(5) Viewing the twentieth century as a whole, we can say that, if not with steady consistency, yet in stages, and by midcentury definitively, the US, as anticipated in early twentieth-century Americans' thought, did move from being a hemispheric-regional ("isolationist") power, adhering to the older Washingtonian tradition of no entangling alliances, to becoming a world power with multiple, globe-circling alliances, and a leading participant in the United Nations and numerous other international organizations and agreements. This corresponded with a strong trend, by the end of the twentieth century, toward the receding of the ages-old history of the cyclical rise, fall, and succession of empires, and the recurrent shift in the seat of empire, and toward the strengthening of global cumulative-evolutionary development in human history. A not insignificant sign of this was that the dissolution of the huge Soviet empire and its replacement by numerous independent or separate states, and also the assumption of genuine independence by eastern European and the Baltic states, did not involve, as would be expected in the past, wars and protracted revolutions, but rather were accomplished, by and

large, through peaceful change. That is, it was largely a process of creative destruction and reconstruction by civic and political means that did not recapitulate the cyclical rise-and-fall pattern of the past, but blended with the cumulative-evolutionary pattern of the global open system.[6]

(6) As anticipated in early twentieth-century Americans' thinking, developmental investment acted as a constant driving force in twentieth-century world affairs, begetting both progressive change and retrograde, often monstrous, results or reaction. The principal agency of development investment was the large corporation (including finance and banking) operating more and more transnationally, although governments and intergovernmental agencies, directly, or indirectly in connection with corporations and other entities, played significant roles as well. By the end of the century, large corporations (both nonfinancial and financial), and even some not so large corporations or enterprises, were increasingly acquiring multinational staffing and management, and decreasingly a singular national identity, and similarly with nonprofits and NGOs. The more the global open system spread and developed, the more it was characterized by shifting trade, investment, employment, and production patterns, moving toward having multiple centers, instead of a fixed seat or geophysical center. Whereas by the 1890s–1910, the Britain–Germany rivalry and the Japanese challenge were the salient points in *great power* relations, no similar clear-cut nation-vs.-nation conflict of worldwide proportions was clearly identifiable at the end of the 1990s. (The pan-Islamist imperialist challenge was worldwide, but of a different order, hence eliciting new kinds of strategic responses, and will be addressed in (7) and Part Four below.)

The comic book saying that after the end of the Soviet system there remained only one "superpower" – the US – in effect recognized more the prospective absence of warring great power conflict than an actual presence of a "superpowerdom" in real-world history. If by 2000, the US was widely regarded, whether favorably or unfavorably, as world leader – or "indispensable nation," or "Hegemon," or "Global Empire," or "Leviathan-Colossus," or "Infidel-Crusader" – nevertheless it was neither as a Rome with its empire of centuries ago, nor as an Arab or Ottoman Empire in medieval and post-medieval centuries, nor as a Britain with its empire of less than a century ago, nor as a Soviet empire of the twentieth century. At the end of the twentieth century, modern development was increasingly transnational, less and less geo-centered, in accordance with the "superpower's" (the US') own long-pursued objectives evolving since the beginning of the century. The US, the "superpower," that is, was acting as a leading participant in a global open system, and given its large advanced economy and military capacities, in large part as its guarantor, in which people and enterprise within and across societies may have variable shares of worldwide development, in proportion to their tangible and intangible productive, investment, technical, and organizational capacities. Germany, Japan, and Italy found greater prosperity, internal development, and shares in world development, not to mention prestige, esteem, and respect, in the US-championed open system than in their previous attempts at closed-empire, state-command systems, which on the contrary led to national ruin and disaster for themselves and others.

By the opening of the twenty-first century, Russia, other former Soviet states, eastern European nations, China, and India, chose to move into the global open system, with strong developmental consequences. China entered upon the road to becoming one of the world's greatest economies, with corresponding political-strategic ramifications. India entered upon a similar road to an economic pre-eminence and with similar ramifications. The US–UK intervention in Afghanistan and Iraq, and the attempted installation there of protomarket-parliamentary systems, sought to reinforce and invigorate the trend. By 2000–2008, the leaderships of many less developed countries were abandoning the closed state-command model of development for the open-market model. Cuba, Zimbabwe, Iran, Syria, and North Korea remained significant exceptions to the trend, joined to some degree by Venezuela, Bolivia, and Ecuador, with cognate tendencies in Peru, Nicaragua, Argentina, and Mexico. Overall, however, as the open-market system spread and developed in the world, and as anticipated in early twentieth-century Americans' thinking, so did, less quickly, consistently, or completely, but persistently, principles and institutions of rule of law, individual liberty, elected representative government, and acknowledgment of universal human rights and standards – in short, "modernization."

(7) The special US–Britain relation continued tightly in the Kuwait–Iraq war of 1990–1991, and in the Afghanistan and Iraq wars of 2001–2008, when the open-system West–Asia connection, and prevention of a land-based greater Eurasian system – France, Germany, Russia maneuvering, with China closely watching – were put to strong tests. The tests were met by the resolute US–UK intervention in Afghanistan and Iraq, and engagement in Central Asia more broadly, pulling France, Germany, and Russia back from moving definitively toward a land-based Eurasian revival, while reassuring China and India of the open system's viability and staying power, and in the process holding Pakistan (precariously) in the system, fostering India–Pakistan and China–India rapprochements,

pressing for change in the Iranian closed-system state-command despotism, seeking to strengthen pro-Western electoral-democracy trends in the Balkans, Georgia, Ukraine, Kyrgyzstan, Azerbaijan, and Armenia, working to reorient, or reinforce a reorientation in, Libya, Lebanon, Kuwait, Qatar, Bahrain, UAE, Yemen, Saudi Arabia, and Egypt, and reassuring Morocco, Algeria, Tunisia, South Africa, and Nigeria.

The states of eastern Europe and Central Asia rather strongly supported the US–UK policies, because they did not want entrapment in a closed Eurasian or Islamist system subjecting them (as during the World War I–II, Cold War, and previous eras) to Russian, German, French, Persian, Turk, or Arab domination, but did want to be part of a larger, global open system that promised for them greater independence and modern development. NATO and EU expansion eastward, with its "New Europe"/"Old Europe" dimension, roiled sensibilities, but helped to raise and animate eastern European spirits and deter revived French–German–Russian Eurasian proclivities, and to keep the three powers "contained," for the time being, in the global open system. The Bush administration's response to the events in Central Asia and the Middle East, 2001–2006 and after, was deeply rooted in long-term twentieth-century US foreign-policy "institutional memory," "core principles," and objectives, that is, in the US open-system quest, and in the universal cumulative-evolutionary movement of humanity to greater modernization – in Hegelian and Marxian, as well as in Whig-Liberal and modern Judeo-Christian, terms, *freedom*: or, the Age of Liberty, as President Bush called it, and gave it further expression in his Second Inaugural, and as Secretary of State Condoleezza Rice pointedly reaffirmed in her Paris address of February 8, 2005.

(8) It is consistent with the universalist principles of the global open system that the monumental conflicts of the twentieth century have included the struggles against, and the great victories over, racism as a policy of state, and as an institutional system of domination and exploitation – for example, the defeat of Nazi Germany, the civil rights revolution in the US, and the ending of apartheid in South Africa. The continuing struggles for women's equal rights and opportunities run on the same universalist road, with strong US–UK backing. As anticipated in the Americans' thinking, the tendency is growing for a pluralism of cultures, societies, and nations, contributing to, and enriching, an increasingly common global society-type, not as yet, if ever, *one* global society, but acknowledging principles of a universal humanity, inscribed in the principles of the Charter of the United Nations (1945) and its *Universal* Declaration of Human Rights (1948), while adapting them to various cultures and

historical traditions. Evidence of an emergent global society-type can be seen in a spreading of economic development along market lines, in transnational business and financial institutions and relations, in transnational class formations and social stratifications, in large and ongoing transnational migrations, in political and governmental policies, practices, and institutions, in urban technostructures and cultures, in higher education and skills, in science and engineering, in TV, cinema, the performing arts, entertainment and recreation, in the Internet and the computer culture, in journalism and the news media, in transportation, travel, and telecommunications, in patterns of fashion and dress (e.g., the ubiquity of jeans, T-shirts, and monogrammed attire), and in culinary tastes and habits: evidence, in short, of the dawn of a post-imperialism and universalist age in human history.[7]

(9) At the end of the twentieth century and opening years of the twenty-first, global development strategies and the stability, growth, and health of the open system turned to a large and decisive extent on relations between the transatlantic West and Asia. By 2000, even more so than at 1900, China, India, and Asia as a whole, given their ever-mounting and probably irreversible intercourse with the West (high-tech and otherwise), and thus major and growing role in the world-political economy, stood at the center of world affairs and world politics. The twain were met.

Notes

1. A corollary question was, would the end of the Cold War system release smaller national and ethnic groups (as it did, e.g., in the Balkans, parts of central and eastern Europe, and former Soviet lands) from restraints that had prevented numerous conflicts among them after World War II? In addition to this, the fear of a powerful Germany, and of a German–Soviet entente, spread among Europeans, including especially in the British (Thatcher) and French (Mitterand) governments. A rather dramatic press discussion of this appeared, for example, in A. M. Rosenthal's *New York Times* column as early as in May 1989, "Fear of Soviet–W. German Power Bloc Is Hidden Factor in Europe Today," in which he stated (in part): "Nobody is telling the truth. In weeks of arguments and pronouncements about West Germany, NATO, the Soviet Union and short-range nuclear weapons, no diplomat, politician or national leader has had the courage to say plainly what lies beneath it all. It is this fear: West Germany, already the dominant economic power in Western Europe, will use the Gorbachev openings to become the dominant economic power in Eastern and Central Europe as well. Huge amounts of West German money and technology will pour into the Soviet Union and its allies, leading to a West German–Soviet economic and political alliance . . . Even before

unification [of West and East Germany], Western Europe will face its nightmare come to life – a mighty Germany working in tandem with a rejuvenated Soviet Union. The Soviet–German alliance will not have to use military power to get its way in the world: economic and political strength should do nicely." As reprinted in the Harrisburg, PA *Patriot-News*, May 3, 1989. See also, on these fears, George Bush and Brent Scowcroft, *A World Transformed* (New York: Vintage Books, 1998), chs. 8–11. Nine years later, by 1998, even with the Soviet system gone and China opening and changing, deep fears remained over whether Germany and Russia would be strongly part of the global open system, or in alignment themselves and with France and China, seek to build a Eurasian system. See, for example, Steven Erlanger, "Germany Sits in with a New Team," *New York Times*, April 12, 1998, which reported (in part): "The problem with labeling yourself the world's 'indispensable nation,' . . . is that you become hypersensitive if other nations, less convinced or more uneasy, start meeting without you." "Late last month in Moscow, the French, Germans and Russians had their very first summit meeting, and Washington did not take the prospect calmly. Senior American officials like the Deputy Secretary of State, Strobe Talbot, were feverishly interrogating their French and German counterparts about what such a meeting might encompass and what it might mean." In addition: "Russia's President, Boris N. Yeltsin, and China's President, Jiang Zemin, have already held summit meetings." "Mr. Kohl went out of his way to stress that this 'big troika' was not aimed at the United States – much the same message that the Americans so often try to send the Russians about NATO expansion. 'This meeting is, naturally, not directed at anyone else,' he said, and he made sure the agenda stuck to continental, rather than transatlantic, issues." [Par.] "Even more striking, senior German diplomats immediately telephoned senior American officials at the State Department, as soon as the meeting was over, to give a readout of what happened there, without waiting for the Americans to ask. And both French and German officials briefed the British." "Since World War II, Germany has always looked to Washington for both connections and protection, wanting to insure that the United States remains tightly bound to Europe and European security. The American presence keeps not only French ambitions in check, but German ones, too – something of a relief to those Germans who are suspicious of their own impulses." "And a French official urged Washington to calm itself. 'The main purpose is to try to show Moscow that EU and NATO enlargement is not aimed at Russia,' the official said. 'Regional initiatives will happen in a globalized world. We don't, as in the past, systematically interpret what the Americans do in foreign policy as directed against us, and we hope the Americans won't assume that all we do is directed at them.'"

2. Concerning the eastward expansion of NATO in relation to managing Germany's role, and reinforcing the US role in guaranteeing the stability of greater Europe and Russian security within it, see Strobe Talbot, "Russia Has Nothing to Fear," *New York Times*, February 18, 1997; Jane Perlez, "Blunt Reason for Enlarging NATO: Curbs on Germany," *New York Times*, December 7, 1997; also, Warren Christopher (secretary of state, 1993–1997) and

William J. Perry (secretary of defense, 1994–1997), "NATO's True Mission," *New York Times*, October 21, 1997; here Christopher and Perry referred to NATO expansion and the NATO–Russia Founding Act (Partnership for Peace, Russian Associate status) as engaging "a critical constituency in the formation of the new Eurasian security order: the Russian military," and affording "practical cooperation dealing with real-world problems of mutual concern." Russia's government leaders understood this; whatever the rhetoric they may have felt necessary for reassurances, or for undercutting nationalists in domestic politics, the Russian government has not seriously opposed NATO's expansion. Russia's associate status with NATO is a further indication of this understanding by both the Russians and the NATO members. See, e.g., Michael R. Gordon, "NATO Is Inching Closer, But Russians Don't Blink," *New York Times*, May 2, 1998.

3. See, for example, David E. Sanger, "Greenspan Sees Asian Crisis Moving World to Western Capitalism," *New York Times*, February 13, 1998, reporting (in part): "Alan Greenspan, the Federal Reserve chairman, told a Senate panel today [February 12] that one of the most fundamental effects of the Asian crisis was a worldwide move toward 'the Western form of market capitalism,' instead of the competing Asian approach that only a few years ago looked like an attractive model for nations around the world." [Par.] "'What has happened here is a very dramatic event towards a consensus of the type of market system which we have in this country,' Greenspan said before the Senate Foreign Relations committee." "'We saw the breakdown of the Berlin wall in 1989,' he added, 'and the massive shift away from central planning towards free market capitalist types of structures. Concurrent to that was the really quite dramatic, very strong growth in what appeared to be a competing capitalist-type system in Asia. And as a consequence of that, you had developments of types of structures which I believe at the end of the day were faulty, but you could not demonstrate that so long as growth was going at 10 percent a year.'" The term "free market," so commonly used, denotes not the old competitive market system of, say, the late nineteenth-century US, but a market system of the modern type both administered (regulated) and competitive, but free of state command. The lead headline on the story (above) accurately summarized Greenspan's words, but the headline over the continuation of the story on an inside page is, I believe, more accurate about the situation: "Greenspan Sees Asian Crisis Moving World to West's System" (instead of "to Western Capitalism"). This may be indicated in Greenspan's own qualified wording elsewhere in his testimony: "'a consensus towards the, *for want of a better term*, the Western form of free-market capitalism as the model which should govern how each individual country should run its economy'" (emphasis added). See also, regarding the impact and outcome of the Asian crisis: Alan Murray, "New Economic Models Fail While America Inc. Keeps Rolling: Why? Asian Fallout Is a Triumph of Wall Street . . ." *Wall Street Journal*, December 8, 1997.

4. The critics of the IMF were probably right that its policies, instead of stabilizing currency values, contributed to continued instability. But that was beside another point, which was an IMF intent to manage, rather than quickly to

end, the crisis, in order to push countries into larger reforms. For example, Sanger, *New York Times*, February 13, 1998: "Mr. [Robert E.] Rubin [Secretary of the Treasury], Mr. Greenspan, and Lawrence H. Summers, the Deputy Treasury Secretary, argued today [February 12] that the IMF had succeeded in using its bailouts to force nations to open their markets and transform their economies – a step, they suggested, toward more democratic government." Also, Mark Landler, "Rubin Defends IMF Policies and Continues His Asian Tour," *New York Times*, June 30, 1998. The same may be said for Secretary Rubin's delayed intervention in support of the Japanese yen. See, for example, Jonathan Fuerbringer, "Deliberately or Not, Rubin Set Up a Fall" (in the yen), *New York Times*, June 18, 1998; David E. Sanger, "US Joins Japan in Surprise Move to Shore Up Yen," *New York Times*, June 18, 1998; and Bob Davis, "Rubin Prescribes Tight Money for Asia: US Treasurer Backs Policy of IMF Despite Protests of Choking High Rates," *Wall Street Journal*, June 30, 1998. Note also, the assessment of the IMF's Indonesia policy by the international currency expert, Professor Steve H. Hanke of Johns Hopkins University (Letter to the Editor, *WSJ*, June 2, 2005, p. A13): "The IMF actually launched a regime-change program that succeeded at the price of devastating the Indonesian economy. As former US Secretary of State Lawrence Eagleburger put it: 'We were fairly clever in that we supported the IMF as it overthrew [President Suharto]. Whether that was a wise way to proceed is another question. I'm not saying Mr. Suharto should have stayed, but I kind of wish he had left on terms other than because the IMF pushed him out.' Even the former managing director of the IMF, Michel Camdessus, could not find fault with this assessment. On the occasion of his retirement, he proudly proclaimed: 'We created the conditions that obliged President Suharto [in 1999] to leave his job.'" On the revised IMF-World Bank roles, after the currency crises of the 1990s, in the years 2001–2006, in extending and strengthening the global open-market system among developing countries, see John B. Taylor (former US Treasury under secretary for International Affairs, prof. of economics, Stanford University), "Loan Ranger," *Wall Street Journal*, Op-Ed, April 19, 2006, p. A12. One of the important reasons, among many others, for the failure of US efforts, early in the twentieth century, at Chinese currency reform – to put China on a gold-exchange standard, a system similar to that installed by the US in the Philippines, and to the later currency board system of Hong Kong – was that the US insisted on corollary structural and fiscal reforms in the Chinese government, under Western supervision (a function of the IMF today), which the Chinese government (both the Imperial and the successor under Yuan Shih-kai) refused to accept.

5. Indicative of the staying power, in the 1990s, of Eurasian closed-system outlooks in Russia and China, and of the continuity of certain threads running through twentieth-century world politics, are the following two items: (i) In a statement that appeared on the *New York Times* Op-Ed page, February 1, 1996, Gennadi A. Zyuganov, the head of the Russian Communist Party, said, "Our foreign policy priority would be to maintain continuity with the foreign policies of pre-revolutionary Russia and the Soviet Union. We would seek to restore our state's unique role as the pivot and fulcrum of a Eurasian

continental bloc – and its consequent role as a necessary balance between East and West." (ii) The official Chinese Communist Party newspaper, the *People's Daily*, stated, as reported in the *New York Times*, April 27, 1996: "The strategic objective of the United States is to dominate the world . . . [The United States] will not tolerate the emergence of a strong nation on the Eurasian landmass that would threaten its dominant position." Also, Steven Erlander, "Germany Sits in with a New Team," *New York Times*, April 12, 1998, reporting that at the summit meetings between Russian President Boris Yeltsin and Chinese President Jiang Zemin, "they took turns denouncing the dangers of a 'mono-polar' world," and that at the German–French–Russian summit in March 1998, "Mr. [Helmut] Kohl [German Chancellor] looked uneasy during . . . [Yeltsin's] disquisition on the summit as a milestone in the creation of a 'Greater Europe,' which, he predicted, 'will be the dominant power.'" On a different note, about Georgia's important role, under pro-Western President Eduard Shevardnadze, in tying Eurasia into the global open system, "linking China and Central Asia with Europe," see James A. Baker III, "America's Vital Interest in the 'New Silk Road,'" *New York Times*, Op-Ed, July 21, 1997.

6. I think this is a fair characterization, even in view of such violent conflict in the 1990s as in the Balkans, Romania, Chechnya, Georgia, and Azerbaijan-Armenia. US, NATO, Russian, and UN efforts to contain and end these conflicts, including a degree of cooperation between Russia and the US and NATO, especially significant because not without abrasive frictions, would seem to corroborate this characterization, as would Russia's subsequent acquiescence in the eastern expansion of NATO and EU, and the changes in Georgia, Ukraine, and Kyrgyzstan in 2004–2005. Other violent conflicts elsewhere in the world there were aplenty, in Africa, the Middle East, Latin America, southeastern Asia, but they were apart from the dissolution of the Soviet empire. Cf. Charles S. Maier, *Among Empires: American Ascendancy and Its Predecessors* (Cambridge: Harvard University Press, 2006), p. 124: "only one empire has allowed itself to expire peacefully, without invasions from outside the frontiers, warlordism and upheaval within, or the military lashing out at rebels and invaders: the Soviet Union between the late 1980s and 1991; and at different points in the process, whether in Leipzig or Lithuania, violence might easily have been triggered. The Soviet sphere aside, expiring empires have proved sites of repetitive battles and often prolonged violence."

7. Post-imperialism as a description of international relations, as periodization in distinguishing historical eras, and as theory of structure and dynamics in world politics, is informing a growing body of scholarship. The pioneering work is Richard L. Sklar, *Corporate Power in an African State: The Political Impact of International Mining Companies in Zambia* (Berkeley: University of California Press, 1975), esp. ch. 6, pp. 179–216; and developed further by R. L. Sklar in subsequent work, including: "Postimperialism: A Class Analysis of Multinational Corporate Expansion," *Comparative Politics*, 9: 1 (1976), pp. 75–92; "The Nature of Class Domination in Africa," *Journal of Modern African Studies*, 17: 4 (1979), pp. 531–552; "Developmental Democracy,"

Comparative Studies in Society and History, 29: 4 (1987), pp. 686–714; "Postimperialism: Concepts and Implications," Occasional Paper, John Sloan Dickey Center, Dartmouth College, 1997 (with useful bibliography); and see *African Politics in Postimperial Times: The Essays of Richard L. Sklar*, ed., Toyin Falola (Trenton, NJ, and Asmara, Eritrea: Africa World Press, 2002). See also the important collection of essays by various scholars in David G. Becker, Jeff Frieden, Sayre P. Schatz, and Richard L. Sklar, eds., *Postimperialism: International Capitalism and Development in the Late Twentieth Century* (Boulder, CO: Lynne Reinner Publishers, 1987); and in David G. Becker and Richard L. Sklar, eds., *Postimperialism and World Politics*. See also David G. Becker, *The New Bourgeoisie and the Limits of Dependency: Mining, Class, and Power in 'Revolutionary' Peru* (Princeton University Press, 1983); D. G. Becker, "Business Associations in Latin America: The Venezuelan Case," *Comparative Political Studies*, 23: 1 (1990), pp. 114–138; D. G. Becker, "Beyond Dependency: Development and Democracy in the Era of International Capitalism," in *Comparative Political Dynamics*, eds., Dankwart A. Rustow and Kenneth Paul Erickson (New York: HarperCollins, 1991), pp. 98–133; Scott R. Bowman, "The Ideology of Transnational Enterprise," *Social Science Journal*, 30:1 (1993), pp. 47–68; S. R. Bowman, *The Modern Corporation and American Political Thought* (University Park: Pennsylvania State University Press, 1996), esp. ch. 7, pp. 286–304; Parrini, "Charles A. Conant, Economic Crises, and Foreign Policy"; Keith A. Haynes, "Dependency, Postimperialism, and the Mexican Revolution: An Historiographic Review," *Mexican Studies/ Estudios Mexicanos*, 7: 2 (Summer 1991), pp. 225–251.

CHAPTER 9

American Century Fulfilled and Revoked, or Nullified: From Empires to a Universal Humanity? Or, Cycles Forever?

(1) Consistent with its own open-system principles, and not without internal dislocation, discontent, and dissent, the US assumed the paramount leadership role in the global open system. It disowned "exceptionalism," in accepting and adapting to a relatively declining share in world trade and investment over the decades after World War II, and in helping others acquire and increase their shares, while the world economy, and for many countries, absolute share sizes, steadily and massively grew. In so doing, the US persistently fostered cooperative international prodevelopment organizations, however much for good or ill they may be judged, ranging from the IMF, IBRD (World Bank), GATT, the UN, and the ECA in the immediate postwar years, to the OECD, OSCE, European Union, G-7, G-8, WTO, EDB, IADB, ECB, NAFTA, G-6, ASEAN, APEC, CAFTA, and others. In assuming its strong open-system leadership role, the US both *pushed* development by exporting and transferring to others surplus capital, goods, services, and know-how, and *pulled* development by importing all these from others, and, by the 1980s, by running substantial annual trade and current account deficits. This was in contrast to Britain in its late nineteenth- to early twentieth-century imperial heyday, which ran trade deficits but overall current account surpluses. In each category, push and pull, from 1945 to the early years of the twenty-first century, the US remained the world economy's single largest shareholder, yet also eventually becoming the single largest world "debtor," on an unprecedented scale, again in contrast to imperial Britain, which was the great creditor nation before World War I (as was the US after World War I until the 1980s), and yet, again, the US sustaining a flat, or a *relatively* declining, share of world trade, production, and investment (at around

25 percent), as other national economies grew, and the prospect of the US losing its Number One position in the world economy as the new century wore on.

(2) In general, since the early twentieth century, US leadership, in effect, has chosen international development over national-imperial aggrandizement in relations with other developed countries, and it has promoted a transnational post-imperialism that, as it has evolved, is antiracist, antiethnicist, and antireligious chauvinist, and that affirms national sovereignties and cultural differences as the basis of a universalist-transnational order. The emerging transnational system can be thought of as a kind of Madisonian-Hamiltonian federalism globally applied: as in the US, where vigorous state and local governments serve as the basis of interstate economic, political, associational, civic, cultural, and social relations, and hence as the basis of a strong national system and a strong national government, so in world affairs, vigorous nation-states, and their subdivisions, may serve as the basis of a thriving transnationalism, and of international institutions of cooperation, management, and regulation – both governmental and nongovernmental. Indeed, strong national governments are, and for a long historical era will remain, essential to the establishment, development, and very survival of an authentic transnationalism, or "globalism," because without them, as some salient current tendencies show, transnationalism will in all probability devolve into plutocracy and class warfare, national and ethnic conflicts, chaotic and massively destructive activities by rogue states and sub- and supranational nongovernment organizations, and, in consequence, the reversion to the old cyclical history of empires, as nations and other social-political entities coalesce for protection, security, welfare, aggression, and aggrandizement, in rival imperial systems: hence, the strong "nation-building" commitment evident in US foreign policy, whatever the campaign rhetoric in election seasons.

Those who pit "nationalism" against "transnationalism" or "globalism," as mutually exclusive opposites, or as in fundamental conflict, may have in mind traditionalist, antidevelopment, or "mercantilist" nationalisms, and past imperialisms. But in the historical reality of the post-World War II world, strong and more numerous nation-states (notwithstanding the weak, failed, and "rogue" ones) and "globalism" have been mutually engaged and reinforcing, each the condition of the other, and will remain so as (and if) human history continues to move into, and sustains, a post-imperial age. Indeed, failed states, "rogue" states, and sub- and supranational operations (e.g., Somalia, Sudan-Darfur, FARC, Mexican "coyotes" and narco-gangs, North Korea, Muslim Brotherhood, Al-Qaeda, Iranian pan-Islamism,

Hezbollah, Hamas/PLA) pose serious threats to modernizing globalism. Tendencies in a retrograde cyclical direction could be seen in the international divisions over the Afghanistan and Iraq wars of 2001–2006, in the crises associated, for example, with Bosnia, Kosovo, Chechnya, North Korea and Iran (nuclear weapons/missiles), the Pakistan–India conflict, the Kurds, Sudan (South, Darfur), the Israel–Palestine–Lebanon–Syria–Iran war, the Russian intervention in Georgia (2008), and pan-Islamist (Arab/Iranian) imperialist programs, actions, and warmaking. Nevertheless, outcomes attained or pending in some of these instances indicate at least a probational strength of the transnational or "globalism" trend. Among the implications of the foregoing, the following may be mentioned:

(3) As the global open system spread, so did the surplus-capital problem – commonly referred to, by the late 1990s, in the media and in business and government circles, as the problem of "excess capacity," "gluts," "asset inflation," "excess liquidity", and "price deflation" (or lack of "pricing power"). This was also a central concern in late nineteenth and early twentieth-century Americans' thinking. Although the capital surplus-problem has been chronic throughout the twentieth century, the situation of the 1980s–1990s bore some particular similarities with the era of price deflation and explosive growth of the 1870s–1890s (but without the deep and prolonged depressions of the 1870s and 1890s): tremendous growth in both output and productivity, related as it was to epochal technological innovation, intensely competitive market conditions, deep socioeconomic restructuring, and massive human migrations, drove the expansion and recurrent crises in the transatlantic system then, and in the much larger transnational system 100 years later. As in the 1870s–1890s, so in the 1980s–1990s, the spreading of the capital-surplus problem accompanied the expansion and quickening of the globalization impulse, along with the companion impulse of social democratic reform. Unlike 100 years earlier, however, late twentieth-century transnationalism and international cooperation, long promoted by US policy, replaced the imperial rivalry among the developed countries that in the past had led to wars among them. In addition, of the three great post-World War II closed systems, the Soviet empire dissolved, and China and India opened. Russia, other ex-Soviet states, China, and India effectively joined the global open system. Accordingly, and together with similar dispositions of a growing number of other nations, especially in East Asia (South Korea, Taiwan, the Philippines, Indonesia, Malaysia, Singapore, Thailand), incomparably greater areas and larger populations of the world became ready, willing, and able to receive the effective deployment of development capital.

These conditions permitted the continued and new engagement of capital-surplus sectors of the world in the development of capital-scarce sectors, on a scale not available 100 years earlier – China, East Asia, India, Russia and other former Soviet republics of Europe and Central Asia, eastern Europe, the Baltic states, the Balkans, some of the Persian Gulf states, northern Africa, South Africa, and a growing number of other nations in sub-Sahara Africa.[1] By 2005, so broad and vigorous had global development work become that energy sources (oil, natural gas, coal, nuclear) and commodities, including steel and other metals, began moving from chronic relative oversupply to temporary relative scarcities and substantially rising prices (and vendor "pricing-power"). Managed with care and fairness, by the late 1990s and after, there was more than enough development work to be done in the world to continue, for a long time to come, deploying surplus capital on the basis of the "Open Door" principle of variable *shares* and international cooperation, and hence to sustain and extend the post-imperialism age in ensuing world history. An interruption or reversal of this trend could come, however, from the action of antimodernizing political-military adversaries (governmental and supragovernmental), e.g., pan-Islamist imperialism, as well as from modernizing rivalries over scarce-supplied resources, or national/regional efforts to protect, employ, or export surplus labor and productive capacities, or a full-blown reversion to *modernizing* imperial rivalries drawing precisely upon transnational enterprise capacities.

(4) No more than the economies *within* the developed and developing countries is the emergent transnational economy a "free market" system, nor is it simply a "capitalist" system. Rather, as with the national economies, the transnational economy is an *administered* market system – that is, a regulated market system, regulated both by intramarket agencies (e.g., corporations, banks, exchanges, cartels, cooperatives, unions, hedge funds), quasi-government agencies, e.g., central banks, governmental agencies (national and international, including the WTO, IMF, WB, EU Commission, OPEC), and NGO operations, and it is a mix of capitalism and socialism. To conceive the transnational, or global-open, system as "free market" and simply capitalist in character is not only empirically inaccurate, but it obstructs the thinking and dispositions necessary to managing both the normal functioning of the system (e.g., in forums, policies, and operations of G-7, G-8, EU, EMU, ECB, FRB, NAFTA, APEC, ASEAN, IMF, IBRD, EDB, USAID, WTO), its crises (e.g., the 1994–1995 Mexican, the 1997–1998 Asian, the 1998 Russian, the 2002 Argentine), and crisis-bearing special problems (e.g., 2005–2008 oil and natural gas

prices, yuan revaluation, and the breakdown of the WTO Doha round in 2008). Just as with the national political economies of the developed and developing countries alike, so the transnational political economy is best understood as consisting of a mix of public and private authority, of production, distribution, and consumer interests, of profit-making investment and social-programs investment, or, in traditional political-economic terms, a capitalism-socialism mix.

Nowhere by itself has either a pure-and-simple "free market" capitalism, *or* a state-command socialism, yielded successful, sustained modern development. Successful development in the twentieth–twenty-first century has been achieved in those societies that have combined regulated markets and rule-of-law liberalism with an adequate evolving balance of the capitalism-socialism mix, as compared with those societies that from doctrine or historical circumstance have not. In the global open system, the capitalism-socialism mix is to be found within nations, transnationally, and in international institutions and agreements. In "taking on" market relations, China, Russia, and other former Communist-governed countries began relinquishing state-command economies, but they were not adopting "free markets," or exchanging socialism for capitalism. Rather, they have been moving away from state-command systems and toward the "Western" system of administered (regulated) markets, and increasingly toward liberal rule-of-law contractual and political practices, as the basis of an evolving, prodevelopment capitalism-socialism mix. The mix-characteristics of the global open system – nationally, transnationally, and internationally – were understood, with more or less clarity, and whether or not they personally liked it, by such political leaders in the "West" as US Presidents Ronald Reagan, George Bush, William J. Clinton, and George W. Bush (and many of their top senior officers), UK Prime Ministers Margaret Thatcher and Tony Blair, French Presidents François Mitterrand, Jacques Chirac, and Nicolas Sarkozy, and German Chancellors Helmut Kohl, Gerhard Schroeder, and Angela Merkel; such leaders in developing countries as South Africa's Presidents Nelson Mandela and Thabo Mbeki; and such leaders in the "East" as China's Chairmen-Presidents Deng Xiaoping, Jiang Zemin, and Hu Jintao, and India's Prime Ministers A. B. Vajpayee and Manmohan Singh. It was also grasped by the Soviet Gorbachev-Shevardnadze leadership, and the subsequent Russian Yeltsin and Putin leaderships.[2] In other words, the capitalism-socialism mix had a global political standing corresponding with its presence in the global economy.

(5) The global open system has meant, or at least needs, the emergence and functioning, not of fewer or weaker, but, whether more or less in

number, of stronger, independent nation-states that are hence capable of becoming *inter*dependent nation-states. It also, therefore, means that the emergence of "new" strong nation-states, playing larger roles in world affairs, is to be expected as normal to the health and development of the transnational system – for example, such nations as China, India, Pakistan, Indonesia, Malaysia, the Philippines, Iran, Iraq, Egypt, Brazil, South Africa, and Nigeria, to name a few. Each such nation will naturally expect to engage in world affairs as one among sovereign equals, whether in matters of equitable shares in the world's development and wealth, or of prestige, or of national-strategic security – which has meant nuclear weapons proliferation. This means, further, that national leaderships in a post-imperialism era, if the world is not to revert to the old empire systems, and risk catastrophic war, will need to foster acceptance of, and adaptation to, strong nation-states, including the "newcomers" among them. Precisely because of this, they will need to establish, maintain, and develop strong international and transnational institutions of cooperation, management, and regulation (governmental and nongovernmental), building upon and *reconfiguring* those that already exist (such as has been happening with NATO and EU, and under discussion concerning the UN), and adding new ones as appropriate. As all this implies, there will also be need for the reformulation of old, and the articulation of new, principles of collective security among the nations, including rules of proper and improper, legal and illegal, behavior in war and peace by nations, their alliances, and their subdivisions, and by NGOs and individuals operating within and across them, as well as principles, rules, and procedures of deterrence, enforcement, and punishment – pending the international formulation and implementation of which, particular governments and regional pacts (e.g., NATO, CIS, African Union, US, UK, Australia, Spain, Colombia, Russia, China, the Philippines, Pakistan, India, Indonesia, the new Iraq and Afghanistan, Israel, Nigeria) have been obliged at times to assume.

(6) The twentieth century may be thought of as the "American Century," insofar as the course of world affairs has accorded, to a large and significant extent, with the expectations and objectives in the thinking of early twentieth-century US policy makers and their successors. Yet, although it has meant the US assuming to a world leadership role, it did not turn out to mean a sole dominant role, because after World War II, its power and reach were limited (aside from the finitude of its own capacities) by the "check and balance" of its allies (people and governments), and of the rival Soviet-China closed-empire system(s). The "American Century,"

into which the post-Cold War world has been entering in the twenty-first century, is a world in which sole domination by the US, or by any single nation or group of nations, is so difficult as to be practicably impossible. This has become clear in the Afghan-Taliban, Al-Qaeda, and Iraq conflicts, and in relations with North Korea and Iran (2001–2008), no less to American leadership than to others. Some commentators have mistaken *shifting patterns* of multilateralism and transnationalism for US unilateralism. Hence, the "American Century" would realize itself in its negation as the "World Century," or as the British editor said to Vanderlip in 1901, "A United States of the World" – if that may be taken to mean something like an evolving quasi-federal commonwealth of nations, rather than some centralized "One World" government.

Along these lines, the American-championed open system and its outlook (including an evolving capitalism/socialism mix within the framework of a rule-of-law democracy) have, so far, proved superior to the closed, state-command system in material, moral, and spiritual terms,[3] and their acceptance has in general become prevalent among the world's active political leaderships and elites, whatever the "anti-America" and "antiglobalism" rhetoric.[4] The antination (or supranation) pan-Islamist-empire war against the open system and its developmental modernization confirms the prevalent trend, while posing a lethal threat to it. If the global open system is to survive and develop, it will need not only elite acceptance, but also popular acceptance, and accordingly, careful tending and cultivation, that is, the exercise of deliberate human will and reason in a framework of an ecumenical ethic – what may be thought of as the broadening and deepening development of a progressive human self-government worldwide, or in philosophical terms, freedom, or, the workings of *Geistische Vernunft* in human history: the essence of Pope Benedict XVI's Regensburg University address of September 12, 2006, and, it should be added, of the policies and themes embraced in Presidents Reagan and George H. W. Bush's "New World Order," President Clinton's "Indispensable Nation" and "Bridge to the 21st Century," UK Prime Minister Tony Blair's Social-Democratic Internationalism, and President George W. Bush's "Age of Liberty."

(7) If there is to be a model of world politics fitting the potentialities and realities of modern world affairs as they have been moving into the twenty-first century, it is that of the global open system vs. restricted closed systems, with the salient fundamental conflicts being: (i) those among prodevelopers – promodernizers – about the *pace* and *quality* of development, and the *distribution* of its work and fruits; (ii) those between prodevelopers and antidevelopers, or between promodernizers

and antimodernizers. Such conflicts run *within* and *across* national, ethnic, religious, and "civilizational" lines, rather than *along* them. If not the "Clash of Civilizations" paradigm for explaining the "Post-Cold War World, What?" the answer *in* actual history has been the "clash" of Empire-Cycle/Closed-System vs. "American-Century"/Global-Open-System – a cumulative-evolutionary explanation of universal human development that is cross-civilization in understanding, that is transhistorical in explanatory power, and that, accordingly, has applied to the pre-Cold War, Cold War, and post-Cold War eras alike, and to imperial and post-imperial epochs of human history.[5]

Notes

1. Concerning surplus capital and its global spread in the 1990s, the following example of press discussion is one among legions: Louis Uchitelle, "Global Good-Times, Meet the Global Glut," *New York Times*, November 16, 1997, which states, in part: "The Asian financial turmoil may be the first stage of a developing worldwide crisis driven mainly by a phenomenon called overcapacity: the tendency of the unfettered global economy to produce more cars, toys, shoes, airplanes, steel, paper, appliances, film, clothing, and electronic devices than people will buy at high enough prices. [Par.] 'There is excess global capacity in almost every industry,' Jack Welch, chairman of General Electric, said in a recent interview in the Financial Times of London . . . The inflation rate in the United States has fallen in part because of global overcapacity, and business people everywhere complain that they can't raise prices." "East Asia has been the main source of the world's overcapacity in recent years. Since 1991, countries like Thailand, South Korea, Indonesia, Malaysia, and the Philippines have accounted for half the growth in world output, primarily manufacturing, according to David Hale, chief global economist for the Zurich Insurance Group." ". . . the fresh blow of a bank default would make Japan even more eager to export its unsold goods – its overcapacity – to the United States. With that in mind, Treasury Secretary Robert E. Rubin publicly urged the Japanese Government last week to spur domestic consumption." See also, on Japan's surplus capital or oversaving and the need to raise consumption: Marc Chandler, "Poor Japan Has Too Much Capital," Global Forex [foreign exchange] Strategy, Deutsche Morgan Grenfell, April 24, 1998 (Chandler emphasized Japan's need both to raise consumption and export capital in the form of development investment in developing countries, instead of in the form of more savings in portfolio investment, e.g., in US bonds); and Wayne Angell (chief economist of Bear, Stearns, and formerly a Federal Reserve governor), "How to Save Japan from Oversaving," *Wall Street Journal*, Op-Ed, June 22, 1998.
2. See also my discussion of the capitalism-socialism mix at *United States as a Developing Country*, chs. 1, 7, and "Capitalism and Socialism in the Emergence of Modern America," and "Thoughts on Capitalism and Socialism: Utopian

and Realistic." Many articles in the press in the late 1990s, especially about Clinton and Blair, seem to corroborate the mix formulation, e.g., Thomas B. Edsall, "Clinton and Blair Envision a 'Third Way' International Movement" [of the "center-left"], *Washington Post*, June 28, 1998. The same article, in quoting Seymour Martin Lipset and Gary Marks on "The Failure of Socialism," etc., indicates how little many intellectuals (especially in the US) are able to understand this, because ironically they are so much in intellectual thrall, it seems to me, to what I call the Leninist Captivity in the understanding of socialism as a state-command system, an understanding originating among political elites in less developed society, and which by the early twentieth century was already becoming virtually obsolete in application to the more highly developed, advanced-industrial Western societies (as "modern" socialists understood – e.g., Marx, Eduard Bernstein, William English Walling, Morris Hillquit, Iulii Martov), although permeating many minds in the West with apparently long-term indelible effect. A reader may be thinking now – Aha! He's citing "revisionists," the "not really" socialists, the "renegades" (except Marx, maybe); and this, of course, confirms the point about the Leninist Captivity: that is, understanding socialism exclusively as Lenin (and "Leninists") defined it – a political and utopian, or reactionary, definition (as Marx would say), not a historical ("scientific") understanding; or, to make the point a little differently, like understanding Christianity as exclusively that of the Russian Orthodox Church. Edsall's article, in also quoting William Kristol, editor of the *Weekly Standard*, and Adam Myerson, editor of the Heritage Foundation's *Policy Review*, stating the other side of the coin – the victory of Thatcherism, Reaganism, and Kohlism as a victory of "free-market" capitalism – shows that "conservatives" are no less smitten by the Lenin romance. Lenin may be passé in Russia (and China), but he seems alive and well among many Western intellectuals on left and right alike.

3. Regarding material progress, see, e.g., the annual A. T. Kearney/*Foreign Policy* Globalization Index, fourth annual index: "Measuring Globalization: Economic Reversals, Forward Momentum," by *Foreign Policy*, A. T. Kearney, March/April 2004, accessed at www.foreignpolicy.com.

4. See, e.g., the op-ed article by Supachai Panitchpakdi, director-general of the World Trade Organization: "Brave New World," *Wall Street Journal*, February 26, 2004, p. A10, which states, in part: "More than any other country, the United States of America was instrumental in the creation of the global trading system. Indeed, the US has been the driving force behind eight rounds of multilateral trade negotiations, including the Uruguay Round, which created the World Trade Organization. The recent [US] initiative . . . to re-energize the current Doha Round of negotiations . . . is yet another reminder of how essential US leadership is to multilateral progress . . . Since the final dark days of World War II, trade has helped to lift millions in Asia, Latin America and Africa out of poverty, and millions more have new hope for the future." "The world is a very different place than it was in 1947, when the foundations were laid for the WTO and the global trading system we know today . . . continued US leadership . . . is indispensable to the system's success . . . strengthening the world trading system is key to America's wider objectives. Fighting

terrorism, reducing poverty, improving health, integrating China and other countries into the global economy – all of these issues are linked, in one way or another, to expanding world trade." "If the Doha Round is allowed to drift, what is the alternative? A fragmented world of hostile trading blocs? A world of greater poverty, marginalization and uncertainty? This is surely the world of the past, not the future – a world that our forefathers turned away from after 1945, and one that we should reject just as decisively today." See also the articles by two Chinese intellectuals and senior CCP leaders, and a leading Singapore scholar, all in *Foreign Affairs*, 84: 5 (September/ October 2005): Zheng Bijian, "'Peacefully Rising' to Great-Power Status," pp. 18–24; Wang Jisi, "China's Search for Stability with America," pp. 39–48; Kishore Mahbubani, "Understanding China," pp. 49–60; and see also Norton Wheeler, "Modernization Discourse with Chinese Characteristics," *East Asia*, 22: 3 (Fall 2005), pp. 3–24. See also Taro Aso (Foreign Minister of Japan), "Japan Awaits a Democratic China," *Wall Street Journal*, Op-Ed, March 13, 2006, p. A18 (in part): "Democracy in Asia is spreading ... [Par.] China's turn is imminent, and I am positive on the prospects for this evolution. Citizens of Japan, South Korea and Indonesia can all attest that prolonged economic development creates a stable middle class, which in turn provides a spring-board for greater political representation. The question is no longer 'whether,' but 'at what speed' China will metamorphose into a fully democratic nation. I can assure our friends in China that Japan is committed to China's success to that end. [Par.] My hope is that China recognizes that there is no longer a place for an empire. Rather, the guiding principles in today's world are global interdependence and the international harmony that can engender."

5. See Chapter 5, note 2.

PART FOUR

BRINGING HISTORY BACK IN

CHAPTER 10

History in the US; the US in History

I

"Bringing History Back In" is a play on the title of a volume of essays published in 1985, "Bringing the State Back In."[1] The essays were intended as a corrective response to politicalizing trends, today still strongly current, among professedly "radical" writers of social history. Those trends posed "social" history ("bottom-up" history) *against* political/legal/institutional ("top-down") history. They deemphasized, rejected, or ignored the study of matters of state – government, politics, and law – as an ideological privileging that prefigured historical understanding, and thus at best as insufficient or irrelevant, and at worst as antithetical, to an authentic historical understanding. Politicalizers of historiography were "socializing," by "depoliticizing," history.

These social-history or "radical"-history trends, however, were themselves an ideological privileging, indeed an ahistorical aberration, of not comprehending that both "top-down" and "bottom-up" studies entail social history, that both are integral to historical understanding, that each kind is better understood in context of the other, usually inextricably, and that matters of state are themselves profoundly matters also of social history, indeed of "radical" (root) significance, no less than other aspects of history, and that by 1985 many historians had for some long time understood such things. Applied to US history, the social-history trends were also lacking in an adequate thinking about periodization: in times and places of a rising bourgeoisie, developmental capitalism, market-class relations, and nation-states, such matters as government, law, and party politics are of fundamental historical – and social – significance, on both empirical and theoretical grounds.

In other words, professedly "radical" historians were displaying less a dissenting or innovative challenge to "conventional" perspectives and theory than a craft-deficiency, or, the way it is sometimes put, reinventing the wheel – but still having it square or in some shape not yet round.[2] Renewed study and research are proper and necessary to the disciplined pursuit of knowledge, and professedly "radical" historians have contributed a respectable share, but this was a case of driving out and "Bringing Back In" what for many experienced inquirers (including some "radicals") was never properly "Out."

But what can it mean to say, "Bringing *History* Back In," in the understanding of twentieth-century US society? Has it ever been "Out"? Is not the question, rather, how the history itself may bear different *interpretations*? Conceding this, and acknowledging some tongue-in-cheek parody, we can consider the meaning intended here: bringing history back in as a *discipline* of inquiry and knowledge about the twentieth-century US, as a society evolving in time, and in the broader context of human evolution and world history, instead of *doing* history, as a political "struggle" in the present – radical or otherwise – for justification, salvation, career, or power.

Among historians, including the best of them, the temptation is very strong, and hence the tendency, to make themselves the keepers, purveyors, and sometimes the creators, of the preferred party lines, true faiths, or sacred stories, and to place themselves among the articulating partisans and denominational leaders in the party, faith, and story wars. As with matters of state, so more broadly, "Bringing *History* Back In" is meant to raise the question of choosing historical method, instead of choosing a politicalization of history-writing in an ahistorical allegiance to party, faith-based, or ideological callings. It is meant also to acknowledge that this is a problem for historians across the board, from left to right, not only for "radicals," and not only for those in the American Historical Association, the Organization of American Historians, and their affiliates, but also for those in more recently formed associations, like The Historical Society, which presents itself as dissenting from the politicalization of the older establishments.[3]

The question of politicalization is not simply one of committing departments, curricula, or professional associations (and their publications, meetings, and conferences), to political causes or positions, or making them arenas and instrumentalities of political agendas (including religious, ideological, or interest-group agendas), as if the departments, curricula, associations, conferences, were surrogate political clubs, or movements, or parties, or faiths. The question of politicalization meant here does include this kind of activity, but also, and more essentially, the inclination, in the very history we write and teach, to serve and vindicate, or disserve and refute, past or current morals, politics, movements, interests, ideals, or selected ideological trends: history as pastor, acolyte, therapist, censor, or judge, instead of history as disinterested discipline.

II

In a variation on George Santayana's famous aphorism, it is said that those who don't *know* their history are doomed to *repeat* it. But it is not so sure that the doom does not also attach to the knowing, and maybe the more so. It seems to me that many among us historians – including, at least at times, myself and numerous esteemed colleagues of my personal acquaintance – those who supposedly *know* history the most, or *read* in history the most, outdo others in *repeating* it.[4] It even seems that they are determined to know or study history *in order* to repeat it, that is, to "bring back in" a past or an aspect of it – and this on both the left and the right, and points in between – not in the entirely appropriate service of healthful memory, reflection, or correlation with current circumstances and trends, but in the spirit of combat or "struggle," and with a hankering, or a nostalgia, or a *need*, for bygone times and ages, bygone alignments, conflicts, loves, and hatreds: a determination less to understand them than to resuscitate, perpetuate, and *repeat* them. To revitalize, as it were, the dead hand of the past. On the left, for example, in the US context, the retrieval of the "good" world or the good cause (real or idealized) of the equalitarian artisan or yeoman farmer, the pristine republican, the pre-market or antimarket communitarian, the antimonopoly populist, the labor-radical, the public welfare progressive, the Debsian socialist, the benevolent Communist, the Movement activist; and the "bad" world of plantations, robber barons, "gold bugs," "Social Darwinism," business unionism, patriarchalism, racism, imperialism, McCarthyism, Vietnam (quagmire). On the right, e.g., the "good" world of the Old South of mint-juleps-magnolias-and-strange-fruit, the nineteenth-century free market, the Anglo-Saxon prevalence, minimalist government in market affairs, maximalist government in moral affairs; and the "bad" world of jacobins, anarchists, silverites, populists, progressives, communists, new dealers, hippies, new leftists, feminists, secularists, liberals, Vietnam (cut-and-run).

In these inclinations, on both left and right in the US today, may be observed a common disdain for, and a disaffection from, current US society – a society, a people, derelict, deprived, and degraded, needing the instruction of the correct sacred stories as told by the correct storytellers. Hence, historians and ideologues, on the right and on the left, have fought over The History Standards for school instruction. Are they to be standards of historical study of the US? Or are they to be "true stories" or true story *lines* – the very essence of the politicalization of historical inquiry: a battle over the *learning* from history, or the *repeating* of history, by those most engaged in "knowing" it. Which is which? And how to tell?

III

There is another adage: "History is lived forwards but it is written in retrospect. We know the end before we consider the beginning," as C. V. Wedgwood phrased it in her biography of (aptly enough) William the Silent.[5] For example, we know the outcome of a past war as those entering it, and fighting it, could not.

True enough, and upon reflection, there is more to it than that. We may ask, do we *know* the end, the outcome, the later in time, or the present? We know it imperfectly, and even that may be an overstatement. To know the end better – whether the outcome of a past war, or more generally our own present times – to know *what* it is all about, *what* it means, *how* and *where* it is tending, do we not have to reach back to the past to discover how and why the outcome, or the present, came to be, so that the more perfect understanding of the *what* and the *how*, and their tendencies, are a matter of an ongoing interplay of past and later, or present, inquiry, past and later, or present, circumstances, events, and trends? One of the points, among others, of the study of history is our starting with the awareness that we know the end, an outcome, or the present, not well enough, that we need to keep studying the past to know an outcome, or the present, better.

The future we anticipate, moreover, is relevant to our understanding of the past and present, and may be relevant as well to *what* the past and present *caused*. The meaning of living history forward, but writing it in retrospect, therefore, further depends upon our frame of mind.

We can start *from* the present, for example, and interpret and judge the past under the direction of present-day sentiment and patterns of thought. This includes sentiment and thought ascribed to the past and held today. Or, we can seek to understand the present and the beckoning future as an evolving (or a devolving) *from* the past, acknowledging both a causal and a volitional framework of interpretation, which includes components of necessity, choice, and chance, and hence invokes a discipline of both inductive and deductive inquiry and reasoning, without pretensions to predictive certainties, but with openness to predictive feasibilities and probabilities.

One of the more powerful strains of starting from present-day views and judgments, and retrofitting them upon the past, is a way of thinking about society that has strong modern roots in the *utopian* Enlightenment and its Romantic progeny, including their Nietzschean antihistory culmination – arraying static, ahistorical archetypes such as the Noble or Natural Person, the Noble or Natural Soul, the Noble or Natural Community, the Noble or Natural *Volk*, against current history and the currents of history. It has yielded profound insights and perspectives, and some of the currents too, but when claiming an explanatory authenticity, the Utopian-Romantic temper strikes an attitude of escape from, denunciation and erasure of, history, that is, what it regards as the *bad* institutions, customs, and people oppressing, profaning, and misdirecting the present. It involves a yearning for a future – and a present – located outside of history, in an idealized past, or a coming Kingdom of God, or a True Community, Nowhere just now or just yet. Those of the Utopian-Romantic temper inevitably grasp the present as Dystopia, and conceive it in a static and ahistorical way: short of the Utopia, change there may be, but it only leaves everything "basically" the same, or is of no "essential" consequence, except as it serves (wittingly or unwittingly) the utopian fulfillment. Utopian-Romantics have peacefully renounced or denounced the world, or at length, whether cynically or sincerely, condemned and murderously sieged it. Like others, they have helped change the world, but not as they professedly intended, indeed if in power, or exerting effective powers, quite the contrary, over and over again, from the "left" and the "right" alike, and often over countless dead bodies. (Vide: millenarians, Inquisitionists, Jacobins, race- and *Volk*-purists, Nazis, Marxist-Leninists, Maoists, '68ers, greeners, Third-Worlders, Khmer-Rougers, Liberationists [Theological, Anti-Hegemon], Jihadi-Islamists, *et al.*)

On the other hand, studying the past either simply from an interest in it, or the better to understand the present, that is, studying it forward in time from the earlier to the later, is a method with modern roots in the *historical* Enlightenment and its evolutionist progeny of nineteenth-century social science:[6] it consists of viewing people, in their social relations and modes of consciousness *in the world*, as making and remaking their history, their situations and circumstances – their reality – in an interplay of choice, chance, and necessity, of the subjective and the objective, of alternatives and limits, living and moving in an evolutionary continuum that may nevertheless include discontinuities and new departures, as well as the interplay of conflict and consensus, retrogression and progress, or as in some cases, impasses and dead ends.

In general, the *historical* or evolutionary temper tries to read history forward from the past to the present and the future, observing and explaining the past in its own terms, and then also, where appropriate, an evolutionary pattern in social relations and thought (including applied thought), but in any case, seeking to discover the necessary as well as the contingent connections between earlier and later events, between past and present, or, in different words, acknowledging causality in time, and time in causality.[7] With an implicit or articulated use of standards of verification and refutation, the historical temper looks for, observes, and explains, temporal change, development, or *progress*, or its absence, if not retrogression. It reads contextually, and assumes an objective or a tragic-comic perspective, as against reading extracontextually and assuming an adoring, disaffected, cynical, comical, or melodramatic perspective.

Like some other disciplines recognizable as modern sciences, history in this key, although having sturdy pre-modern roots as well, is strongly based in the cumulative-evolutionary conception that emerged in the Enlightenment and came to a first maturity in the nineteenth century. In our modern times, not unlike in those of Herodotus, Thucydides, and Polybius, historical writing not in this key, including that of the highest literary merit, tends strongly, if not inexorably, to yield monumentalist (role-model) or utopia-dystopia pleadings, partisan propaganda, sacred stories, idiosyncratic dispositions, or a present-minded prejudice common to the incoherence of arbitrary subjectivity. There is a reason in the Foucault-minded post-modernist repudiation of cumulative evolution, its disdain for history as such, its displacing history with "semiotics" and "hermeneutics," and its posing social science *against*, rather than intertwined with, history: it releases present-day thoughts for ahistorical (in effect, Utopian-Romantic) judgments of past and present without the rigors of context and research. It may be thought of as less post-modern than pre- or supraresearch, and in a way, a triumph, or revenge, of the C *history* student (however otherwise exquisite the student may be). In the name of a timeless objective relativism in matters of truth, it renders a presentist subjective absolutism in matters of history. A Triple-Meta: A Meta-Physics of Meta-Research in Meta-History.

IV

Especially in regard to post-Civil War and twentieth-century US history, prevalent historical understanding has been permeated by static-presentist categories and labels originating not in historical inquiry itself, but with political partisans, ideologues, and journalists. The permeation profoundly affects historical understanding, as is the case of names, labels, and categories in human language and cognition in general. Think, for example, of leading categories – or labels – routinely in use among historians (myself included) in writings, textbooks, lectures, conference discourse, and public venues, although they usually remain in their use static abstractions, without historically grounded, historically precise, meaning: Gilded Age, Progressive Era, Progressive Movement, Progressivism, Normalcy, New Deal, Cold War America, Cold War Liberalism, The '60s, The Movement, Reaganomics, Conservative, Neoconservative, Liberal, Fascist, Radical, Left, Right, Christian-Right, Mainstream, Hard-liner, Moderate, Superpower- (Hyperpower-) Hegemon, Empire, Third World, and so on. There are many others – each can add to the list. We historians should be aware of, and resist, a careless deployment of static, ahistorical, and a priori categories, labels, and terms, and their antihistorical effect upon our work, no less upon our historical imagination. Too often, we allow ourselves to be led by the nose by the *chic* of the partisans, ideologues and journalists, or the cheek of the C students, those making phrases, labels, and presentist judgments, in place of historical evidence, study, and context. Too often, our thinking, teaching, and writing about the twentieth-century US is dominated by the ahistorical categories and labels, past and present, of partisans, ideologues, and journalists – and journalists are, all too often, barflies at the lounges of the partisans and the ideologues.

True: history is at once the most thematically heterogeneous and the most politically contested of the social sciences and humanities, and therefore perennially vulnerable to ideological intrusions, distortions, and deformations streaming from all sides: party allegiances, interest groups, and religions; everyday custom, habit, taste, and prejudice; passing fads, fashions, and rages; respectable – and iconoclastic – theories and phrasings from the various social sciences and humanities.

In modern times, the ideological invasion has waxed in proportion as historians have grown in numbers, and have wanted, not implausibly, not only to be providentially or cosmologically connected, but also civically relevant, and as they have more systemically supplied the schools and colleges with instructional material. The tendency is normal and all the more magnified, and hence all the more in need of being guarded against, with the incessant growth of the Democratic Ethos in education, which has included the ever-widening accessibility and popularization of higher education. While not itself new, the politicalization of history on the modern large scale of production is indeed a signal mark of progress in the broadening of people's access to knowledge and technique, especially since World War II, in the US and elsewhere. But it is something, there-fore, to be acknowledged and dealt with appropriately, in maintaining the scientific spirit and substance of the discipline. Instead, today, many of our academic historians, on both left and right, however much with altruistic intent, take a pride in their ideology as a badge not only of their honor but of their profession, rather than recognizing it as a weakness, or a debilitating addiction, to be remedied and overcome.

In modern times, if more so in the US than elsewhere, history has become an essential discourse, as with myth and religion since earlier times, in establishing social (including personal) identity and its tendency or destiny. Myth and religion still continue strongly to inform and shape historical understanding, to its enrichment and its detriment, while history informs and *desacralizes* myth and religion with like mixed effect. Knowledge of the present as an outcome of the past, or at least as causally connected to the past, and as a causative condition of the future, in short, *historical* knowledge, is of even more contentious interest, because it is a distinc-tive characteristic of the modern mind to see the shaping of the future as something to which thinking and acting in the present make a difference, and to view knowing as essential to intentional shaping, and the shaping as constitutive and reconstitutive of the knowing; and to assume to know-ing better than before, in short, to *progress*. To do, to make, is to know. To do, to make better, is to know better: the grand Western philosophical and scientific tradition, especially since the Enlightenment, and magnified among Americans with their particular commitment to a history-centered identity. Hence, modern-style history has become central to the dialogue and controversy with, and about, the past in the contest for the future, and thus in the contest for defining the present and for power in it. This is the mundane essence of the idea of Reason as the quest for human freedom in time. History, therefore, precisely in its character as a disciplined method and a science, cannot escape implication in the "sacred stories" of society, any more than physics, astrophysics, and evolution could in the times of Galileo, Newton, Darwin, Einstein, or Hubble.

All the more reason that historians not acquiesce in the superficial-ists' axioms that history can be nothing other than, or mostly, ideology ("sacred stories," "party lines"), and all the more important, whatever historians may do as citizens, that as *historians*, they not become the partisans, or the purveyors of the partisans' professings, programs, predispositions, prevarications, peeves, and prejudices. Of all this partisanship there is abundance in surfeit in historical (and other) writings. Instead, all the more committed should historians be to seeking to *understand* the partisans, not join them, and move thought beyond theirs, or at any rate differently from theirs, in pursuing a dialogue with and about the past that may *dispel* ideology with scientific discipline, based in research, and in both inductive and deductive reasoning, and that may inform our understanding, and elevate our perspective, with objective knowledge, in the contention over the past and future, and thus over the shape of the present. A tall order, not easily attained, and precisely so, all the more needing the effort.

V

If the quest for objective knowledge is not the task of historians, if in Carl Becker's phrasing, "Everyman his own historian," in the sense that every effort at thinking about history (whatever the literary elegance or conceptual power) is as valid as any other, which Becker himself did not believe, then in all honesty, we should close down or spin off the history departments in the colleges and universities, embrace (even if fighting over) indoctrinating civics in higher education, stop fussing over whether there is substantial difference between faith, fiction, myth, movies, and history, and throw in the towel to "post-modernists" and "deconstructionists," those whom historians (including sophisticated Marxians) used to consider vulgarizers, simplistifiers, and sectarians.

Historians holding to history as a scientific discipline have strongly contributed to identifying the defining characteristics of our evolving social relations and their tendencies, in both their subjectivity and objectivity. They have thereby informed and deepened our thinking about the substance and interplay of such vital elements of human evolution as freedom and necessity, choice and limitation, rights and obligations, liberties and coercions, and the interrelations of all these; hence also, the evolving variabilities, probabilities, and feasibilities, on the one hand, and the invariabilities, improbabilities, and impossibilities, on the other, in the various historical trends.

This kind of historical work is especially called for at the opening of the twenty-first century, when the US, many other countries, and the world in general, are moving into a new epoch of human evolution, not without lethal reaction, as in past times, but now at a vastly accelerated pace, and not without bitter conflict over the terms, or acceptability, of the transformations, as in the past, but now with massive ecological implications, and unprecedented prospects alike of improvement and devastation.

The epochal passage has been prepared for by the post-Columbian sixteenth- to twentieth-century techno-economic and demographic revolutions on a global scale, and equally important, and intimately related, religious, cultural, and political revolutions, involving an enlarged and more inclusive *popular* participation in the making and shaping of public affairs – that is, in the making and shaping of history – *across* class, national, racial, ethnic, religious, sexual, and generational lines: a movement, richly varied as it is, toward nevertheless a human universalism, philosophically (and theologically) anticipated, and arduously advocated, in the past, but now becoming a reality in the practical affairs of political economy, government, law, culture, and everyday life, within and across societies, and in international relations. Yet, it is just at this time that many historians, thinking themselves radical, or iconoclastic, or realistic, and joining with parochial and utopian ideologues, have chosen to emphasize, in order to *repeat* and perpetuate, human particularity, insularity, and locality, especially along lines of ethnic, racial, religious, or "civilizational" identity (whether archaic or of recent design): aka "multiculturalism," i.e., multiple *mono*culturalisms, and "post-modernism," really an academic neo-premodernism – with scarcely sufficient serious attention to the human-universalizing currents, tides, and trends, although often disdaining or denouncing them as "empire," "imperialism," "hegemonism," "super-(hyper-)powerism," "free-market capitalism," or just plain "globalization," not to mention "obsolete objectivity."

VI

What does it mean to speak of history as a scientific discipline? It is by now broadly understood that it does not mean an iron determinism, a quantitative reductionism, or either a retrospective or a predictive certitude, so often *erroneously* equated with science. As with all sciences, and as, indeed, with art, history as science I take to mean a disciplined method of inquiry, learning, and display. (History, from the Greek, ἱστορία, inquiry; science, from the Latin, *scire*, come to know, learn.) The old puzzle of whether history is a science or an art may be held moot, or at least in abeyance. Art is scientific, and science has its art.

Each partakes of the other, and expresses and deploys the other, in expressing, deploying, and developing itself. One may say art is a kind of science and science is a kind of art. Just as there are different kinds of art, some more precise, arithmetic, structural, than others, so there are different kinds of science: physical sciences, social sciences, evolutionary and nonevolutionary sciences, more exact and less exact sciences, predictive and nonpredictive or quasi-predictive sciences. A field – e.g., history, or geology, or astronomy, or architecture, or sculpture – encompasses several sciences and arts, an explanatory, methodical, and displaying plurality, just as with a particular science or art as such. Hence, in speaking of history as a scientific discipline, I wish to be understood as meaning that it is composed of various sciences and arts. In and through them, it anchors itself in empirical research, and engages in incessant questioning, hypothesizing, and theorizing, proceeding in both inductive and deductive modes of reasoning, yielding certainties and uncertainties, and presented overall in discourse both analytic/synthetic and narrative. As with other sciences, intuition plays an essential role, as do imagination, chance findings, and random discoveries, especially as theory or a framework of interpretation, in its role of guiding and defining "normal" or acceptable research, may overdetermine or obstruct empirical inquiry. Openness to variability is essential to science and art alike. In general, history is among those sciences that ultimately derive explanation or interpretation (or law or theory) from, and repeatedly test it against, empirical evidence, and thereby seeks, as with all sciences, to disclose objective knowledge, as distinguished from opinion, prejudice, or ideology. By corollary, as with other sciences, history assumes, and seeks to disclose, an ever-evolving, ever-revised body of knowledge, and hence errors and deficiencies always at hand, and being found, hopefully dispelled.[8]

VII

Is history as a science necessarily *amoral* or nonethical? Indeed, we may ask, conversely, is history, or any science, necessarily *moral* or ethical? This is an essential question, and a difficult one, inviting acknowledgment, and while not presuming to its being treated adequately here, I offer the following in aid of the present discussion, as food for further thought, and as a good-faith disclosure of some of my own thinking.

The science of history resides in its subject, humanity, which is by its nature *artificial*, that is, by its nature cognitively conscious, volitional, and social, and hence distinctively evolutionary.[9] Change and adaptive variation may be understood as a persistent condition of human volitional cognition, and volitional cognition as the driving force of a cumulative development of knowledge, and hence of a *cumulative* human evolution: if we take *species human* to be inherently cognitive, willful, and social in character, we may also take human-being to be cumulative-evolutionary, or developmental, in character. *In* history, human individuality (hence cognitive and volitional individuality) has resided in, and has been a function of, human sociality. At the same time, the more individuality develops, in quantity and quality, the quicker, broader, and deeper the pace, scope, and variability of cumulative evolution in human sociality. It may be said that individuality is the highest form of sociality, and it drives sociality incessantly to new, if not higher, paths and forms, at times to disorder (chaos). The science of history, therefore, is more about studying and understanding variabilities (or their absence) than about predictions and certitudes, while nevertheless disclosing patterns of cumulative evolution (or their absence, or devolution), and that means, also, causal connections between past, present, and future. Such patterns have been referred to, by some thinkers, as laws of history, that is, causal regularities or probabilities, in time, in modes of cognition and in social relations, even as they involve contingency and uncertainties as well. We may remember that in physical science, *uncertainty* goes hand in hand with laws, patterns, and regularities, and even with some certainties.

Evolution toward what? And via what volition? This is the perennial question, in effect wrestled with since the prophets and thinkers of antiquity: what is the purpose, the destiny, the meaning, the *end*, of humanity? "What hath God wrought?" In my own wrestling, I have come to believe, in the course of studying history, that it is an evolution of and toward an expanding and deepening Reason and Freedom – that is, knowledge manifesting intent, expressed in words and deeds, via a cumulatively developing volition, embodying growing, or increasingly more proficient, human self-government, exercised collectively and individually in variable patterns, in the natural environment and in society. This evolving is the human-universal condition, the paramount transhistorical dimension – the supreme transhistorical imperative – which became the more cognitively conscious and powerfully volitional in thought and social relations in the nineteenth century, and all the more so in the twentieth century, as the cumulative-evolutionary process spread globally and accelerated, a reason perhaps for the twentieth century having been, so far, the most destructively violent, reactionary, *and* the most constructively progressive, century in human history, in terms of cumulative knowledge attained, expressed, and applied.[10] This human-universal condition is also variously known, in such other "Western" philosophical terms, as the laws of nature and nature's God, Spinoza's Substance, Leibniz's Monads, Locke's Human Nature, Kant's Categorical Imperative, Hegel's *Geist*, Comte's Positivism, Marx's Species-Being, Bagehot's Political Physics, and Peirce's Pragmatism – an evolutionary constant, or set of evolving constants, found in some degree in all times and all societies, that is, *universal*, just as, for example, the speed of light is a universal constant, or an evolving universal constant, in the physical world and physical science.

This transhistorical dimension – or transhistorical imperative – is observable in social relations and institutions, and in religious and secular thought and activity, and it may be taken to define the ethical, or the *moral*, in history, and hence in the science of history. It is an ethical essential, a critical universal, that makes history an evolutionary science. It is what makes history a science of – a disciplined study of – not one thing beside another, not one thing after another, not one thing no better or worse than another – but a study of cumulative cause and effect in time, from earlier to later, from simpler to more complex, from less to more knowledge and human self-determination (reason and freedom), from "less developed" to "more developed." Hence, periodization lies at the heart of history as a science.[11] The transhistorical dimension is the great forcing house of humans' *discerning* and making moral choices – not preordaining them, yet ever inciting and rejuvenating the human exercise of reason and freedom: the tree of knowledge bearing fruit both bitter and sweet, lethal and vital, sinful and sublime. Various as they were in substantial elements of thought, thinkers like Locke, Smith, Burke, Benjamin Franklin, Kant, Hegel, Saint-Simon, Comte, Mill, Spencer, Marx, Bagehot, Tönnies, Max Weber, Peirce, William G. Sumner, Lester F. Ward, Thorstein Veblen, John Dewey, Joseph Schumpeter, Hannah Arendt, Friedrich Hayek, Peter F. Drucker, and Milton Friedman shared in this universal constant – or transhistorical imperative – regarding the interplay of human volition, social relations, and the physical world, evolving in the direction of growing human knowledge and self-governing. Hence the enduring paradox – or more accurately the enduring dialectic: on the one hand, science – and art – must insist on the distinction between fact and value; on the other hand, and at the same time, science and art practice and thereby vindicate their ineluctable, if persistently variable and often unstable, intermixture. The thoughts here are in essence a restatement, however inadequately, of the nineteenth-century social-science legacy, emerging from prior Western thought, and bequeathed to us and further developed in the twentieth to twenty-first centuries. It is not new, but it bears, indeed needs, reaffirmation, if history is to be understood and plied as an evolutionary science, or, as a disciplined search for objective knowledge with an ethical dimension rooted in human-being, whatever the role ascribed, or not, to the Divine.[12]

The failure of the historical imagination, that is, of holding fast to history as at once an evolutionary and an ethical science, and the inundation of scholarly history writing by that of partisans, faith-keepers, and ideologues, especially those in the utopian and antihistorical modes, are apparent in some telling historical distortions presenting themselves in historical writings about the US, and in broader public discourse, as uncontested assumptions, or, might we say, the conventional wisdom. Let me here address a few of these distortions under three headings: (1) The Idea of the Left (and Right); (2) Transvestiture of Left and Right; (3) An Ahistorical Syndrome Regarding the US in the Twentieth Century.

VIII

Distortion 1. The Idea of the Left (and Right)

In recent US public discourse, routinely in usage by the late 1990s, the term, "Left," has been effectively conflated with "Liberal"/"Big Government," and the term, "Right," with "Conservative"/"Free Market"; also, "Left" with "Secularist," and "Right" with "Traditional-(Christian)-Religious" ("Traditional-Islamist," tends to get a pass, if not erroneously conflated with "Left" or "Right.") This term-conflation has been largely practiced by partisans and journalists across the political spectrum, and adopted without much resistance or reflection by the intelligentsia, including historians. But the conflation is lacking in empirical foundation and historical substance – in real life, Liberal, Conservative, Government/Markets, Secular, Traditional-Religious, cut across lines of Left and Right.

The term-conflation, however, is a variation on previous usage, which still runs with and through the newer version. In this previous and still current usage, the idea of *The Left*, among scholars, journalists, and just about all other manner of writers and commentators, whatever their own standing along the spectrum from left to right, is that The Left (or the left) is synonymous with doctrinal, sectarian, and selected issue-plying, party-going, or "movement" elites, groups, personages, and views, so that reference made to The Left (or the left) is to these doctrinal, sectarian, and selected elects, and their views, however their views may have changed from time to time, and however incongruous at any time. Upon some historical reflection, however, as well as empirical inquiry, and with all due respect to my colleagues' studies, it is clear that the doctrinal, sectarian, select-elect left is to be distinguished from the *historical* left, that is, from the left, or left-side, in actual history: the doctrinal, sectarian, select-elect left has been a segment, and a relatively small segment, of the *historical* left.[13] In the Western world, and including especially the US, the *historical* left has in modern times (in the US since the pre-national colonial times of the seventeenth century) encompassed a very large part of the population. Although it is not necessary to the point being made here, nevertheless let me suggest that this very large part of the population has usually been the majority, but in any case, not some nobly heretical, heroically dissenting, or victimized, minority. Whether or not Americans believed themselves born free (Louis Hartz), it may be close to the truth to say that most of them were born, and lived, on the left (wherever geophysically they were born). This may dismay doctrinal and select-elect leftists, particularly in the US, who like to think of themselves as special and uncommonly anointed, messianic in etymological terms – as a moral minority, the exception to American Exceptionalism – but psycho-dismay, messianic presumption, or moral sanctimony cannot be, or at least should not be, a standard of historical study.

The doctrinal, sectarian, select-elect left is neither typical nor coterminously representative of the historical left, but a small, however loquacious and munificent, component of it, and ought not to be called, or thought of as, *The Left*, but rather as a small, often fringe, if influential, part of it – and, splintered as elects, doctrinaires, and sectarians usually are, more accurately, small and fringe parts of it.[14] This same point is to be made of the Right, except that the historical right in the US (and some other parts of the Western world), although like the historical left a very large part of the population, has been, *unlike* the historical left, usually not a majority. Governments of the right in the modernized West in the twentieth century have either governed to the left, or, if doctrinal-sectarian, have governed tyrannically and murderously.[15] (In political-economic affairs, policies for and against state-command and markets, respectively, are a major source of confusion regarding left/right designations of parties, movements, and governments, and will be addressed in Distortion 3 below.) In transatlantic liberal democracies, governments of the left have not governed tyrannically, and have not needed to, and neither have they been *doctrinal/ sectarian* left governments.

Doctrinal/sectarian leftists have usually directed their strongest invectives and adversarial energies against leaderships of the majority (historical) left, more so than against rightists or "conservatives," because it is precisely the majority (historical) left that has been "the competition," and that has most effectively contained, limited, and marginalized the doctrinal/sectarian left. Hence the repeated complaints by doctrinal/sectarian leftists about "cooptation," or "sellout," etc., against majority-left positions, actions, leaders, and governments – and similar complaints may be regularly observed on the right by doctrinal rightists against historical rightists (as also with doctrinal/sectarian Islamists vs. Muslims of historical Islam). At the same time, in the competition *between* left-side and right-side in US politics (and elsewhere), note the standard practice of leaders on each side to identify the other with its own doctrinal/sectarian segments or fringes ("far left," "far right," "out of the mainstream," and other terms to like effect), in order to diminish each other's legitimacy and vote-getting among the majority (historical) left and right sides; and note the equally standard practice, in general elections, of political leaders on each side "distancing" themselves from their respective doctrinal/sectarian fringes, nevertheless courting them in primaries and party affairs where the doctrinal/sectarians, being activists, have disproportionate votes and influence, and appeasing or harnessing them with offices, grants, and contracts.

IX

(*Distortion 1*. The Idea of the Left – continued)

What, more precisely, is meant by *historical left* and *historical right* in modern times (in the Western world, since about the seventeenth century)? A common distinction, of provisional value, identifies the left with favoring equality at the expense of liberty, and the right with favoring liberty at the expense of equality, with shadings in between. In history, in the US as elsewhere, it is not quite so clear-cut.

In the US, the *historical left* is the side (or set of sides) in society that has favored the trinity of liberty *and* equality *and* progress (progress alias growth, improvement, development), pushing toward a broadening and ultimately universal inclusion in the application of the trinity, and people's participation in it, across class, race, ethnic, sex, and other lines – in short, the American Dream. It has embraced and championed republicanism, widespread suffrage, the sovereignty of the people, separation of church and state, and the supremacy of the society (the people) over the state, as against monarchy, aristocracy, plutocracy, or autocracy, and as against the supremacy of the ruler, the state, or the clerisy over the people or society. In activity and impact, the historical left has both advocated, and incrementally attained, the reshaping of market- and property-liberty to the requirements of increasingly inclusive universal human rights and entitlements, increasingly understood more broadly. In this sense, it is valid to say (as I have long believed, written, and taught), that the US has been a historically left-wing society, at particular times, and in general trend, and whatever else it may be, it is not historically a right-"conservative" society, although it may be in general a *left*-"conservative" society.[16]

The *historical right*, in the US, is the side (or set of sides) that has favored liberty, or *special* rights or identities, *against* equality of rights and opportunity (or, against equal liberty), and either against development, or against a universal participation in the shaping of development and in the sharing in its fruits – e.g., privileged market- or property-liberty, birth-based or race-based liberty or power, or special identities and privileges *against* universalism. It is in this sense that it is valid to say that the US is not historically a right-wing society, although it may be validly considered a mixed left/right society, but in which the left side has tended to be the larger among the people and the stronger in general trend. It is in this sense, too, that we may understand race-based slavery and post-slavery race-based inequality as having been the longest-running, intensively engaging matter of conflict, and moral scandal, in US history, precisely because such inequality has run against the prevalent left-wing grain. In a truly right-conservative society, as may be observed in such societies elsewhere or in other times, movements against such slavery and inequality would have weakly resonated, if having a significant political presence at all. Similar observations may be made about class-based and sex-based inequality.[17] The historical right is today in the US rather small and getting smaller. Indeed, if not for many American activist "multiculturalists," "affirmative-actionists," "speech-policers," "environmentalists," "anticonsumerists," and "antiglobalists," who in these respects are historical rightists, but erroneously, and ahistorically, think of their works as on the left, the right would be even smaller. (See Distortion 2, below.) In real history, left and right cut across both party and capitalism/socialism lines, and across lines of race, ethnicity, sex, and class, and are not synonymous with "liberal" and "conservative," or "secular" and "religious," respectively; both left and right contain liberals, conservatives, Democrats, Republicans, independents, secularists, the religious, and various mixtures of these characteristics and others (such as radical, moderate, libertarian, traditionalist, commercialist, rich, poor, and so on).[18]

With respect to the left in the US in the twentieth century, it is of some clarifying value to specify its plurality. There are those of the in-the-world lefts (much the larger part), and those of the other-worldly, utopian lefts (the smaller); religious lefts and secularist lefts; workers on the left, capitalists on the left, farmers on the left, small-business enterprisers on the left; philanthropists, teachers, professors, students, administrators, civil servants, on the left; doctors, lawyers, judges, clergy, journalists, bloggers, talk-show hosts, think-tankers, members of the military, on the left; artists, musicians, entertainers, actors, athletes, producers, publishers, on the left; and so on – all these, not to mention people engaged directly in government, party politics, interest groups, and political action committees. The same goes for the right. In addition, many individuals, including sophisticates, and many groups, will be found (as in the past) to have, at one and the same time or serially, within their own minds (or organizations' principles and practices) both left and right ideas, inclinations, values, and interests. Persons of the twentieth-century left in the US have variously thought of themselves as socialists, communists, anarchists, pacifists, progressives, populists, Democrats, Republicans, radicals, nationalists, feminists, liberals, laborists, trade-unionists, antiracists, civil-rights and civil-liberties advocates, environmentalists, secular-humanists, social Christians, Christian socialists, and so on, as well as some combination of such categories.

Lists like these (or historical inventories) help visualize more concretely in the mind's eye the diversity and breadth of that part of the political-cultural universe we call the left (and again, similarly with the right) in modern society, and make it more understandable when we say that the left is a very large and pluralist swath of the population of a modern society, and especially of the US. It also means that to use the term, the Left, and to think it refers only, or primarily, to doctrinal, sectarian, utopian, elite, or select-elect persons, groups, ideas, or trends, is to miss most of the left in real history, in modern times, and to refer only to a small part of it quantitatively, and to an atypical part of it qualitatively. This is misunderstood, and so is much else, not only about the left, but also about modern society and modern history – and in this, the US is no "Exception." Our historians and journalists (and others) miss, and misunderstand, all too often.

It may be recalled that Richard M. Nixon, in effect, acknowledged the majority standing of the historical left in the US, not because he was "tricky," but because he was both a *post*-1930s Republican practitioner (with strong roots in pre-1933 "progressive" or "TR" Republicanism) and an astute political observer. As he said, after becoming president, "I am now a Keynesian." It may be apocryphal, but descriptively accurate, that Nixon remarked that to win the GOP presidential nomination, he had to run to the right, but to win the general election, he had to run back to the center, and to *govern* the US, he had to govern on the left (at the same time, seeking to identify his Democratic party adversaries with the "far left," and seeking to keep "far rightists," especially "dixiecrats" – north and south – in the electoral-democracy fold under the GOP tent), all of which Nixon as party leader, candidate, and president did in matters both of domestic policy and foreign affairs. (Woodward and Bernstein may well have been assisted – perhaps used? – by disaffected rightists pushing a leftist, and vulnerable, Nixon out of the presidency.[19]) Over thirty years later, much if not all of these things President George W. Bush also did: running in GOP primaries on the right, running in general elections as a "moderate," and governing on the left as a huge entitlement-expander (Medicare drug program), a health-clinics multiplier and funder, an education-federalizer, a massive housing-subsidizer, a record-breaking public-works and public-relief provider, and a deficit-spending, jobs-growth-stimulus Keynesian, as well as with a "multicultural" cabinet;[20] and in international affairs (like FDR and Churchill in the past), uniting with Blair and Britain against the reactionary right in world affairs (this time round, against Islamist, and Arab national-socialist, fascism), and seeking alignment with Russia and China (just as, also, Nixon and Kissinger reoriented US policy toward the Soviet Union and China), and with modernizing-democratic forces in eastern Europe, Asia, Latin America, Africa, and Arab countries. President Reagan, too, it might be noted, out-lefted the left with "super-Keynesian" deficit-spending, strengthening Social Security funding and coverage with six payroll-tax hikes, installing Medicare price-controls on providers, amnestying illegal immigrants, moving toward nuclear disarmament, and (again, in strong unison with Britain – the Thatcher government) friendship with what was still the Soviet Union under Communist Party rule – but now undergoing change (fitfully) *toward* market-modernizing development and political democratization. Such policies and moves, it is often not remembered especially by many invoking him as a conservative paragon, brought upon Reagan, at the time, strong criticism and denunciation by prominent professing conservatives. In sum, in Western liberal democracies, and in the US in particular, the "center" is usually standing more to the left than to the right of center, whatever the ostensible complexion of the head of government or the majority party in the legislature.

It is empirically observable, perhaps more readily from outside than inside academia or the media, that in the world there is no such thing as *The* Left or *The* Right: each encompasses a plurality of trends, associations, organizations, publications, personages, views, and principles, the one often intersecting or blending with the other at the center and at the extremities. In the same sense, there is no *The* Feminism, *The* Radicalism, *The* Conservatism, *The* Liberalism, *The* Secularism, *The* Socialist, *The* Capitalist, *The* Black, *The* White, *The* Hispanic, *The* Asian, *The* Christian, *The* Muslim, *The* Jew, *The* Hindu, *The* Buddhist, *The* Atheist, and so on. Each is a plurality. Yet, a plurality, upon reflection, can have also a broad identity, and plurality and identity are intersecting matters of reality, as are order and disorder, certainty and uncertainty, that historians are called upon, as are those in other sciences, not to ignore or deny, but to study and understand.

In modern history, conflict goes on *within* the left and *within* the right (and the other categories) as much as between or across them, often more so, and consensus contains conflict *within* and *across* them in constituting the ongoing normal relations and institutions of society and government, in contrast with those times known as abnormal, sometimes involving civil war, when intractable and disintegrative conflict may occur, and often, if not quite apart from left vs. right, cutting across left and right (and the other categories). In history, left and right may be so intricately intertwined as not easily to be disaggregated. Yet the distinction retains meaning. For example, in pre-Civil War US history, significant elements not only of the right-side, but also of the left-side, in American politics and culture, correlated strongly with slavery. When, however, the left-side broke definitively with slavery, it was the end of slavery. The only period in US history when the right-side – slaveholders and their allies – held the national government, and *governed*, strong-headed/strong-handed, on the right for a sustained period, *c.* 1853–1861 (during the Pierce and Buchanan presidencies), the outcome was a mobilization and empowerment of the republican, free-soil, free-labor left, a transformation of party politics, civil war, and the utter destruction of the slave-property system, of the slaveholder class, and of the right-side it dominated.[21] A "new right" had subsequently to emerge, along with a "new left," corresponding with changes in modes of production, property–labor relations, and the constitutional order, and both left and right maintained lines of continuity with the past even as they proceeded to evolve along new lines as well.

Neither "The Left" nor "The Right," in the meaning as purveyed by doctrinaires and sectarians, and thence by many academics, think-tank analysts, and journalists, is a valid analytical, interpretive, or historical category, but rather a *political* construct (as is "Marxist," "Feminist," "Liberal," "Conservative," "Neo-Conservative," "Secularist," "Christian-Right," "White," "Black," or "Hispanic," etc.), that is, an instrument serving adversarial purposes of vying for power, influence, budget-making, marketing, and careers, not least in struggles or rivalries between and among leftists themselves, and on the other side, between and among rightists (and similarly with the other constructs). Yet historians and other intellectuals, of all persuasions, have by and large adopted these political constructs as if they were valid analytical, interpretive, or historical categories. Regarding the idea of the Left (and the Right), the Western intelligentsia has long been caught in what may be called a Leninist Captivity – in effect acquiescing in and repeating Lenin's and Leninists' static-ahistorical political constructs as a matter of course. The same Captivity may be said to prevail for "Capitalism" and "Socialism." (See Distortion 3 below.) The Leninist Captivity is rather stunning in its hold on the minds of historical and political thinkers dealing with the modern world, and across the spectrum from left to right. Hermeneutics caged.[22]

X

Distortion 2. Transvestiture of Left and Right

The binary distortion in historians' (and others') ideological understanding of Left and Right has disabled them from identifying, distinguishing, and tracking the historical characteristics of Left and Right in recent times. It has resulted in their not discerning, while commonly embracing, a transvestiture of professedly Left and Right – or, might we say, of professional Left and Right – in the US and elsewhere. Let me explain.

Some people who appear, and present themselves, in society, academia, the media, and politics, in *dress* and *labels* of the left, and are taken by historians (and others, including themselves) to be of the left, or to be The Left, are actually, in their substantive views, historically of the right. Let me offer an illustrative listing (or inventory) of some such historically rightist views presenting themselves in dress and labels of the left:

- Affirmation of a static relativism (custom, mores, culture) against a plastic and evolving human-universalism.

- Affirmation of ethnic, race, and gender identity against a human-universalism, and of *Volk* or nation or culture against internationalism (globalism).
- Affirmation of subjectivity, ideology, static archetypes or paradigms, and of perennial genetic, subconscious, or irrational characteristics of human nature (e.g., "male" predator, "female" virtue, "white" racist, "black" victim, in general, bio-oppressor/bio-victim) as against an evolving rationality, objective knowledge, objective behavior, and objective reality.
- Favoring *Gemeinschaft* (traditionalism, communalism, custom, "organicism") against *Gesellschaft* (associationalism, citizenship, civil society).
- Disdain for modern economic development and growth, and for applied science and technology, with a correlated suspicion of "Progress," or outright hostility and opposition to it, and a pessimism about the future.
- Favoring or glorifying the pastoral or pristine ("green") against the urban-industrial or developmental.
- Favoring declining or superseded, against rising or superseding, productive forces, modes of production, classes, and class relations.
- Favoring an abstract, or aristocratic, austerity against rising consumption – that is, austerity for others besides oneself, alias "anticonsumerism," "anticommercialism," "environmentalism." (We may remember that in historical-left thinking, rising consumption – wages – is a working-class principle, and implies a democratization of the market economy and the broader culture, an abundance requisite to a modern socialism, and an overcoming of production alienated from social and individual human use.)
- Valuing noblesse oblige, condescension, and induced or protected dependency, over workers' employment, independence, and self-governance.
- Favoring *special* rights, liberty, entitlement, or privilege against *equal* rights, liberty, and entitlement, equality at law, and equality of opportunity. (This includes favoring a corporatist dispensation of rights, liberties, entitlements, or privileges – e.g., by birth, status, gender, race, ethnicity, religion, or previous social condition – as against universal application to citizens or persons as individuals.)
- Favoring elite superiority over the people, with an elite self-regard as a moral minority opposed to, or specially designated to reorient, lead, or "save," a supposedly wayward, degraded, sinful, falsely conscious, misguided, apathetic, ignorant, or selfish people.
- Contempt for, opposition or indifference to attaining, electoral democracy, universal suffrage, and representative institutions.

- Favoring appeasing, aiding, or not proactively opposing, the power and aggressions of secular or clerical fascism, or retrogressive imperialism, in world affairs (as promoted in the US by the "American Firstism" of the 1930s).
- Favoring order and stability over social and political democratization, and a formal state-sovereignty over a democratizing internationalism.
- Favoring elite-, clerical-, party-, or state-directed orthodoxy, propriety, or authority, against popular liberty, popular freedom of expression, and popular "profanity" or "vulgarity."

These views have been very largely, even if not always and absolutely, associated historically with those on the right in modern society, and have been usually and strongly rejected and opposed by people of the left. Yet, historians (and others) have come to acquiesce in identifying people holding or professing these views (in whole or in part) as on the left (or "left-leaning"), or as The Left. The dress and labels may *appear* of the left, but the views, beneath the dress and behind the labels, are historically of the right.

On the other side, some people who appear, and present themselves, in society, academia, the media, and politics, in *dress* and *labels* of the right, and are taken by historians (and others, including themselves) to be of the right, or to be The Right (e.g., "conservatives," "neoconservatives," "libertarians," "free-marketers," "evangelicals"), are actually, in their substantive views, historically of the left. Let me, once again, offer an illustrative listing, of some such historically leftist views presenting themselves in dress and labels of the right:

- Affirmation of universalism and internationalism, and of a common human identity, as against *Volk*, ethnic, exclusive religious, race, and gender identities.
- Affirmation of universal human rights and liberties, and the universality of the principle of the sovereignty of the people – not of the ruler, or the Leader, or the party, or the clergy, or the state.
- Affirmation of life against death-cults, and against bigoted "eugenics" based on race, ethnicity, gender, class, or disability.
- Affirmation of an objective historical reality, objective knowledge, rationalism, and science, as against arbitrary, ahistorical, utopian, or antiscience subjectivity or irrationalism.
- Favoring associationalism, pluralism, and civil society, against traditional or authoritarian hierarchy, communalism, custom, or "organicism," whether religious or secular.

- Favoring modern economy, applied science and technology, development and growth – embracing "Progress."
- Favoring rising and superseding, against declining and superseded, productive forces, modes of production, classes, and class relations.
- Optimism about a future better than the past and present, favoring a progressive-pragmatism of people actively engaging in making change in institutions and human behavior through laws and programs (aka Reason) – as against a rejectionist creed of vested "rights," "unchangeable human nature," ingrained custom, tradition, habit, and mores, or inviolable nature.
- Favoring equal liberty at law, equal opportunity, and universal civil liberties and rights, regardless of race, religion, nationality, or sex.
- Favoring electoral democracy, representative institutions, and universal suffrage, and opposing autocratic, theocratic, bureaucratic, or oligarchic authoritarianism or despotism.
- Favoring the people's bearing of arms (or, an armed people) as against arms-bearing restricted to a privileged aristocracy or group(s), or to the state or effective state (or party-state, clerisy-state) units: a corollary of the sovereignty of the people, as against sovereignty of the state or of tyrannical or oligarchic power.
- Favoring internationalism and an international economy ("one world"), and proactively opposing nationalistic, racial, or religious exclusiveness, bigotry, censorship, or intolerance, and in the twentieth to twenty-first century in particular, opposing racism, male-supremacy, anti-Semitism, and fascism (clerical or secular), in world affairs.
- Favoring countercyclical and prostimulus, progrowth fiscal and monetary policy, including "deficit-spending," as against fiscal austerity, monetary parsimony, and perennially balanced or surplus-accruing government budgets.

These views by and large have been, again even if not always and absolutely, associated historically with those on the left side of politics and culture in modern society, and with democratizing change and dynamics, not with "rightist" conservatism, traditionalism, or reaction, and indeed have been usually strongly rejected and opposed by people of the right. Yet historians (and others) persist in identifying those with such views as on the right, or as The Right. People of the transvestite left, including historians, professional analysts and commentators, journalists, special-interest activists, entertainment celebrities, religious ethicists, philanthropists, and politicians, have been condemning many, if not all, of these views, and complaining of their "hegemony" in the US and globally. But this is good evidence, which may be added to other substantive evidence, of the dominance, even if not the definitive triumph, of the historical left in the US and in other parts of the world, the electoral victories in the US (and, e.g., in western Europe) of professedly, or dressedly, rightist parties and candidates notwithstanding, or more accurately perhaps, withstanding.

Much of the political debate – as well as historical debate – current in academia, the media, and among "activists" in party politics in the US (and elsewhere), has been a quarreling between transvestite left and transvestite right, crowding the discussion and debate of the citizenry at large, including the broader range of people of the *historical* left and right: little wonder at the massive resort to a more open, less prefigured, less structured, less strictured, less cross-dressed alternative media, in print, radio, cable TV, and the Internet. It would be of some value, for retrieving historical understanding, to divest actual views so prominent in media, politics, and academia, of the dress and labels in which they parade, for assessment in historical perspective.

Louis Hartz once observed that US historians have more replicated than explicated American political history: "our current historical categories reflect but they do not analyze the American political tradition."[23] It is true that left and right have changed in history, as for example, in the US during and after the Civil War, and that such change has signified a closing of one historical era and the opening of another, as seems also to be the case of the 1980s–1990s and onward. Instead of tracking the change and elucidating it, however, historians have tended strongly to take at face value, and themselves acquire and put on the dress and the labels (a hefty "consumerism," no less) displayed and purveyed by the partisans, doctrinaires, sacred story-tellers, and journalists, in effect, acquiescing in the doom of replicating history instead of explicating it: knowing your history and repeating it, too.

XI

Distortion 3. An Ahistorical Syndrome Regarding the US in the Twentieth Century

Industrializing capitalist society emerged late in the course of the development (1500s–1800s) of a transatlantic market system that intertwined self-employed, wage-earner, slave, and peonage, labor systems with their corresponding property relations and sociocultural characteristics. In the

1830s–1880s, coincident with a great wave of capitalist industrialization, slave-labor was ended in the transatlantic world (not yet in Africa itself), by law and by war, especially the US Civil War. Peonage succeeded to slavery in the US, and continued there (as elsewhere) well into the twentieth century, codeveloping with the wage-labor and self-employed labor systems, which themselves underwent great changes in extent and in kind. In these and other ways, industrializing capitalism, as it developed and spread during the nineteenth century, quickened and deepened by steam railroads, oceangoing steam-shipping, and telecommunications, embodied both a *continuity* of historical evolution from the past, and great historical *departures*.[24] It intensified and accelerated the already ongoing spread of money-market exchange relations, in goods, land, and labor, and the concomitant desacralizing and secularizing trends in social and political relations, as well as in religion itself. It thus brought on an incessant shifting from kinship-centered to interest-centered, or associational, relations – from *Gemeinschaft* to *Gesellschaft*, from the rigidities of status to the fluidities of class, from "traditionalism" to "modernity": continuity *and* departure, transformative change in and through history, not beyond or outside or erasing it – revolution *in* evolution.

These trends were already robust in the pre- and early-industrial transatlantic world, but by the latter part of the nineteenth century, industrializing capitalism brought them on, in some areas, with an overwhelming force. In addition to the secularization of social-political relations, the market-associational trends, combined with industrialization, represented a basic departure in another way: they brought the passage from a scarcity-replacement economy, slowly and extensively incremental, to an abundance-surplus-developmental economy, rapidly and intensively incremental, which broadened and deepened the associational and secularizing trends, and also began an epochal passage from society intricately engaged with nature and precariously at risk to scarcity, to society both exploiting nature and becoming (for better or worse) increasingly detached from its rhythms and rigors, and in a chronic state of abundance and surplus of supplies and capacities, including labor-power: hence, the emergence of the "modern" society, and, after the ending, by a great revolutionary civil war, of slavery and the obstructive power of the slave-owning class, nowhere more strongly than in the US by the 1870s–1890s – something more than a "Gilded Age," and something other. Evolution *through* revolution (the US Civil War and aftermath).

This was a society that while still moving in the grip of the seasonal cycles of nature was ever loosening that grip by a Promethean development of productive, transport, distributive, communicative, applied-science, engineering, and managerial-organizational capacities. It was a society also now moving with greater regularity – modifying or displacing the cycles of nature – in a *business* cycle of expansion and contraction of production, exchange, and employment: a human-made cycle, an "artificial" cycle, that nevertheless acted as if it were a force of nature beyond human control, or was widely understood as an unalterable law of economics. The historical departure also meant, accordingly, that "hard times" came less from physical shortages, natural catastrophes, and seasonal change, than from the capacity-supply-demand disequilibriums of progressive development itself (Marx's transformations of values, Schumpeter's innovation and creative destruction, the vernacular's "booms-and-busts"), which periodically disrupted and subdued market activity and left large numbers of people destitute in the midst of plenty, or unemployed in the midst of plenty to do and with the know-how and resources with which to do it: the quintessential "free-market" society, industrializing capitalist society, the mobile, ever-variable, modern society.[25]

If humanity could modify and displace cycles of nature, could it not modify, tame, and redirect the artificial, human-made cycles of business? This was a question being raised with a growing urgency, in the course of the late nineteenth and early twentieth century, not at all only by self-identifying "socialists," but also by social philosophers, promarket economists, political leaders, farm and labor leaders, and not least of all by capitalists themselves, the latter both in their thinking and in their practical business activity in the offices and the marketplaces (e.g., Andrew Carnegie, Lyman J. Gage, Elbert H. Gary, Franklin MacVeagh, J. P. Morgan, Sr., George W. Perkins, John D. Rockefeller, Sr., Theodore N. Vail, Frank A. Vanderlip, and Paul Warburg). By the early twentieth century, industrializing capitalism and its techno-economic revolutions (shorthand for saying the people and society doing these things) brought along vast *socializations* of market and production organization and relations: think of factories, railroads, steamship lines, telegraph and telephone, central power plants, department stores, catalogue retailing, corporations, insurance companies, commodity and capital (securities) exchanges, trade unions, cooperatives, trade associations (business), trades councils (union-labor). They brought, along with urbanization and suburbanization, vast *socializations* of civil society: think of civic, professional, and religious associations, settlement houses and other social service organizations, urban public and parochial schools, philanthropic organizations, colleges and universities, the new specialized graduate schools and research centers, public libraries, museums, and parks, mass transit, office buildings, autos and roads, bridges and tunnels, tenements and street life, mass media and advertising, theater and amusements, sports and recreation. Industrializing capitalism and its techno-economic revolutions brought along also vast *socializations* of government functions: think of public health and sanitation facilities, police and fire departments, resource conservation programs, regulatory policies and agencies, pensions and social insurance, countercyclical fiscal and monetary operations, public enterprise and contracting.

Industrializing capitalism, in other words, especially as it moved into a corporate stage of reorganization and development, brought with it modern socialism, not as ideally, romantically, dyspeptically, or schematically conceived by either procapitalism or prosocialism partisans, doctrinaires, or utopians, but in everyday market, civic, and governmental affairs, and in activity and outlook across class lines: the trends may be understood, historically, as conveying socialism, not only in the sense (above indicated) of growing socializations of production relations, civic affairs, and government functions, but also in the sense of a growing working-class power in market relations and public-policy making, rising real-wage/salary income, and rising investment (absolute and as a share of the economy), by both capitalist and noncapitalist persons and agencies, in social goods, public goods, and social services – i.e., investment "for use," as well as "for profit"; also in the sense of a growing corporate, associational, and governmental management, direction, and planning of the market (administered markets) and of the economy as a whole, moderating the business cycle, matching more closely savings, investment, and consumption (no great depression between 1897 and 1929, and none after the 1930s to the end of the century and after); also in the corollary sense of increasingly making markets and the overall economy socially serviceable and accountable, and politically integrated into the quest of civil society for the expansion, deepening, and universalizing of human rights (in earlier times, alias "industrial democracy"), which necessarily involved the reconceptualizaton and reformation of property rights along the lines of social goals and principles.[26]

The period of the 1890s–1920 saw the early stages of this capitalism-socialism mix. Along with the continuing development of the capitalist components, the socialist components enlarged and intensified during World War I, they continued their codevelopment in the 1920s, and the mix grew into a sustained stage of maturity in the manifold reforms and restructurings during the Great Depression of the 1930s, and continued to develop, in scale and scope, in the reforms and restructurings during World War II and the post-war years of 1945–1960s, and in the civil rights, sexual, entitlement, and digital-IT revolutions of the 1960s–1990s.

All these changes became telescoped within, and further magnified by, another historical departure, the passage from industrial to "post-industrial" society. This passage began in force in the US in the 1920s, in advance of all other societies, and better explains the onset, length, and depth of the Great Depression in the US, 1929–1941, than fiscal, monetary, regulatory, or tariff policies, world trade barriers, or previous conditions of the business cycle: that is, a convergence and combined impact of the long-term "post-industrial" trend with shorter-term cyclical and geopolitical trends.

"Post-industrial," in *this* historical context of the twentieth-century US, refers to goods production in general – agricultural, extractive, as well as manufactures – and designates not declining production (i.e., not "deindustrialization," "outsourcing," etc.), but on the contrary, rising goods production with the employment of less of society's labor-time (embodied in plant, energy, equipment, materials, and current labor), not only relatively but absolutely. With the continuing evolution of the modern mode of production (including managerial, organizational, and investment know-how and technique), the condition of *rising* and higher-quality goods production became *declining* labor-time required for it: new investment meant fewer hours of work or fewer jobs; rising goods production meant less or negative net investment. In other terms, the "post-industrial" trends meant a phasing out of capital accumulation in *rising* goods production, indeed, its *disaccumulation* in rising goods production, and the reallocation and accumulation of capital and current labor-time in nongoods production ("services").[27]

The disaccumulation of capital in the "post-industrial" context brought the diminishment and eventual abrogation of the investment-consumption conflict that had been vital to the accumulation process, and the easing and reconfiguration (not yet the elimination) of capital-labor class conflict. It made this class conflict increasingly negotiable in the spheres of contractual relations, party politics, law, and public policy, and reinforced the socialist trends. It brought, indeed, a growth of production, production capacities, and productivity, through consumption itself – that is, from rising consumer demand and consumer revenue streams, the dissolving of lines between consumer and investment goods (e.g., sewing machine, typewriter, telephone, automotive vehicle, camera, radio, TV, sport-recreational equipment, computer, cell phone), and from skills and enablements acquired in consumption (including education), as well as those acquired on the job or in training (all this later called "human capital"). Consumption also became a growing *outlet* for allocation and investment of savings (individual, business, institutional), for example, in consumer and home financing, in funding employees' and shareholders' consumption at higher standards of living, in funding the consumption and care of the nonemployed (retired, disabled, disemployed, children, indigent), as well as in funding rising consumption of education, health-care, and recreational products and services, and in funding expanding public programs and employment. (Say's Law revised and reversed: consumer demand creates more production.[28]) Hence, especially in the US by the 1980s–2000s, and all the more strongly as computer-driven rising productivity and disaccumulation took hold and spread in the services sectors by the 1990s, the modern economy increasingly exhibited the combined characteristics of "low savings rates" ("low" by older measuring rods) yet vigorous growth; lower tax rates on trade, income, and capital, yet rising government revenues; rising public spending and sustained fiscal deficits (ranging low as percent of GDP), yet low interest rates and low or moderate price inflation, nevertheless with strong growth in jobs and relatively low unemployment rates (or, repeal of the "Phillips Curve") – in a nutshell, the coming-of-age of "supply-side" economics. Economic theory, as well as central-bank policy, strained to catch up with all of this.[29]

As with industrialization, so too, the "post-industrial" disaccumulation trend, in other words, meant still more restructuring and re-formation leftward of social relations, of government and its functions, and of society as a whole: in effect, a century of "permanent revolution," or revolutionary evolution, in the US.

XII

(*Distortion 3*. Ahistorical Syndrome – continued)

At the outset of the twentieth century, W. E. B. DuBois said that the problem of the twentieth century was the problem of the "color line." DuBois was himself a great practitioner of the nineteenth-century social science discipline, and in self-conception, a socialist and revolutionary. His axiom made a strong claim of validity in the cumulative-evolutionary perspective. But DuBois's axiom, if taken literally (i.e., as *the* problem and *the* line) was much too limited – ironically, one might say, American-parochial – and in any case, all too modest an anticipation. In US history, and in that of much of the world, the twentieth was the century of the multiline crossings – the number of lines, and the *kind* of lines, in so relatively short a period of time, in one and the same society, and across so many societies, without historical precedent, and thus corroborative of a great departure in a universal-human cumulative-evolutionary, and hence revolutionary, trajectory.[30]

I offer a provisional list of lines crossed in the US in the twentieth century, and some of the sublines, as follows (let us begin with DuBois's color line):

- *The Color Line (Race Line).* The *peaking*, and then the defeat, of racism as a legal or state-imposed system of exploitation and power: the war against Nazism and its defeat in Germany and Europe; the war against Japanese religio-racist imperialism and its defeat in Japan and Asia; the US civil rights revolution; the end of apartheid in South Africa; self-government and growing role and power in world affairs of nations of Asia, Africa, and Latin America.[31]

- *The Sex Line.* Equalitarian revolution in women's role, status, participation, and power in the family, society, the economy, and body politic; similarly with homosexuals; most completely in the US and other Western societies, much less so but with movement in an equalitarian direction elsewhere, in some direct proportion to modernizing trends.

- *The "WASP-American" Culture Line.* Interacting with Americans of Anglo-Euro-Protestant heritage, a steadily growing engagement of urbanizing African-Americans and immigrants (Irish- and Euro-Catholic, Euro-Jewish, Hispanic-Catholic, Chinese and other Asian) in the making, reshaping, and transformation of American politics, the labor force and broader economy, and culture (literature and letters, arts, music, education, journalism, fashion, cuisine, film, radio, TV, etc.) – a process beginning forcefully by the 1890s–1914, and continuing throughout the century.

- *The Electoral-Power Line.* Universal suffrage in the US – women, African-Americans, 18-year-olds – and in most other nations. In the US, rising power of workers, women, African-Americans, Asian-Americans, Hispanic-Americans, homosexuals, in society, the economy, politics, and public-policy making.

- *The Education Line.* In the US, universal primary and secondary school education; mass higher education, with mobility impact on occupations, income, status, and class.

- *The Empire Line.* Dissolution of empires (Austro-Hungarian, Ottoman, czarist Russian, German [twice], Japanese, Italian, British,

French, Dutch, Belgian, Portuguese, US [in the Philippines, Cuba, Panama Canal Zone], Soviet); by 2000, national-government in about 190 nation-states, over two-thirds of which did not exist in 1900.

- *The National-International Line.* At the same time as the multiple flowering of nation-states, the emergence of a working internationalism, to a large degree institutionalized, in economic, monetary, governmental, military, media, educational and other sociocultural affairs: e.g., transnational corporations, securities and currency exchanges, interrelations of central banks and currency boards, universities and research centers, think tanks, international press editions, satellite TV, film/DVD, the Internet, and in approximate chronological order since the 1940s, IMF, IBRD (WB), UN, GATT, OAS, ECA, NATO, Warsaw Pact, SEATO, CENTO, IAEA, IADB, OECD, OSCE, EU, G-7, OPEC, G-7/8/9, NAFTA, OAU/AU, EMU, ECB, EDB, CIS, WTO, CAFTA, APEC, ASEAN, ADB, IEA, G-20, revised IMF/WB/WTO.
- *The Property System Line.* The corporate reorganization of enterprise and of the market system; from individual to associational (socialized), and from unified to separated, ownership/management, and investment/ profit-disbursement; from privatized to socialization of business risk, liability, and hazard ("moral" and otherwise), in limited-liability, bankruptcy, tort, regulatory, insurance, central-bank, government-treasury, GSE, stimulus, and subsidy, law and administration;[32] from mostly individual to increasingly intermediary and institutional ownership of stocks and other securities.
- *The Class Relations Line.* From workers as factors of production paid according to standards of commutative justice, to collective bargaining, labor laws (wages, hours, working conditions), income transfers via both the contract-price system and the tax system; hence, a spreading of distributive-justice standards, at first reinforcing and supplementing collective bargaining, and later displacing it; from strongly rising trade union power and membership to their steady decline (except among government workers and higher-paid professionals); rising stock-ownership by workers, pension funds, and unions; more and more intersecting of investor and labor interests with rising workers' income (current, deferred, retired) not only from wages and benefits but also now from capital gains, and from profits via interest and dividends; decline of class-formation and politics based on the older capital-labor, investor-producer distinction.[33] Interrelated with this line-crossing, the crossing of:
- *The Production-Communications-Investment Line.* From industrial to post-industrial society; from capital accumulation to disaccumulation;

from goods production to services and information/knowledge production as dominant in occupations; from typewriters and "business machines" to computers; from analog to digital; from wired to wireless in telecommunications; from print media and broadcast to cable, satellite, and Internet; from diminishing returns on rising investment to rising returns on diminishing investment (especially in digital software and related goods and activity); from oversupply/lower-value to oversupply/higher-value (knowledge with digital networking); revival of self-employed investment in, and production of, goods, services, and information, with exponential impact on innovation, individuality, and sociality of old and new kinds. Correlatively, the crossing of:

- *The Investment-Consumption Line.* From investment and consumption being mutually antagonistic as a condition of growth, to their becoming more and more mutually reinforcing; growth of consumption itself as a massive investment field; consumer-revenue streams becoming a rising component of savings/investment streams; growing workers' participation in investment and capital gains as sources of current and deferred income, and in the context of rising productivity, bringing a softening of upward wage pressure and a superseding of the older "wage-price" inflation. (Cf. note 33 and related text, above.)
- *The Occupation-Status Line.* From birth-determined, to chosen, occupation and status; from "doing" what your parents did, to "doing" differently, and better, or happier; from occupation-for-life to multi-occupations over a life span; from "one person, one life," to "one person, many lives" (a modern realization of Marx's more pastoral anticipation).
- *The Health-Demographic Line.* Public health programs vs. disease; mass access to health care and medicine; rising longevity; growing retired population consuming without producing, and in the US moving from age group with highest to lowest poverty rate; quadrupling of US population (*c.* 76m to *c.* 300m) and of world population (*c.* 1.5bn to *c.* 6bn), in one century, 1900–2000.
- *The Energy Transmission Line.* From coal-steampower-electricity-hydro-electricity, to also oil-internal combustion, natural gas, nuclear, electronic.
- *The Travel-Space-Time Line.* From horses, railroads, and steamships, to also autos, trucks, highways, commuter mass transit, airplanes and airlines.
- *The Materials Line.* From older to new technologies in steel, alloys, and copper, and from agri-goods and alkaloids to petrochemicals-synthetics-plastics, pharmaceuticals, biotech engineering, silicon-chip-fiberglass.

- *The Exploration Line*. From all over the earth, to above and below the earth's surface, to outer space.
- *The Multiple Science-Revolution Line* (integral to many of the foregoing). Relativity (macro-), quantum (micro-), DNA-genome, nano-tech.

These lines crossed count to eighteen (plus sublines). Doubtless, others could be added, and those rendered here are certainly subject to revision or reconfiguration.[34] Taken all together, they might bring us back to affirming DuBois's axiom, in the sense that they tend toward a crystallizing of a universal-human identity, and corresponding social relations, on a world-historical scale, which in effect has meant a global crossing of the color line (although not quite yet of the tribal, ethnic, and religio-racism line). So, in an appreciative sense, we may say with DuBois that the problem of the twentieth century was the problem of crossing the color line, but as integral to many other interactive line-crossings, and the crossing of lines still leaves many steps to go, and may not be irreversible; lines not yet crossed remain, and the future will bring many other lines to cross. Barring the biblical apocalypse or a cosmic catastrophe, the end of history is not quite near.

It is evident, nevertheless, that the twentieth has been a century of unprecedented changes, in number and in cumulative-evolutionary substance, and in all of which the US – its people, society, and government – has played a leading and decisive role. It is not that historians (and others) are by and large unaware of these changes and their correlated trends, although perhaps with some differences in terminology, nor that they have not produced substantial bodies of work about them, particularly specialists in economic, technological, military, management, demographic, IT, and other such focused fields. It is, rather, that an awareness and knowledge of these trends remain dissociated from the treatment of the larger political and socio-cultural history of the US and its role in the world, and hence also from the treatment of world history. It is as if historians were saying, Yes, the trends have been happening, but in effect above the American people's heads and behind their backs, or in spite of them: that is, all this dynamic, world-historical change has been going on in the US, and much of the change is "progressive" in substance, and "leftward" in direction, but the American people and government mostly are "conservative" and "rightward" just the same. Yes, people make their own history, but apparently not the American people in the twentieth century; their history kept changing, but quite regardless of them. Yes, a techno-economic determinism ("objective conditions") independent of what people are thinking and doing is unacceptable as an interpretation of history, except for the ("conservative") American people and government in the twentieth century – another "American Exceptionalism." Yes, the US has been *the* "Superpower," or global "Hegemon," but all this world-historical change in the US, and increasingly elsewhere, is apart from world history and the US role in it:[35] Cognitive dissonance as critical dissidence. Concerning the American people and the US, and their role in world affairs, in the twentieth century, historians suspend the usual standards of their discipline, or to paraphrase another Marx (Groucho), they waive the rules. It is a case not of American Exceptionalism in real history, but of historians' exceptionalism in their historiographical practice.

Without comprehending, interpreting, and assessing twentieth-century US society, and the character of its people's thinking, activities, and culture in the context of human history, and in that of basic historical trends of their own making – that is, the passage from *Gemeinschaft* to *Gesellschaft*, from a scarcity-replacement to an abundance-surplus-developmental economy, from natural-cycle to business-cycle, from industrializing capitalism to a capitalism-socialism mix, from industrial to post-industrial society, from capital-accumulation to disaccumulation, and the related civil rights, sexual, entitlement, and digital-IT revolutions – our historical studies, our historical understanding, about the US and the wider world, will remain in a crucial degree ahistorical.

Each of these trends marked major turning points, and together epochal change, in human history, in all of which the US and its history, that is, its variable *people*, its evolving *society-type*, and its changing modes of *government*, especially from the mid-nineteenth century on, played a major role, and continue to do so. Most of our historians in the transatlantic world, however, and their historical work about the US, its role in world affairs, and accordingly about world humanity, have been caught in the grip of an ahistorical – a Utopian-Romantic – syndrome. The US society and the world have been constantly changing, but the categories remain the same: evolution in the straitjacket of a "static equilibrium." It was capitalism ("free markets") then, it is capitalism today (triumphant, in crisis). It was socialism (government ownership, state command) then, it is socialism today (failed, coming-back). It was Empire/Imperialism then, it is Empire/Imperialism today; rich and poor then, rich and poor today; Gilded Age then, Gilded Age today; Progressivism then, Progressivism today; racism then, racism today; Big Business (corporate interests) then, Big Business (corporate interests) today; "New Dealers" then, "New Dealers" today; "minorities" then, "minorities" today; cowboys (straight-shooters) then, cowboys (straight-shooters) today; and so on – *plus ça change, plus c'est la même chose*, in the ever-fashionable French. Knowing your history, and repeating it, too. Yet, as Galileo said about the earth, after a religiously correct recantation otherwise, *e pur si muove*. Historians and other thinkers in "emerging" Asia and the East, more than those in "post-modern" US and the West, have grasped the Galileo-moment. (The advantages of "underdevelopment"?)

In the years around the close of the nineteenth and the opening of the twentieth century, Americans along a broad spectrum of social spheres – intellect, business, labor, law, politics, civic and religious associations – with varying degrees of optimism and pessimism, were addressing the epochal departures and turning points in human history brought on, at an accelerated pace, by industrialization (at that time, with steam power, electricity, telecommunications, large-corporate reorganization of enterprise, cooperatives, trade unions, investment banking, and modern securities markets), and its concomitants in urbanization, secularization, productive abundance, business-cycle rhythms, and rival world-girdling imperialisms. They were asking the question, whether this was, in essence, another rise-and-fall cyclical-turning in human history, or a cumulative-evolutionary departure to a new stage of human history, both in social relations within societies and in international relations among them.[36]

One hundred years later, around the turn of the twenty-first century, many learned inquirers have also been grappling with this question of cyclical vs. cumulative-evolutionary history with a renewed urgency and growing amplitude, and now with the advantage of a century of further history that was the unknown *future* to the earlier thinkers, and that is an experienced *past* both accessible to our study and a part of our knowledge. Yet, with all its resurgent prominence, the question is only tangentially, or vaguely, if at all, and not *integrally*, brought by historians into our understanding of twentieth- and early twenty-first-century US history, the US role in world affairs, and world history as a whole. The twentieth century cascading, alike of hellish conflict and manifold progressive change, in the US and the world, may have so bedazzled as to have benumbed the American (and transatlantic) historical mind. Especially among professional (academic) historians, historical thought seems to be caught, in an ahistorical syndrome, between the Utopian push into "end-of-history" stasis, and the Romantic pull of cycles-of-empires and civilizations clashing, rising, and falling, with little room left between for perspectives on the implications of twentieth-century historical developments for a universal-human cumulative-evolution in US and world history. Such evolution, in effect, remains regarded in the prevalent public discourse of US (and transatlantic) historians and other intellectuals, whether in triumphalism, animosity, embarrassment, or troubled fatalism, as "American Empire," or as a "Western," or "American," or "Anglo-American," hegemony, or as imperialist "corporate" transnationalism, or in shorthand, abstractly, as "globalization."

XIII

US and World History in the Twenty-First Century: Cyclical or Cumulative?

In little more than a century, since the 1890s, the world has passed from various empires, nations, cultures, and societies interacting in belligerence or amity, to various nations, cultures, and societies intensively interacting, intermixing, and moving toward a universal-human civilization, consisting of variations and variabilities: one might say, allegorically, from "Clash of Civilizations" and rivalry of closed empires, since ancient times, to the modern-society, "Open Door" world, or globalism, of the "American Century."[37]

* * *

Pan-(Jihadi)-Islamism of the 1970s–2000s, bicentered in Arab and Iranian politics, in both rivalry (at times lethally violent) and collaboration, has appeared to be, in some respects, a defensive "last stand" of a professing traditionalism against modern society. But in its essential characteristics, it is an aggressive-expansionist imperialism, on a global scale, and, as of 2006–2010, with a rising Iranian salience, subject however to continuous oscillations in the balance of power between Arab and Iranian sides.[38] In its dual formation, Pan-Islamist imperialism represents a counterglobalism to that of modern-secular, social-democratic ("capitalist") society. Its policy-commanders intend a worldwide renaissance of distinctive "civilizations" (with some clashing), in effect, dissolving, or otherwise subduing or destroying, the modern-society, "Open Door" world, of the "American Century," and thereby provisionally restoring a multipolar world of closed or restrictive empires, pending the ultimate establishment of its own one world empire.[39] This dispensation would interdict a further unfolding of the modern-society cumulative-evolutionary trend. An ironist of history might call it the Anti-Liberal (Islamist) End of History.[40]

Pan-Islamist imperialism may also be viewed, from a perspective of comparative world history, as a remnant, or an attempted rejuvenation, of a great trans-society empire-type of the human past (Persian-Arab-Ottoman); the others of the West, of this type, are gone. (See XII. The Empire Line, above.) It may be that, in some degree, Pan-Islamism comprises such a remnant or rejuvenation, but it is also something other and something more. It appeals, *within* the Muslim world, to territorial or cultural revanchism, with a strong victim-pathos voice, as well as to an Islamist chauvinism, and to other national, ethnic, or tribal chauvinisms, and to a broad range of current economic, militarist, and ideological-institutional interests. Its propaganda organs anathematize modern-liberal-commercialistic ("bourgeois" or "social-democratic") Western society as such, and also as embodying an imputed satanic combination of Judeo-Christian heritage, seductive pagan decadence, and exploitative capitalistic imperialism of global reach. It appeals, *outside* the Muslim world, to both *realpolitik* maneuverings, and populist-statist or totalitarian movements and their strategies, against Anglo-American power, among government and military policy makers, intelligentsia, particular interests, and broader publics, in such "greater" powers as Russia, China, India, Japan, France, and Germany, indeed also among such circles in the US and UK themselves, and in such "lesser" powers as Italy, Spain, Sweden, Denmark, the Netherlands, Belgium, North Korea, South Africa, Zimbabwe, Cuba, Venezuela, Bolivia, Ecuador, Argentina, Colombia, Peru, Nicaragua, Mexico (i.e., much of Latin America), and Canada.

Pan-Islamism has access to empire-scale finance, and to modern technologies of energy, mobility, communications, and massive destruction.[41] It is a party-state (or clerisy-state) in political configuration, it is state-command, leader-cult, terror-coercive, and totalitarian, in mode of social organization and governing, and it is committed, in principle, against modern democracy, and to the use of violent force to make gains. All these characteristics (in this and the previous paragraph) suggest parallels and analogies with the three major forms of twentieth-century European state-command socialism, i.e., with the Mussolini-Fascist party-state, with the Hitler-Nazi party-state (here including the racism against Jews), and with the Lenin-Stalin Communist party-state; also with the religio-racist Japanese Shinto-state. It was not coincidental, but a matter of historical circumstances, that Hitler waxed interested in a putative Islam, and also a Japanese Shinto, as an authoritarian religion suited for the German "Third Reich" (remember – as had Hitler himself – the genocide in the World War I- and pre- and post-war years by Muslim

Turks against Christian Armenians, including mass deportations *in railway cars*, and also mass deportation of Greeks). Nor was it merely from a geopolitical opportunism, but also from an ideological affinity, that pan-Arab nationalists (Ba'athists) and resurrectionist Islamists had, variously, strong relations with European Fascism and German Nazism, and with the Nazi state, in the 1920s–1940s, and with the Soviet state, "Marxist-Leninists," and "Maoists," after the demise of Nazism.[42]

Pan-Islamist imperialism, building steam in the 1970s–1990s (e.g., in Iran, Afghanistan, Pakistan, Kashmir, Saudi Arabia, Yemen, Egypt, Syria, Lebanon, Palestine, Jordan, Iraq, Algeria, Sudan, Somalia, Turkey, in parts of the Balkans, in parts of Central Asia, Chechnya in Russia, Uighur region in China, in Southeast Asia [e.g., Indonesia, Malaysia, Thailand, the Philippines], and in emigrant colonies in central and western Europe, Britain, Canada, parts of Latin America, and the US), has brought on a protracted conflict, which may prove massively destructive, within and across societies, or "civilizations" (not *between* them), and of world-war proportions – again, analogous with the civil-war characteristics and revolutionary upheavals of World Wars I and II, in the twentieth century, brought on by an aggressively expansive German/Italian and Japanese imperialism challenging an attenuated Anglo-American global hegemony, just as an aggressively expansive Arab and Iranian Pan-Islamist imperialism has claimed to be doing since the 1970s–1980s, and by 2010 the Turks. After World War I, the world seat of empire remained in flux, not at all settled in the US, nor, as after World War II, dually in the US and the Soviet Union/China. In the later years of the Cold War and after it, the world seat of empire again came into flux, in a process of either dissolving in a universal globalism, in accordance with "American Century"/"Open Door" principles, or moving (back) to Asia, and pending one or the other outcome, yielding once again (analogous with the years before and between World Wars I and II) portents and outbreaks of war, civil war, insurrectionary upheavals, revolution and counterrevolution, across the globe, not excluding within the US itself.

Pan-Islamist imperialism is, in principle, supranational and opposed to the all-sovereign nation-state. It seeks control of national governments not as instruments of imperial sovereignty as such, but for securing bases of operations and training, for imposing by law and police-terror preferred Islamist practices, and thereby also for suppressing opposition thought and activity.[43] Pan-Islamist imperialism seeks control of national governments, also, for accessing revenues, labor, and know-how; for developing geopolitical, logistical, financial/investment, and diplomatic muscle; for acquiring armed forces and nuclear weapons and other WMD along with delivery systems – in all these ways accumulating not only the physical might, but also the growing prestige and leverage, of a World Power; and last and far from least, for controlling a lion's share of world oil and natural gas supply, upon which modern society, as now known, depends. The authority of imperial *sovereignty* itself, in this schema, resides in a transsociety, transnation, and supragovernment apparatus – part vanguard-party-state, part clerisy-state, part proto-Caliphate, pending a Caliphate proper.[44] Precisely the supragovernment transnationalism, the "globalism," of the modern political economy, the vast oil-derived riches of that global political economy accruing to the Islamic *umma*, and a renewed geopolitical multipolarity, palpably if still inchoately emerging in international affairs since the end of the Cold War, have become the realistic ("material" and "diplo-political") basis for the resurrection of the pre-modern model of territorial-sacred empire: The modern world itself assures that the Caliphate will rise again (or the Hidden Imam): negation of the negation.[45]

In its major strategic thrust *at this point* in its history, in addition to diplomatic, economic, and indoctrination/propaganda operations, Pan-Islamist imperialism has targeted, and *by choice* engaged with violent force, not the military might en masse of its adversaries. Rather, deploying out-of-uniform assault units in missions such as organized bombing and rocketry, arson, hijacking, eco-pollution, cyber-attack, demonstrations, rioting and vandalism, abductions, death threats, and public murder, it targets and engages with violent or otherwise disruptive force (legal, extralegal, and illegal), its adversaries' open-market economies, modern infrastructure systems (transport, communications, energy, health, security), public places, press-speech-religious freedoms, women's human rights and equality with men, civilians' lives and security at work, education, and recreation, and public edifices of liberty, power, and wealth – in sum, the essential components of modern pluralist/democratic society as such. It also targets for bombings, execution, or hostage-taking, from time-to-strategic-time, highly vulnerable singular political, diplomatic, military, and NGO persons and units of its adversaries, such as embassies, UN mission-leaders, diplomats, political leaders, religious leaders, journalists, intelligence officers, aid workers, military personnel, merchant and naval ships in port or at sea, military land convoys, and aerial auxiliaries.

Besides its own higher state organs[46] (de jure, de facto, or prospective, e.g., Al-Qaeda executive [Salafi], Muslim Brotherhood executive [Salafi],

Saudi high Wahhabi councils, Ba'ath party executive, Muslim World League executive, Hezbollah executive, Hamas executive, IRGC/Quds executive, Supreme Guide and Council of Guardians/Assembly of Experts), Pan-Islamist imperialism's major organizational nodal points and command centers remain at present of two types: (1) small, mobile, and dispersed units, communicating by cell phone, Internet, public media, travelers, and otherwise, including those embedded in selected embassies, consulates, mosques, charitable institutions, exchange and finance networks (including banks and racketeering), business organizations, civic associations, media entities, institutes, universities or their departments or Studies Centers, and clandestine cells, all of which draw sustenance and cover, variously, from state agencies, governments, resident populations, and emigrant colonies; (2) where effective and feasible, at the head of larger units operating as armed irregulars or militias (as in Lebanon, Palestine, Iraq, eastern Afghanistan, western Pakistan, Kashmir, Thailand, Indonesia, the Philippines, Somalia, Sudan-Darfur), and simultaneously or alternatively, as social service organizations and religio-political movements, fronts, or parties. All the world's a battle stage. Every society's a theater of war. Mundane time is not of the essence.[47]

Pan-Islamist imperialism may succeed in establishing itself as a world power. Or, it may be contained and gradually dissipate, or be definitively defeated, as and if the universal-human/cumulative-evolutionary trend spreads and deepens in strength, stamina, resolve, self-esteem, and vitality. No small as or if.

Notes

1. Peter Evans, Dietrich Rueschemeyer, and Theda Skocpol, eds., *Bringing the State Back In* (New York: Cambridge University Press, 1985). See also William E. Leuchtenburg, "The Pertinence of Political History: Reflections on the Significance of the State in America," *Journal of American History*, 73: 3 (December 1986), pp. 585–600, and works cited in Leuchtenburg's notes.

2. Cf. M. J. Sklar, "Periodization and Historiography: Studying American Political Development in the Progressive Era, 1890s–1916," Steven Hahn, "Response to Sklar," M. J. Sklar, "Discussion with Steven Hahn," *Studies in American Political Development*, 5 (Fall 1991), pp. 173–223; also M. J. Sklar, *United States as a Developing Country*, chs. 1, 2, 7. For similar wheelwrighting in the field of US labor history, see, e.g., Howard Kimmeldorf, ed., Round Table Discussion: "Bringing Unions Back In (Or Why We Need a New Old Labor History)," *Labor History*, 32, Winter 1991, pp. 91–129; and the interesting discussion of the matter by Richard Schneirov in "William English Walling: Socialist and Labor Progressive," Introduction to new edition of

William English Walling, *American Labor and American Democracy* (New Brunswick: Transaction Publishers, 2005), pp. xi–xli, at pp. xxviii–xxix; and for yet again similar, more recent, wheelwrighting in general political history, see Sean Wilentz, *The Rise of American Democracy: Jefferson to Lincoln* (New York: W. W. Norton, 2005), "Preface," pp. xvii–xxiii, and Jill Lepore's discussion of the book, dealing with issues addressed here, in *The New Yorker*, October 24, 2005 (LXXXI: 33), pp. 80–84.

3. Full disclosure: I was among the founding members of The Historical Society, Program Co-chair, with Professor Alan Charles Kors (University of Pennsylvania) of the society's first National Conference, Boston, 1999, a charter member of the society's Board of Governors and Executive Committee, 1998–2002, and substantially aided in the drafting and adoption of the society's by-laws (in which not all of my suggestions were included). I was also a member, from its founding to June 2005, of the Editorial Board of the *Journal of The Historical Society*. This chapter further develops a presentation I gave at the society's second National Conference, Boston, June 3, 2000. That is, the presentation was composed from materials I had been developing during previous years, pre-Historical Society, and publicly delivered on various occasions "pre- 9/11."

4. Santayana's words were (*The Life of Reason*, vol. I): "Those who cannot remember the past are condemned to repeat it." In his weekly column ("Wonder Land," *Wall Street Journal*, August 26, 2005, p. A12), Daniel Henninger wryly observed: "Maybe Santayana was misquoted. Maybe what he meant to say is those who *remember* history are condemned to repeat it. And repeat it, and repeat it." It might be added that knowing history may not be the same as knowing the past; and also that in some cultures, and in some circles or "movements," the purpose of "knowing" the past is precisely to repeat it, and to enforce its repetition.

5. C. V. Wedgwood, *William the Silent* (London: Jonathan Cape, 1967), p. 35. To similar effect, Sören Kierkegaard's words are: "Life can only be understood backwards; but it must be lived forwards."

6. Cf. Ernst Cassirer, *The Philosophy of the Enlightenment* (Princeton University Press, 1951; Beacon Press paperback edn., Boston, 1955), ch. 5: "The Conquest of the Historical World," pp. 197–233.

7. Cf. Stephen Kern, *A Cultural History of Causality* (Princeton University Press, 2004), esp. chs. 7, 8; Paul K. Conkin and Roland N. Stromberg, *Heritage and Challenge: The Theory and History of History* (Wheeling, IL: Forum Press, 1989), ch. 10 (by Conkin).

8. Elsewhere, I have discussed periodization as essential to scientific method in history. See note 2. See also Walter Dean Burnham, "Pattern Recognition and 'Doing' History: Art, Science, or Bootless Enterprise," ch. 3 (pp. 59–82) in Lawrence C. Dodd and Calvin Jillson, eds., *The Dynamics of American Politics: Approaches and Interpretations* (Boulder: Westview Press, 1994); and Richard Schneirov, "Thoughts on Periodizing the Gilded Age Capital Accumulation, Society, and Politics, 1873–1898," *Journal of the Gilded Age and Progressive Era* (*JGAPE*); 5: 3 (July 2006), pp. 189–224; and see Schneirov, *Labor and Urban Politics*, Introduction, pp. 1–15.

9. *Artificial*: making by art or the arts (craft, skill, preconceiving and conceptual, hence with intent or will), in this case, interpersonal, i.e., social; e.g., tool-making, language-making, thought-making, self-making, world-making (society-making); all this, whether or not the cognition and the volition or will are taken to be free, or determined, or some intermixture. In any case, the *distinctive* quality of human evolution is that the human species, via its volitional cognitive and social characteristics, participates in determining or shaping its own evolution: a natural-artificial selection.

10. Regarding the violence, cf. Charles S. Maier's estimates: "Probably no period of history will make so many subject populations hostage to the reciprocal terror and atrocities of rebels and rulers as the twentieth century. The collations of statistics . . . converge around a total of 170 to 190 million victims of politically motivated carnage . . . Of the hundred million or so killed in wars during the twentieth century, about thirty to forty million perished in Europe through 1945, and the rest perished outside Europe: perhaps ten to twenty million in Asia during the Second World War, and perhaps another forty to fifty million in the second half of the century." Maier, *Among Empires* (Cambridge: Harvard University Press, 2006), pp. 131–132. Regarding the twentieth-century combination of unprecedented progress and destructive violence, cf. Niall Ferguson, *The War of the World* (New York: Penguin, 2006) pp. xxxiii–xli, 647–654. Marx once said, "Human progress [resembles] that hideous pagan idol, who would not drink the nectar but from the skulls of the slain." Little did he know (or did he perhaps suspect?) how much more this would apply to the twentieth than to any preceding century. Will the twenty-first century exceed the twentieth in this respect? And will it come more with retrogression than with progress? Or instead of progress?

11. See notes 2, 8.

12. Cf. Hegel's comment: "Science alone is the theodicy; it keeps one both from looking at events with animal amazement, or ascribing them, more cleverly, to accidents of the moment." Hegel to C. G. Zellman, January 23, 1807, in Walter Kaufmann, *Hegel, A Reinterpretation* (Garden City, NY: Anchor, 1966), p. 321. Cf. Pope Benedict XVI, UN General Assembly Address, NYC, April 18, 2008, discussing with strong approval the UN Universal Declaration of Human Rights as an agenda to be fulfilled (and rejecting what he had earlier called the "dictatorship of relativism"): "As history proceeds, new situations arise, and the attempt is made to link them to new rights. Discernment, that is, capacity to distinguish good from evil, becomes even more essential . . . [and] since important situations and profound realities are involved, discernment is both an indispensable and a fruitful virtue." Discernment facilitates disclosing "human rights . . . principally rooted in unchanging justice," "rights and the resulting duties . . . [which are] the fruit of a commonly held sense of justice . . . [and] valid at all times and for all peoples." The pope also affirmed and emphasized this universal-human principle as the essence of "natural law" given by God. It and the discernment corollary correlate with what is here referred to as the "universal constant" and the "transhistorical imperative." "Full Text: Pope Benedict XVI's UN

Speech," www.wcbstv.com, 6 pages, at p. 4. Also, the pope's University of Regensburg lecture, September 12, 2006, Catholic World News.com.

13. Until sometime after 1991 (demise of the Soviet Union), it was a widespread habit to equate "The Left" with Communists, with socialists and other self-identifying leftists or "progressives" who were not anti-Communist, and with those professing to be anti-US, anti-Western imperialism, and pro-"Third World." Still, in more recent years, to the present, that habit retains a potent staying power: for example, the book published in 2005 (Encounter) about Communists and allies in the film industry, 1930s–1950s, *Red Star Over Hollywood: The Film Colony's Romance with the Left*, by Ronald Radosh and Allis Radosh, interesting, informative, and historically sophisticated as it otherwise is, effectively equates Communists, the CP, and allies, with "the Left," an equation largely taken for granted by reviewers and readers. The book is indeed about film people's engagement in or with CP activity, but to be historically accurate, not about a "romance," and not "Hollywood's," "the film colony's," or the film industry's, but rather about some serious politics of some (including powerful and influential) people in the film industry, an industry in which many of the others, perhaps most, although they were not CP members or allies, or were positively anti-Communist, were nevertheless people of the left in politics, ideas, values, or sympathies.

14. This would include such latter-day "parts" as Code Pink, ACORN, Air America, TIDES Foundation, Apollo Project, Midwest Academy, CAP, MSNBC, MoveOn.org, DailyKos.org, MediaMatters.org, DemocraticUnderground. org, and HuffingtonPost.org, in whole, or in postings- or operational-parts.

15. E.g., modern or quasi-modern Fascist (Mussolini) Italy, Nazi (Hitler) Germany/Austria, Vichy France, Franco Spain, Salazar Portugal, and some Latin American countries.

16. But, see note 17 and related text, below. Historically understood, the *trinity* is the "American Dream," not a house, secure income, or fame and fortune, "making it," etc. (none of which is peculiarly "American," and each of which would be reductively materialistic), but the bringing together – liberty and equality and progress – what the Old World presumably denied or put asunder. The "American Dream," in other words, is of and on the left. This, of course, is entirely at odds with the conventional view, held on the left and right alike, and reiterated, e.g., by *The Economist* editors John Micklethwaite and Adrian Wooldridge, as in their Op-Ed essay, "Cheer Up Conservatives, You're Still Winning!" *Wall Street Journal*, June 21, 2005, p. A16: "The biggest advantage of all for conservatives is that they have a lock on the American dream. America is famously an idea more than a geographical expression, and that idea seems to be the province of the right . . . If the American dream means anything, it means finding a plot of land where you can shape your destiny and raise your children." (See also their book, *The Right Nation: Conservative Power in America*, New York: Penguin, paper, 2005.) My comment: if, however, this means a universal-equalitarian *right* to land ownership, it was in its origins a "left-wing" idea. Otherwise, it is more an Old World, pre-modern, plot-of-land-peasant "idea" than the American

Dream, still less *the* modern (or peculiarly) American idea, and note how the authors immediately bury the "idea" in "a geographical expression." In pre-Civil War US, the "plot of land"–"shape your destiny" was the *reality* of most white Americans, the *dream* of most black Americans, the nightmare (menace and nemesis) of most American Indians, and the back-home grave-yard to most immigrant, and *urbanizing*, Irish-Americans. After the Civil War, the plot of land was a reality from which white Americans fled in droves the better to *shape* their destinies and *follow* their dreams. Black Americans, in the meantime, were forcibly held to plots of land, in peonage, until the 1910s–1950s brought the boll weevil, the 1927 Mississippi flood, AAA acre-age allotments, the mechanical cotton-picker, massive black *urbanization*, and then (1950s–1970s) the civil rights revolution – "I Have a Dream." It may be unfair to expect editors of *The* (London) *Economist* to understand properly the American Dream, although their illustrious editor-forebear Walter Bagehot might have. Also, to be fair, Americans have not been doing much better on this. For example, former President William J. Clinton and California Gov. Arnold Schwarzenegger collaborated to say: "The American dream is founded on the belief that people who work hard and play by the rules will be able to earn a good living, raise a family in comfort and retire with dignity." (Co-authored Op-Ed, "Beyond Payday Loans," *WSJ*, January 24, 2008, p. A17). But this is more a German-Austrian/American-Gothic *gemütlichkeit*-norm, a modern update of the idealized old peasant ver-sion, than the American Dream, and certainly not descriptive of the authors' own Dream-life-trajectories. This update-archaic version was reiterated by Sen. Barack Obama, campaigning in the Pennsylvania primary (Wilkes-Barre, April 1, 2008, PA Public Affairs TV Channel), and by Sen. Hillary Rodham Clinton, addressing the Democratic Party National Convention (August 26 2008, news.Yahoo.com.), each themselves also enjoying a dif-ferent Dream-life-trajectory. Peggy Lee might be heard singing, "Is that all there is? Is that all there is . . . ?" For two other American examples of the update-archaic version (both on the left), see the interesting books by Barbara Ehrenreich, *Bait and Switch: The (Futile) Pursuit of the American Dream* (New York: Henry Holt and Co., 2005), and Robert B. Carson, *The Missing Link: Recalling the Forgotten Generation of American Dreamers* (Victoria, BC: Trafford Publishing, 2005), esp. ch. 26, pp 370–390. The update-archaic (peasant) version appears more on the "left" than on the "right" in current US politics – a type of "forward-to-the-past" outlook, what Marx might have included in his "feudal-socialism" category, or what the early twentieth-century American socialist W. J. Ghent referred to as a benevolent industrial feudalism, although now we might dub it a post-industrial feu-dalism, and with social workers, "community organizers," lawyers, "activ-ists," professors, journalists, and party leaders the fief-chiefs and the lords. (See Distortion 2. Transvestiture of Left and Right.)

17. It is also in this sense that the slave South was a right-wing society (with a left that was largely enslaved and otherwise suppressed), and the Civil War may be understood, inter alia, as in general a left-vs.-right struggle, in which the majority left-nation prevailed over the South, but not within it.

The failure to establish universal citizenship, equal liberty in the rule of law, and modern market relations in the South, after the Civil War, kept Southern society a right-wing enclave (with a suppressed and disfranchised left) within the larger nation for the next 100 years, and always acted as an obstruction to the left in the larger nation. Hence, the huge leftward surge in US politics, society, and culture, coincident with the civil rights revolution, mid-1950s and after. Martin Luther King's great impact in US political life and social relations resided in his understanding of the nation's left-prevalence. It was the "right-wing" President Reagan who signed into law (1983) "Martin Luther King Day" as an official national holiday, commenting (accurately), as he signed, that King was a socialist. Also indicative of this US left-prevalence was President Lyndon B. Johnson's moving simultaneously, and hence successfully, on both the civil rights and the social-programs ("Great Society") fronts, making him America's greatest twentieth-century left-wing president (in the sense of expanding and deepening the liberty-equality-progress agenda, whether deemed well- or ill-designed), or, at very least on a leftward par with FDR; and, arguably comparable, in *institutional impact*, with Washington, Lincoln, and FDR. If not for the bitter divisions over the Vietnam War, it is reasonable to think, this would be a piece of common conventional wisdom, instead of the mixture of nonpersonhood, disdain, and excoriation visited upon LBJ in politics, media, and academia alike. These considerations may also offer some thicker context to Mississippi Sen. Trent Lott's praise, in an unguarded moment of compassionate nostalgia, of South Carolina Sen. J. Strom Thurmond's "dixiecrat" foresight (on Thurmond's 100th birthday), and Lott's sharp repudiation by President Bush and immediate removal by Senate Republicans from the leadership. As LBJ had fully anticipated, the civil rights breakthrough, with decisive congressional GOP support, meant the Democrats losing much of the South to the GOP, but it also meant winning a nation, including the South (and Republicans), moving strongly leftward, and a Democratic House for the next 30 years, and a Democratic Senate for 24 of those 30 years. It has also meant the South gradually, but steadily, moving toward a more normal two-party politics, in elections and public-policy choices, at the local, state, and national levels. Cf. Doris Kearns's aptly titled, *Lyndon Johnson and the American Dream* (1976). (Doris Kearns: subsequently, Doris Kearns Goodwin.)

18. Cf. M. J. Sklar, *Corporate Reconstruction*, ch. 5, esp. pp. 33–40, 361–367; M. J. Sklar, *United States as a Developing Country*, chs. 1, 7; M. J. Sklar, "Thoughts on Capitalism and Socialism: Utopian and Realistic," *Journal of the Gilded Age and Progressive Era*, 2: 4 (October 2003), pp. 361–376; M. J. Sklar, "Liberty and Equality, and Socialism," *Socialist Revolution*, No. 34 (7: 4), July–August 1977, pp. 92–104.

19. This parenthetical conjecture was written by me in manuscript, and offered at times in lectures, some many years before the public confirmation (2005) of "Deep Throat's" identity (FBI deputy director William Mark Felt), a confirmation which could be taken as corroborative of the conjecture, although conjecture it still remains. Cf. Obit by Tim Weiner, *New York Times*, December 19th 2008, p. B11. On Nixon's views more generally, his

leftist policies as president (e.g., substantially expanded funding of "Great Society" programs, price and rent controls, cutting the dollar from gold, new programs like OSHA and EPA, affirmative action in government contracting, southern school desegregation, détente, China initiative), and conservatives' or rightists' growing disaffection with him in 1970–1973, see e.g., Herbert S. Parmet, *Richard Nixon and His America* (Boston: Little, Brown and Co., 1990), chs. 18, 20; the quotation, "I am now a Keynesian," is at p. 618; and cf. Kenneth Thompson, ed., *The Nixon Presidency* (New York: University Press of America, 1987), esp. essays by Elliot Richardson and Leonard Garment; and Daniel P. Moynihan, *The Politics of a Guaranteed Income* (New York: Random House, 1973); and more recently, Ryan Sager, "The Right Rebels," *New York Post*, October 7, 2005, p. 33. See also J. William Middendorf II, interviewed by David Frum, "After Words," C-SPAN2, recorded November 15, 2006, broadcast viewed November 25, 2006, 9–10pm. Middendorf had played a leading role in Barry Goldwater's and Nixon's presidential campaigns, was secretary of the Navy, 1974–1977, and is the author of *A Glorious Disaster* (2006), about the Goldwater 1964 campaign; Frum was an AEI senior fellow at the time of the interview, and had been a speechwriter for President Bush, 2001–2002. See also Dorothy Rabinowitz, "Affairs of State," *Wall Street Journal*, February 9, 2007, p. W4, review of "Nixon: A Presidency Revealed," History Channel, presented February 15, 2007, 8–10pm EST: "the Nixon presidency led to major foreign-policy achievements, not least among them Nixon's visit to China and the beginning of détente with the Soviets. In his domestic policies, Nixon leaned to the progressive . . . Bob Dole delivers perhaps the best last word on Nixon in this admirably thorough documentary when he observes, with characteristic dourness, that Richard Nixon 'could never be the nominee of the Republican Party today – the conservatives wouldn't have him.' He was, Mr. Dole explains, too liberal." My comment: the same was said by "conservatives" and "rightists" about Sen. John McCain (Republican-AZ), and he indeed did become the presidential nominee of the Republican Party in 2008 (just as had the "too liberal" Bush in 2000 and 2004). See also Ryan Sager, *The Elephant in the Room* (New York: Wiley, 2006), on religious and secular, left and right, in the Republican Party, more broadly. Cf. John Fund, "Shades of Gray," *WSJ*, Op-Ed, January 18, 2007, p. A16 (re California Republican Governor Arnold Schwarzenegger's universal health insurance proposal for the state, including coverage of two million illegal aliens, referring to the governor as "Schwarzenkennedy"): "Mr. Schwarzenegger . . . is imitating Richard Nixon's old strategy of throwing rhetorical bones to his right while attempting to appease the left with liberal programs . . . That explains Nixon's dramatic lurches into or toward wage-price controls, a guaranteed annual income and mandatory employer health insurance." [Par.] "Arnold Schwarzenegger used to claim he admired Ronald Reagan most 'because he stuck by his principles when others wouldn't.' But with his Rube Goldberg health plan Mr. Schwarzenegger has demonstrated that at his core he prefers roles more suited to Tricky Dick than the Gipper. Should he succeed, the long-term dream of nationalized health care held by Ted Kennedy, and Hillary Clinton, will be closer to reality than ever."

20. See, e.g., commentary (pre-"Katrina"-"Rita"-"Wilma") of *Wall Street Journal* columnist George Melloan ("Global View," *WSJ*, July 12, 2005, p. A17): "Mr. Bush has few peers among American presidents in his willingness to let Congress spend as freely as it always wants to do. And the Republican Congress has few peers in history in its willingness to take advantage of the president's generosity. A Cato Institute study in May [2005] revealed that total federal government spending rose 33% in Mr. Bush's first term, making him the biggest spender since Lyndon B. Johnson opened wide the spigots 40 years ago and touched off the 1970s inflation." [Par.] "Last year's [2004] drug-benefit addition to Medicare – a huge new entitlement that will kick in next year – suggests a certain nonchalance about the growth of expenditures." [Par.] "The Republicans control both the Congress and the presidency . . . Mr. Bush presides benignly over all this. He hasn't once vetoed a spending bill or used his rescission authority to trim the budget. It's a version of the old political formula, tax-spend-elect except in the Republican book it is borrow-spend-elect." My comment: This "formula," in both versions, used to be the "New Deal" ("Great Society," etc.) Democratic book, or, the left-wing book; it may be more telling to say (again, with Nixon) that being on the right in US politics, and winning *and governing*, means "stooping left to conquer." See also Stephen A. Slivinski (dir., budget studies, Cato Inst.), "Fuzzy Fiscal Restraint," *New York Post*, July 17, 2005, p. 27; Slivinski, *Buck Wild: How Republicans Blew the Bank and Became the Party of Big Government* (New York: Nelson Current, 2006); and, on Nixon-Bush parallels, Sager, "The Right Rebels." Consider also George Will's criticizing commentary (in part): "Conservatives have won seven of [the past] 10 presidential elections [i.e., going back through Reagan and Nixon], yet government waxes, with per household federal spending more than $22,000 per year, the highest in inflation-adjusted terms since World War II. Federal spending – including a 100 percent increase in education spending since 2001 – has grown twice as fast under President Bush as under President Clinton, 65 percent of it unrelated to national security. [Par.] In 1991, the 546 pork projects in the 13 appropriations bills cost $3.1 billion. In 2005, the 13,997 pork projects cost $27.3 billion. [Par.] . . . the government is more undisciplined [in spending] than ever." (George Will, "Dover, PA and the GOP: Punting on Pork," *New York Post*, November 17, 2005, p. 33.) Consider also the following, in 2005, from Dick Armey, Republican House Majority Leader, 1995–2003 ("It's My Party . . ." [sic], *Wall Street Journal*, Op-Ed, November 29, 2005, p. A18): "Today, with Republicans controlling both the legislative and executive branches of the federal government, there is a widening credibility gap between their political rhetoric and their public policies." "President Bush and the Republican-controlled Congress are presiding over the largest expansion of government since LBJ's [President Johnson's] Great Society [Par.] . . . even excluding defense and homeland security spending, the growth rate of discretionary spending adjusted for inflation is at a 40-year high." "What will happen to Republicans if . . . [their disillusioned] grass-roots activists don't show up for work next fall? The elections earlier this month [Democratic Party gains] may be an indication of the answer."

My comment: that is, a further strengthening of the left, and the continued shifting leftward of the US polity. On this latter point, cf., e.g., *WSJ* Editorial ("Incumbency over Ideas"), January 9, 2006, p. A12: "Ohio's Mike Oxley [Republican] has run the [House] Financial Services Committee more or less as Liberal Barney Frank would . . . the GOP has achieved little in the last decade that will outlast the next Democratic majority. [Par.] . . . Republicans . . . think the voters will never turn Congress over to a party run by Nancy Pelosi. But that's also what Democrats and the media thought about Republicans led by Newt Gingrich in 1994. Eventually, voters may grow more disgusted with Republicans who care only about re-election than they are afraid of Ms. Pelosi's San Francisco liberalism." The Democratic party's midterm congressional election gains, resulting in their taking control of both the House and the Senate, did indeed transpire. Note also, the post-election statement by Sen. John McCain that the Republicans in Congress during the Bush presidency "have spent more and increased the size of government more than at any time since the Great Society [of LBJ]." McCain quoted at Robert D. Novak, "McCain's Tax Turn," *New York Post*, February 5, 2007, p. 31. Also, the "conservative" columnist Deroy Murdock commented that during President Bush's two terms, from FY2001 to FY2009, the federal budget rose about 67% from $1.86 trillion to $3.1 trillion, with an average annual spending increase of 8.35%, and that these increases "have cascaded from a Republican presidency and a mainly GOP Congress." ("Slapping the Hand of Greedy Gov't [sic]," *New York Post*, May 19, 2008, p. 29.) Note also, in general, Bush's adherence to "compassionate conservatism" (which may be translated, "big-government conservatism," "left-wing conservatism," or "Rockefeller Republicanism"), and the influential position, as a speech writer and adviser, of Michael J. Gerson, known affectionately, or derisively, in the Bush White House, as "the Christian Socialist." See M. J. Gerson, *Heroic Conservatism* (New York: Harper One, 2007); also, Ross Douthat and Reihan Salam, *Grand New Party: How Republicans Can Win the Working Class and Save the American Dream* (New York: Doubleday, 2008). The widely assumed "conservative triumph," or a "Reagan Revolution" rooted in and fulfilling a "Goldwater conservatism" in US politics since the 1970s, is more a matter of wishful consolation, on the right, and sectarian misapprehension, on the left, than of the empirical record, or the historical reality.

21. After the assassination of President Abraham Lincoln, President Andrew Johnson's attempt at a rightist restoration in the national government resulted in a recharged left's mobilization of Congress, the Army, popular action, and public opinion, in Johnson's own impeachment and, without conviction, his immobilization, and in a reconstruction campaign in the South that made African-Americans citizens and voters well before ratification of the 14th and 15th Amendments of the Constitution (a status lost not long after ratification). May it not be emblematic of historical left-prevalence in the American political culture that Presidents Franklin Pierce, James Buchanan, and Andrew Johnson are invariably, and uncontroversially, found at the bottom of president-ranking lists? – and accordingly, e.g., that John F. Kennedy, in a show of sophomoric savvy, included Andrew Johnson among

his "Profiles of Courage," for going against the Reconstruction-Republicans (against the left) as Johnson did?

22. Leninist constructs: Left = Socialism, Right = Capitalism; Left = Government, Right = Markets. Socialism = State-Command/Government, Capitalism = "Business," Markets, Corporations, Corporate-Interests (old-style: "Monopoly"). Socialism = Party, Movement, Capitalism = Mode of Production. Left = Communists (and Designated Equivalents), "Fellow-Travelers" (allies, pro-Communists/DEs), antiCommunists/DEs, Anti-US-led/style-Capitalism, Right = Everyone Else. Left = "Third World," pro-"Third World," Anti-Imperialist, Anti-West, Anti-US, Right = "First World," West, Pro-West, Pro-US. Left = "Radical" (US-new-style: "Liberal/Secular-Progressive"), Right = "Conservative" (US-new-style: pro-Traditionalist-Christianity, anti-Traditionalist-Islam). Some corollary Leninist syllogisms: (1) Capitalism is bad/US is Capitalist/US is bad. (2) Anti-Capitalism/US is good/X (government, leader, person, "Third-World") is anti-Capitalism/US/X is good. (3) Anti-Capitalism/US is Left/X is anti-Capitalism/US/X is Left. (4) Pro-Capitalism/US is Right/X is pro-Capitalism/US/X is Right. Regarding Leninist Captivity, cf. M. J. Sklar, "Thoughts on Capitalism and Socialism," p. 375; M. J. Sklar, "Capitalism and Socialism in the Emergence of Modern America: The Formative Era, 1890–1916," in *Reconstructing History*, p. 310; M. J. Sklar, *United States as a Developing Country*, ch. 7, esp. pp. 215–216.

23. Louis Hartz, *The Liberal Tradition in America* (New York: Harvest Books, 1955), pp. 29, 101, 174; see also, M. J. Sklar, *United States as a Developing Country*, pp. 151–153.

24. Cf. Philip D. Curtin, *Cross-Cultural Trade in World History* (Cambridge University Press, 1984), pp. 251–252: "The most rapid expansion [of total world trade from 1700 to 1914] was a ninefold increase between 1820 and 1880, generated by the spread of the industrial revolution to most of Western Europe and the United States."

25. Over 100 years further along in development, indicative of the "supernatural" characteristic of the modern economy, and the modern society at large, are the following excerpts from three items in the *Wall Street Journal* relating to the aftermath of the US Gulf Coast hurricanes of August–September, 2005: (1) "Hurricane Katrina was of course a big disaster, flooding large numbers of Louisianans and Mississippians out of their homes and businesses, causing an estimated $35 billion in insured property losses, severe damage to the Gulf-centered oil and gas industry and nearly 1,000 deaths. Yet the US economy only hiccupped, as was made plain by last Friday's report [October 7, 2005] of only a slight decline in employment in September." (George Melloan, "Global View: 'I Read the News Today, Oh Boy'," *WSJ*, October 11, 2005, p. A17.); (2) "Katrina, the worst natural disaster in US history, will result in losses of up to $60 billion. Yet, as demonstrated by . . . positive earnings in 2005, the insurance industry was able to handle this enormous burden because substantial historical data on natural disasters has enabled companies to understand and manage their exposure to such large losses." (Edmund F. Kelly [CEO of Liberty Mutual], "When the Next Storm

Strikes," *WSJ*, Op-Ed, May 31, 2006, p. A12.); (3) "The US economy grew at a robust 3.8% annualized rate in the third quarter [ending September 30, 2005], marking the 16th consecutive quarter of growth and confirming that the economy weathered the hurricanes that devastated the Gulf Coast. [Par.] The [US] Commerce Department said . . . that growth in the third-quarter gross domestic product . . . outpaced the 3.3% rate in the second quarter. [Par.] Treasury Secretary John Snow . . . said, 'it really does reflect something powerful [in] the American economy that we can take the blows that hit us in late August and September and continue rolling through it.'" (Joi Preciphs and Jon E. Hilsenrath, "US Economy Marks Solid Growth, Despite Storms," *WSJ*, October 29–30, 2005, p. A2.) The 3.8% growth rate for 2005Q3 was subsequently revised upward by the Commerce Department to 4.1%. "Economic Growth Surges in Summer," Harrisburg (PA) *Patriot-News*, December 22, 2005, p. C1: "The gain was even more remarkable considering that the country was hit by devastating hurricanes and gasoline prices that topped $3 a gallon." The 2005Q4 rate fell to 1.7%, giving a 3.5% rate for all of 2005, but the 2006Q1 rate surged to 5.6%, making the US "one of the world's fastest-growing advanced economies." Reports by Mark Whitehouse, *WSJ*, March 31, May 26 (quotation), 2006, p. A2, and Jeff Bater, *WSJ*, June 20, 2006, p. A5. Subsequently, in 2007–2008, it was not the large-scale destruction and disruptions of hurricanes like Gustav and Ike (September 2008), but the "subprime" financial-credit meltdown of an over-building and underpaid-for (subsidized) US housing sector, that sent crippling shockwaves through the US economy and the entire global economy.

26. On moderating the business cycle, see, e.g., Harvey Rosenblum (Exec. VP and Dir. of Research, Fed. Res. Bank of Dallas), "Fed Policy and Moral Hazard," *Wall Street Journal*, Op-Ed, October 18, 2007, p. A17, discussing Federal Reserve Board FOMC countercyclical operations (guided in the 1990s by the John Taylor Rule), with Table (NBER) showing declining percentage of time spent by the US economy in recession, 1918–2007, as the countercyclical operations became increasingly more proficient: 1918–1836, 41%; 1940–1962, 17%; 1963–1985, 18%; and most impressively, 1986–2007, 6%. On the capitalism-socialism mix, see M. J. Sklar titles cited in notes 18 and 22. See also Marc Chandler, "Creeping Socialism?" *The Nation*, September 4/11, 2000, pp. 38, 39, a review of Seymour Martin Lipset and Gary Marks, *It Didn't Happen Here: Why Socialism Failed in the United States* (New York: Norton, 2000); the review compares the Lipset-Marks view with the Sklar-mix view. The Lipset-Marks book is a representative statement, or restatement, of the standard – Lenin-Captivity – view. See also, e.g., on the capitalism-socialism mix, Richard Schneirov's discussion, "Socialism and Capitalism Reconsidered," *Journal of the Gilded Age and Progressive Era* (JGAPE), 2: 4, October 2003, pp. 351–360, at pp. 354–356 (Special Issue of JGAPE, "New Perspectives on Socialism"); and Schneirov, "William English Walling: Socialist and Labor Progressive," pp. xxxii–xxxiv; also, Schneirov, "Thoughts on Periodizing the Gilded Age"; and James Livingston, "Why Is There Still Socialism in the United States?" (review of M. J. Sklar, *United States as a Developing Country*), in *Reviews in American History*, 22: 4,

December 1994, pp. 577–583. The 2007–2009 financial-credit crisis, and accompanying recession, deep and global, but not yet a "great depression," is a function of the capitalism/socialism mix (or interplay) in the age of disaccumulation (see discussion below).

27. Disaccumulation is not to be mistaken for "decumulation," a term sometimes used to denote deterioration of capital and productive capacities. For the initial use of the term, "disaccumulation," and discussion of its meaning and implications, see M. J. Sklar, *United States as a Developing Country*, ch. 1, esp. pp. 34–36, and ch. 5, esp. pp. 153–170 (ch. 5 reproduces an essay I first published in 1969, in the journal *Radical America*); for subsequent discussion along these lines, based on this earlier work, see James Livingston, *Pragmatism and the Political Economy of Cultural Revolution, 1850–1940* (Chapel Hill: University of North Carolina Press, 1994), ch. 1; Reuben L. Norman Jr., "Smith, Marx, Kondratieff and Keynes: The Long Wave Hypothesis and the Internet," June 6, 1998 (19 pp.), esp. notes 1, 2, 16 and related text; R. L. Norman Jr., "Theories of the Great Depression: Harris, Sklar and Carlo: Secular Stagnation, Disaccumulation, Monopolies-Overproduction and the Long Waves," June 22, 24, 26, 1998 (11 pp.), and "The Internet, Creative Destruction and the Falling Rate of Profit Crisis," February 8, 2000 (22 pp.), esp. Chart 3 and accompanying annotation, p. 8; all at www.southerndomains.com/southernbanks.

28. Also, broadening and deepening a trend, begun earlier during accumulationist-industrialization, of rescinding J. S. Mill's once-famous "Fourth Proposition," based on Say – that demand for goods is not demand for labor. Cf. M. J. Sklar, *Corporate Reconstruction*, p. 65, and 65n29.

29. "Phillips Curve," named for the economist Alban William Phillips. To be fair, and more historically accurate, it may be noted that the principle of higher revenues from lower selected tax rates has long been known and applied. For example, in the 1760s, the British *reduced* the sugar-import tax in the North American colonies to raise more revenue (they kept the tea tax along with granting the East India Co. a monopoly, and lost both revenues and a large tea cargo in Boston Harbor in December 1773). Also, Hamilton's tariff in the 1790s was a *revenue* tariff – to fund the public debt and create an invigorated capital market along with the US Bank – not a high protective tariff. Hence many American "manufacturers" – artisans, mechanics, small-shop producers – deserted the Federalist Party and joined the many other voters already loyal to the Jeffersonian Democratic-Republican Party. The first truly *protective* US tariff came later, in 1816, under the "Jeffersonian" National Republicans. The JFK (Okun/LBJ) tax cuts in the early 1960s, and the 1978 (Steiger-Carter) capital gains tax-rate cut (from 50% to 28%), embodied the same principle of higher revenues from lower selected tax rates. Drawing upon the work of Friedrich Hayek and Milton Friedman in the 1970s Jude Wanniski and Arthur B. Laffer, (with decisive input from Columbia University Professor Robert A. Mundell and *Wall Street Journal* Editor Robert L. Bartley, and Paul Craig Roberts, along with Wanniski working as editorial writer under Bartley at the time), may well deserve

credit, not for originating, but for reemphasizing, as did also in the 1970s British economist (and Labour Party adviser) James Mirrlees, this long-known principle of higher revenues from lower tax rates (via consequent growth), and for framing it in terms of current economic and policy-forming thought, thereby facilitating its explicit adoption as policy by President Ronald Reagan, its implementation by David Stockman and Lawrence Kudlow at Reagan's OMB, and passage through Congress. Appalled at rising deficits, Stockman at length bailed out, decrying the "triumph of politics," and noting the social-democratic preferences (or, majoritarian leftism) of the American people. (*The Triumph of Politics*, New York: Harper and Row, 1986.) Kudlow and Laffer stayed the course, then and to this day, and they have ranked among the more influential of US economic analysts and public-policy advisers. The deeper significance of the Wanniski-Laffer principle (aka the "Laffer Curve"), or "supply-side economics" in general, is that it is *progrowth*, and thus, in an age of disaccumulation, both proinvestor (aroused "animal spirits" and higher net returns) and proworking-class (jobs, rising household income and asset-holdings), and in more specific policy terms, its connecting, *in effect*, sustained fiscal deficits with lower interest rates and lower inflation, as essential pro-growth policy in a context of rising investment and rising productivity. "Supply-side economics" effectively repositioned the Republican Party on the pro-growth-fiscal-deficit left, and the bait-taking Democrats on the anti-growth-budget-balancing (high-tax "Hooverist") right – a "transfer of fortune" (pun intended); and hence a large gain of working-class votes, and formerly left-Keynesian (and Marxian) "neo-con" support, for the Republicans. A reading of Reagan's speeches and writings shows that already in the 1970s he understood these things – in addition, telling working-class audiences during his presidential campaigning that the New Deal lived in him, and abandoning the older Goldwater-GOP hostility to the Social Security system, indeed, while president acting to strengthen Social Security in coverage and funding, and signing on to payroll-tax *increases* in six of his eight years as president. With respect to regaining pro-growth ground on the left, so did President William J. Clinton similarly understand (with the help of Lloyd Bentsen, Roger Altman, Robert E. Rubin, Lawrence H. Summers, and Alan Greenspan), to Republicans' deep annoyance, and to the Democrats' temporary renewal of presidential advantage (although with an effective Clinton-Gingrich partnership; e.g., the 1997 capital-gains tax cut, 28% to 20%), and upon Clinton's departure the Democrats again losing ground to a knowing President George W. Bush (with the help of Karl Rove, Karen Hughes, Richard B. Cheney, and Alan Greenspan) and a knowing, tax-rate-reducing, high-spending Republican Congress (as with the Democratic Congress under Reagan). Regarding Reagan's understanding of "supply-side" principles and thinking by the 1970s, see, e.g., his radio script of October 18, 1977, citing Friedman and Laffer in advocating lower tax-rates for higher revenues, growth, and employment without inflation, in Kiron K. Skinner *et al.*, eds., *Reagan in His Own Hand* (New York: Simon and Schuster, 2001, Touchstone edn., 2002), p. 274. Reagan's chief economic advisers in his 1980 presidential election campaign were Milton Friedman, George P. Shultz, Arthur F. Burns, and Alan Greenspan, a rather imposing, high-powered group, and indicating Reagan's own intellectual strength, confidence, and sophistication. See also George Melloan, "1981," *Wall Street Journal*, Op-Ed, November 14, 2006, p. A20. For the record, and keeping in mind the difference between Keynes's own thinking and "Keynesianism," I think it a mistake to think, as Melloan and others at times tended to do, that "supply-side" economics meant the replacement, obsolescence, or death of Keynesianism; it is, rather, an updated revision and adaptation, just as Keynesianism itself was an updated revision and adaptation of classical and neoclassical economic thought, a revision that actually began with Americans (*c.* 1898–1900s), led especially (not solely) by Charles A. Conant, and that the younger Keynes studied and absorbed. Corroborative of Keynesianism's continuing vital currency, both before and during events associated with the financial/credit/economic crisis of 2007–2009, and supply-siders' (including Melloan's) effective, if grudging, understanding so, see, e.g., *WSJ* editorials, "The Right Stimulus," January 11, 2008, p. A10, "Rubinomics R.I.P.," January 15, 2008, p. A12, "We're All Keynesians Now," January 18, 2008, p. A12, "Managing a Panic," January 23, 2008, p. A24; and Melloan's Op-Ed, "Hillary and Say's Law," *WSJ*, January 23, 2008, p. A25. In the overlapping US presidential primary/ election campaign seasons and the "subprime" financial crisis, of 2007–2008, the Democratic candidates and other Democratic leaders were "anti-Keynesian" in advocating higher taxes, trade barriers, and, in effect, higher interest rates, along with budget-balancing ("pay-go"), in a soft economy, and the Republican candidates and other GOP leaders, including President Bush, Treasury Secretary Henry Paulson, and the Bernanke Fed, were "pro-Keynesian" in advocating, adopting, and implementing "stimulus," recovery, and public investment measures via tax cuts or rebates, interest-rate cuts, massive budget-deficit spending, and deeply intrusive Treasury, Fed, and FDIC operations, including large-scale government engagement not only in broad market relations, but also in ownership and management of enterprises. Who was left? Who was right? Another case of Republicans stealing the march on the left; and Democrats taking the bait on the right. Cf. *WSJ*, Editorial, "Hoover's Heirs," April 3, 2008, p. A14. But thereafter, a case of President-elect Barack Obama, his Clintonist-heavy advisory and appointive "team," along with some congressional Democrats, drawing upon and learning from the Bush/Paulson/McCain Republicans and the Clinton legacy/ legatees, stealing back the march with their own recovery and stimulus add-on plans, raising the ante considerably: "Post-Partisan" Bi-Triangulation "We Can Believe In": a "third-Bush term" combined with a "third-Clinton term." Cf. Sudeep Reddy, "The New Old Big Thing in Economics: J. M. Keynes," *WSJ*, January 8, 2009, p. A10; *WSJ*, Editorial, "The Deficit Spending Blowout," January 8, 2009, p. A14; and, throwing in the towel, George Melloan, "We're All Keynesians Again," *WSJ*, Op-Ed, January 13, 2009, p. A17. In a play on the saying, "No atheists in a foxhole": "No free-market faithful in a stocks-hole (aka market depression)." Also, in a play on "An impending hanging concentrates the mind": "An impending depression concentrates the mind – into a confessional Keynesianism."

30. President Reagan's and President George W. Bush's invocations of world revolution, and of the US as a revolutionary nation with a revolutionary people, are of historic substance, not best understood as empty or propagandistic rhetoric. The same may be said for "New World Order" of Presidents Reagan and George Bush and Secretaries of State George P. Shultz, James A. Baker III, and Lawrence Eagleburger (the latter of whom warned of daunting disorders with the end of the bipolar Cold War system); and for "Indispensable Nation" of President Clinton and Secretaries of State Warren Christopher and Madeline Albright. It is of some significance that although such invocations since the 1980s have been bipartisan, they have come more from Republicans than from Democrats, in US political life, and not at all from the doctrinal, transvestite left, but often from the transvestite right.

31. As this suggests, "color line," or "race line," is not to be taken literally. DuBois and his associates were immediately concerned with the situation of African-Americans in the US, but they were also addressing what they took to be the broader Euro ("white") vs. non-Euro ("colored") conflict – hence, National Association for the Advancement of *Colored* (non-Euro) People. Similarly, in the 1990s–2000s, the Balkans conflicts, the Hutus vs. Tutsis conflict in Burundi/Rwanda, the Muslims vs. Christians and Animists in southern Sudan, and Arab Muslims vs. African Muslims in western Sudan (Darfur), may be understood metaphorically as "racist" (demonization, oppression, mass removal and killing of "the other") without skin color, or race in the strict sense, necessarily being involved, if at all. In a historic departure, or line-crossing, these aggressions and depredations were explicitly opposed as genocidal, however much with little or mixed effectiveness, by governments, the UN, and public opinion worldwide, and, where the opposition has been more effective, with US engagement and leadership. Also, the current (*c.* 1970s–2000s et seq.) Jihadi-Islamism may be understood as a religio-racist imperialism ("kill the Jews, Christians, Hindus, Americans, false Muslims, and Apostates," "restore the Caliphate"), bicentered in (not exclusive to) Arab and Iranian politics, and engendering a worldwide coalition against it (including most Muslims), and again with US engagement and leadership. The "color line," or "race line," of "Euro" vs. "non-Euro" has proven more readily crossed in the US and other parts of the world than the tribal, ethnic, or religio-racist line in Africa, the Middle East, parts of Asia, France, the Balkans, and other parts of Europe.

32. Cf., e.g., David Roche, "Recession Is Inevitable," *Wall Street Journal*, Op-Ed, March 14, 2008, p. A19: "The credit crisis [of 2007–2008] is unfolding . . . more slowly than anticipated, because of the actions taken by central banks (mainly the Fed) and the US government to allay its effects. The wholesale socialization of credit has meant that government and central bank measures account for 70% of new credit since last summer [2007]." (Roche, president of Independent Strategy, a London-based consultancy, is coauthor of *New Monetarism*, Lulu Enterprises, 2007.)

33. Cf., e.g., regarding US implications of the 2008–2009 financial/credit crisis and attendant economic contraction, Mark Gongloff, "Absent from This Downturn: Worker-Investor Dichotomy," *Wall Street Journal*, October 29, 2008, p. C1, 2: "It is one of the oddities of the markets [in the past – actually,

not an oddity, but a regularity] that when unemployment is [was] at its worst, investors do [did] well. [Actually, not always: e.g., 1929–1930s.] This time, investors and workers may suffer together. [Par.] Any industry that depends on discretionary consumer spending, from electronics retailers to specialty apparel stores, will be at risk as long as unemployment is rising. Higher automobile-loan default rates and slumping sales will keep hurting the auto industry. [Par.] 'Take almost any market right now and ask yourself: Is it better off with a rise in unemployment?' said Bianco Research strategist Howard Simons. 'We are in nothing but adverse feedback loops now.'" (See note 28 re Say's Law and J. S. Mill's "Fourth Proposition.") In the 2008 US presidential campaign, the Democratic Party candidate, Sen. (IL) Barack Obama, and most other prominent Democratic candidates and leaders, plied the older-fashioned investor vs. worker politics, suited to a superseded accumulationist mode of production, and in that sense (among others) they were retrograde, or reactionary and antiprogressive. The Republican Party candidate, Sen. (AZ) John McCain, and most other prominent Republican candidates and leaders, plied the updated politics of investor-worker common interests in growth and investment-returns, suited to the currently rising disaccumulationist mode of production, and in that sense (among others) they were progressive. The Obama-camp Democrats' outlook and politics rather consistently embodied, and articulately expressed, a past accumulationist populism and a current "Third-Worldist" antimodernism, analogous to what Theodore Roosevelt dubbed a "Tory radicalism," what Woodrow Wilson called a "retro-reformism," what Karl Marx had earlier called a "feudal socialism," and what later commentators sometimes referred to as "vulgar Marxism," or "backward tyrannical statism." In the opening weeks of the Obama presidency, executive policy and legislation ("stimulus," omnibus spending, FY2010 budget) plied a largely regressive-populism path.

34. We might also note a rather complex *Military Line*: (1) from mass armies (Napoleonic wars, US Civil War, Taiping Rebellion) to mass armies and mass naval power, but now with operations and weapons of massive destruction (US Civil War in part, World Wars I and II, Korean War, Vietnam War, Iran–Iraq War sans large naval power), and then to mobile forces, precision weapons, and minimal destruction (Gulf War, Balkans, Afghanistan, Iraq); (2) from weapons of limited massive destruction (WLMD) to weapons of mass destruction (WMD – nuclear, radiological, chemical, biological); (3) from nation-state-centered armed conflict (including guerrilla war), to supranational "terror"-war with WLMD and WMD, and with "civilian" (out-of-uniform) invasions via legal and illegal migration and infiltration, formation of cell-assault units, and attacks on public spaces and conveyances, for disruption and intended disintegration of modern open-pluralist society, and ultimate imperial conquest of the society's people and wealth.

35. Alternatively, yes, much (if not all) of this change is "progressive" and revolutionary in accordance with long-standing left-wing thought and activity, and those who are opposed to the US and its role in world affairs are, in effect or in fact, right-wing reactionaries, antiprogressives, or counterrevolutionaries, standing firm against all this US-led left-wing change.

36. Cf. Prelude and Part Two.

37. "Allegorically," because the term, "civilization," remains imprecise in historical meaning (however precise in anthropological or dictionary meaning), and because many "clashes" through history, including those between empires, have been intra-"civilizational," especially among those most significant in shaping and changing modern world history, and because, as by this point in the present discussion should be evident, neither "Open Door" nor "American Century" is to be taken literally. Another way of thinking about this, is that, in terms of trend, the "Clash of Civilizations" lies behind us in the past more than before us in the future, short of events of "Dark Age" or Biblical-Apocalyptic proportions, which are not, however, historically unfeasible under present-day circumstances. For a previous discussion of, and demurrer from, Samuel P. Huntington's "Clash of Civilizations" formulation, by me, see "The Open Door, Imperialism, and Postimperialism: Origins of US Twentieth-Century Foreign Relations, Circa 1900," ch. 11 in David G. Becker and Richard L. Sklar, eds., *Postimperialism and World Politics*, at pp. 329n7, 336.

38. As of 2006–2010, the Iranian side rode high, with extensions of power into Arab Iraq, Syria, Lebanon, Palestine, Bahrain, Dubai, Qatar, and UAE, with strong trade and diplomatic relations with Germany, Italy, Spain, Russia, China, N. Korea, India, Venezuela and other Latin American countries, with large oil and gas reserves, sizeable and strategic investments and banking abroad, and a nuclear development program at odds with its nonproliferation-treaty obligations. Still, the Arab side retained vast oil and gas resources, had strong supportive relations with the US and western Europe, Russia, China, and other Asian countries, had great and diversified global investments with major presence in world shipping, finance, industry, and commerce, had extensive influence and power centers, via resident communities, embassies, mosques, schools, universities, cultural, charitable, and propaganda organizations, in western Europe, central, south, and southeastern Asia, Latin America, and the US and Canada, and had a possible future control, in an allied Sunni Pakistan, of nuclear weapons and delivery systems already in place.

39. The "civilizations" and provisional restrictive empires, in this view, would be based, roughly, and respectively, on: Russia; China; India; European Union; US–UK–Japan; Latin America; Sub-Saharan Africa; and Islam (North Africa–Middle East–Central Asia–Southeast Asia). It may be noted that at least some of these, including that designated as Islam, encompass more than one "civilization."

40. And, to an earnest Islamist Iranian, the End of Liberal History: "Mr. [Francis] Fukuyama's real complaint against Iran, [is] that it has failed to conform to his suspect thesis of the end of history and triumph of Western liberalism." Letters to the Editor, *Wall Street Journal*, February 2, 2006, p. A11, letter by Mansour Sadeghi, Counsellor and Head of Press Section, Permanent Mission of Iran to the United Nations, New York. Note also Iran President Mahmoud Ahmadinejad's statement in his letter to US President Bush (May 8, 2006): "Those with insight can already hear the sounds of the shattering and fall of the ideology and thoughts of the liberal democratic system." Quoted at *New York Post*, May 10, 2006, p. 5. Also, on Islamist Iranian views and

broader implications, see Amir Taheri, "'The Last Helicopter'," *WSJ*, Op-Ed, March 29, 2006, p. A18, and Taheri, "About That Letter," *NYP*, Op-Ed, May 11, 2006, p. 41; cf. Francis Fukuyama and Adam Garfinkle, "A Better Idea," *WSJ*, Op-Ed, March 27, 2006, p. A16; and see Fukuyama, *The Great Disruption* (New York: Simon and Schuster, 2000), esp. pp. 279–282.

41. Cf. Philip Bobbitt, *Terror and Consent: The Wars for the Twenty-First Century* (New York: Knopf, 2008), pp. 49–50 et seq.

42. Cf., e.g., Fereydoun Hoveyda, "The Old and the New Middle East: What Is to Be Done?" *American Foreign Policy Interests*, 26: 2 (April 2004), pp. 99–116, esp. pp. 100–102; Amir Taheri, "Fascism in Muslim Countries," ibid., 26: 1 (February 2004), pp. 21–30; Taheri, "The Duel in Islam: Turkey's New Model vs. Iran's," *New York Post*, January 4, 2008, p. 29. In this context, it may be relevant to recall that although in the nineteenth century Britain aligned with (Muslim) Ottoman Turkey against (Christian) Russia, to check expansion of Russian power in Central Asia and the Middle East, Ottoman Turkey in the late nineteenth–early twentieth century aligned increasingly with Germany, and in World War I allied itself with Germany against Britain *and* Russia (and France). The Young Turks had close relations with Italian fascism, and directed the anti-Armenian genocide, but upon Kemal Atatürk's presidency (1923–1938), although the westernizing nationalist-military regime retained Islam as the nation-unifying religion, continued anti-Armenian and anti-Greek policies, and intensively suppressed (Muslim) Kurds' separate national/cultural identity. It also ended the Caliphate (1924), detached Turkey from the former Ottoman-Muslim world, remained neutral in most of World War II, declaring war against Germany in January 1945, and after the war, became a charter member of the UN, allied itself with a liberal social-democratic US, Britain, and western Europe against the Soviet Union (Truman Doctrine, 1947; NATO membership, 1952), remained detached from, or actively opposed to, both pan-Arabism and anti-West Islamism, maintained diplomatic and other consequential relations with Israel (including the military cooperation agreement of 1996), and by the 1990s–2000s sought membership in the European Union as a modernizing democratic nation. But the counterpull of anti-West Islamist imperialism has grown stronger in Turkish society and politics in recent years, with the outcome remaining uncertain. By 2009–2010, the Erdogan government was aligning itself not so much with Arab imperialism as with Iranian imperialism, with a view prospectively to establishing a Turk-Iranian Caliphate-Empire, provisionally if not durably. As the Turk-Erdogan leaders may have been seeing it: with Europe–US/UK in decline, it was no longer advantageous for Turkey to join the European Union, remain allied with the US, stay in an eviscerated NATO, and be westward-oriented, but instead to revive the Islamic Empire as a major player/power in a world political economy increasingly organized "eastward" by China–India–Russia – and Islam. Regarding Turk genocidal depredations against Armenians and Greeks: Michael B. Oren, *Power, Faith, and Fantasy: America in the Middle East, 1776 to the Present* (New York: W. W. Norton, 2007), pp. 292–296, 329–332, 334–339; and Ferguson, *The War of the World*, pp. 174–184.

43. Cf., e.g., Amir Taheri, "Iran's Price for 'Solidarity': Mullahs Seek Useful Marxist Idiots," *New York Post*, Op-Ed, October 12, 2007, p. 31: "The Islamic Republic [of Iran] bans all non-Khomeinist ideologies, but two are specifically punishable by imprisonment or death: [secular] socialism and liberal democracy." Taheri reported, further, in this op-ed column, that at an international conference at Tehran University, convened in October 2007 by President Ahmadinejad's followers, and financed in part by Venezuela President Hugo Chavez, Khomeinist speaker Mortaza Firuzabadi declared, "In this global jihad, we recognize no frontiers"; also, that a keynote speaker, Hajj Saeed Qassem (coordinator of the Association of Volunteers for Suicide-Martyrdom) stated: "Today, communism has been consigned to the garbage can of history as foreseen by Imam Khomeini . . . The Soviet Union is gone . . . Those who wish to destroy America must understand the reality" and "everywhere accept the leadership of our religious pro-justice movement."

44. Cf. Bernard Lewis, *Islam and the West* (New York: Oxford University Press, 1993), p. 136: "For the traditional Muslim, religion was not only universal but also central in the sense that it constituted the ultimate basis and focus of identity and loyalty . . . It was not nation or country that, as in the West, formed the historic basis of identity, but the religio-political community [*umma*] . . . The imported Western idea of ethnic and territorial nationhood remains, like secularism, alien and incompletely assimilated. The point was made with remarkable force and clarity by a grand vizier of the Ottoman Empire [in 1917] . . . 'The Fatherland of a Muslim is wherever the Holy Law of Islam prevails.'" Also, more recently, Ayatollah Ruhollah Khomeini: "We do not worship Iran; we worship Allah. For patriotism is another name for paganism. I say let this land [Iran] burn. I say let this land go up in smoke, provided Islam emerges triumphant in the rest of the world." Imam Ruhollah Khomeini and Hamad Algar (trans. and annot.), *Islam and Revolution: Writings and Declarations* (London: Routledge and Kegan Paul, 1981).

45. Hence, the sensitivity – or strategic salience – of the Dubai World Ports acquisition of the Peninsula and Orient Steam Navigation Co., and such other transnational corporate and intercorporate transactions and operations, including those of "sovereign wealth funds." On empire-types, state-types, and their interrelations, over the course of human history, and their techno-military-economic bases, see Bobbitt, *The Shield of Achilles*.

46. Regarding the term, state, as meant here: in a liberal/constitutional system, the state (the agency of supreme power in society) resides *within* the government and is under the law, or, as we say, subject to the rule of law. In fascist, communist, junta-nationalist, theocratic-totalitarian, absolute-monarchist (e.g., Louis XIV) and such other systems, leaders and members of the state may or may not also be leaders and members of the government, but the state itself resides *outside* the government, is above the government and the law, has the power to dictate to government and to dictate law, and is in effect a law unto itself (the party, the clerical council, the monarchy, the dictatorship, the military command). Without further reference to the examples cited in the text above, and others that may come to mind (including hybrid or transitional cases), recall that when President Reagan began meeting with

Gorbachev in summits of two *heads of state*, Gorbachev held no government position, but as CP general-secretary he was the Soviet head of state. As an indication, or symbolization, that the Soviet Union was moving toward a "normal," or liberal, constitutional system (*perestroika*), Gorbachev gave leadership in amending the Soviet constitution to eliminate the CP's "leading role," and he assumed the office of president in the government, in addition to his office as head of the party. If there were to be a meeting between heads of state of the US and Iran, it would be between the US president and not Iran's president, but Iran's "Supreme Guide," Ayatollah Ali Khamenei (as of 2010, although the "Supreme Guide" would most likely refuse to meet with a mere "politician"). The Arab League and the Organization of the Islamic Conference are intergovernment assemblies and organizations, but not state organs, and they are usually of little or no effectiveness in either policy making or action. It may be remarked here that there is no other religion-based or ethnic-based intergovernment assembly or organization, for example, no intergovernment Organization of the Christian Conference, no intergovernment Anglo-Saxon League, etc., and if there were, it would likely be denounced, and especially by Western enlightened opinion, as racist or imperialist, or both. Intergovernment organizations such as EU, NATO, OAS, AU, ASEAN, APEC are regional/interest associations, based neither on religion nor on ethnicity or race. The EU's efforts at acquiring statehood authority and powers have met with great difficulties and multilayered resistance, and accordingly with a very limited degree of success. The UN is a universal (global) intergovernment association, with limited effectiveness, and with severely limited, nil, or ill effectiveness especially where its acting intersects with, or assumes to, state powers within or across national boundaries; these efforts invariably arouse intense and debilitating controversy, constraint, resistance, and venality. Such efforts, in the cases of violent conflicts, have usually resulted in the UN engaging in relief services or "peace-keeping," the latter basically amounting to observing and often aggression-complicit "neutrality," rather than actual peace-imposing or coercive force on behalf of its stated mission. Hence, intergovernment programs having state powers *and* actual effectiveness, such as the Proliferation Security Initiative, Hezbollah, the US/NATO interventions in Bosnia, Kosovo, and Afghanistan, the coalition interventions in Iraq, the Ethiopian intervention in Somalia, the NATO airlift in Darfur, have been arranged and sustained outside the UN, although the UN may assume a formal authorizing and auxiliary role, whether facilitative or obstructive.

47. Cf. note 34.

Index